# TO TEACH THE TRUTH

# To Teach the Truth

SELECTED COURSES AND SEMINARS

Schubert M. Ogden

CASCADE *Books* · Eugene, Oregon

TO TEACH THE TRUTH
Selected Courses and Seminars

Cascade Books
An Imprint of Wipf and Stock Publishers
199 W. 8th Ave., Suite 3
Eugene, OR 97401

www.wipfandstock.com

ISBN 13: 978-1-62564-944-7

*Cataloging-in-Publication data:*

Ogden, Schubert Miles, 1928–

    To teach the truth : selected courses and seminars / Schubert M. Ogden.

    xii + 212 p. ; 23 cm.

    ISBN 13: 978-1-62564-944-7

    1. Theology. I. Title.

BT65 O38 2015

Manufactured in the U.S.A.

To all who have borne witness to me
when I have tried to bear witness to them

For this I was born, and for this I came into the world,
to bear witness to the truth.

—THE GOSPEL ACCORDING TO JOHN 18:37

# Contents

# *Preface*

To be a Christian is to be called to bear witness to the truth and, in order to bear it validly, also to do theology. This is because doing theology is the form of critical reflection that asks whether bearing witness has been as valid as it claims to be and what it now has to become if it is to keep on being so. But this means that doing theology, as much as any other form of critical reflection, exists entirely for the sake of an activity beyond itself—in its case, the activity of bearing witness to the truth. As a Christian who has pursued the calling to do theology professionally, I have sought to bear such witness, not only implicitly by all of my work as an academic theologian, but also explicitly by doing my best whenever I had "time and opportunity" both to preach the truth and to teach it as a representative minister of the church. This book and a companion volume entitled *To Preach the Truth* are offered as what I hope are fair samples of this other side of my work that the theology I've mainly done has all been intended to serve.

As for my distinction between preaching and teaching, it rests on a significant difference between two modes of bearing witness, which I distinguish as "direct" and "indirect" respectively. It is likely that something of both modes is present in most attempts to bear witness. But in any particular instance, one or the other mode may be sufficiently dominant to warrant classifying the whole accordingly. Any instance may be classified as preaching whose controlling purpose is so to proclaim the truth that God is sheer love as to call the hearer or reader directly for a personal decision: to trust in God's love and to be faithful to its cause. By contrast, any instance of bearing witness may be classified as teaching that calls for that personal decision only indirectly, in that it seeks to clarify as adequately as possible just what it means, intellectually and existentially, to make the decision in a responsible way.

What Christian preaching and teaching, so understood, have in common is that both, by their very nature, presuppose a Christian commitment. They presuppose that the preacher and the teacher alike are themselves personally committed to the truth to which they, in their different ways, are bearing witness. In this, teaching as well as preaching is to be distinguished from doing theology. For, as sure as it is that most persons who do Christian theology are like myself in doing it as a Christian calling, there's nothing logically that requires them to do so—any more than any other form of critical reflection logically requires a prior commitment to the validity of the claims on which it reflects. So it was with reason that I distinguished what is offered in this book and its companion as the "other side" of my work as one who has mainly done theology as his Christian vocation.

The four items selected from my church teaching are typical of the kinds of courses and seminars that I have regularly offered in local churches and other ecclesial communities, including those in whose life and work I otherwise shared and of which my family were, in some cases, members. I think in this connection, with gratitude, especially of Northaven and Casa View United Methodist Churches in Dallas, Texas; of St. Barnabas Episcopal Church in Denver, Colorado; of the Nederland Community Presbyterian Church in Nederland, Colorado; and, not least, of the Stalcup School of Theology for the Laity, now at Brite Divinity School, Texas Christian University, in Fort Worth, Texas. Because it was my custom to begin and end all of my courses with prayer, I have also included such prayers here, along with the statements introducing the courses. The fourth item, Questions and Answers about Faith and Practice, represents a somewhat unconventional way of teaching and learning that maximizes students' initiative in setting the course agenda. I invite anyone intending to participate in the seminar to submit a written question in advance, and I then prepare answers that can form the basis for as much extended discussion as possible by the entire class. Thus, while I have to decide how I am to answer the questions and on the order in which they are to be discussed, I'm indebted to the students for determining what we actually talk about. In the case of the five sessions of such questions and answers included here, I would express my thanks to the members of the two congregations who helped to shape them: Nederland

Community Presbyterian Church and Tarrytown United Methodist Church in Austin, Texas.

I should also acknowledge that, in my citations from scripture, I have in almost all cases depended upon the New Revised Standard Version.

It is a joy once again to express my thanks to three friends who have been particularly helpful in completing a book: Philip E. Devenish, Franklin I. Gamwell, and Andrew D. Scrimgeour. I, of course, remain responsible for the final outcome. But I know, and my readers should know, that it is a better book because of their feedback.

Rollinsville, Colorado
October 2013

# 1

# The Authority of Scripture
## for Christian Existence Today

To exist as a Christian is to exist under authority. Specifically, it is to exist under the authority of God as decisively revealed through Jesus Christ and the Holy Spirit. But from an early time, Christians have generally recognized the unique authority, under God, of holy scripture. Indeed, the mottoes of the Protestant Reformers include not only "God alone," "Christ alone," "grace alone," and "faith alone," but also "scripture alone." Of course, not all Christians, either then or since, have made these mottoes their own. And in the modern period since the Reformation, the question of the authority of scripture has become ever more controversial not only between Christian churches but also within them. We may well suspect, in fact, that the single question underlying most of the many other questions currently in dispute among Christians is, in one way or another, that of scriptural authority. The purpose of this course is to enable an introductory theological discussion of the authority of scripture for our existence as Christians today.

> Blessed Lord, who has caused all holy scriptures to be written for our learning: Grant us so to hear them, read, mark, learn, and inwardly digest them that, by patience and comfort of your holy word, we may embrace and ever hold fast the blessed hope of everlasting life, which you have given us in our Savior Jesus Christ; who lives and reigns with you and the Holy Spirit, one God, for ever and ever. Amen.[1]

1. Adapted by the author from Robert N. Rodenmayer, *The Pastor's Prayerbook,*

## Introduction: Basic Concepts and Terms

### Christian Existence

Of the basic concepts and terms that will be used in our discussion, the first is "Christian existence." To exist in the distinctive way in which any adult human being does is to exist *understandingly*, at the high level made possible by the capacity to use concepts and symbols. One thus has some understanding of oneself and others and of the all-encompassing whole of reality of which both they and oneself are all parts. But, then, to exist in the distinctive way in which a Christian does is to exist with the specific self-understanding and understanding of existence mediated through Christian witness. I say "mediated" through Christian witness because, according to our self-understanding as Christians, we exist "under authority," the faith that we're called to hold being an authorized faith, and the witness that we're in turn called to bear being an authorized witness. Both are authorized, namely, by just that all-encompassing whole of reality that all human beings somehow understand in understanding themselves and others; only now that reality is explicitly understood by us as Christians as the God decisively revealed through Jesus Christ and the Holy Spirit. "Christian existence," then, designates that way of existing humanly, and so understandingly, mediated through the Christian witness of which God, so understood, is the primal authorization.

If we ask now just what way of existing this is, the answer is that it's existing, first of all, in obedient faith in the all-encompassing love of God as decisively disclosed through Jesus and the Spirit; and then, second, in returning love for God and for all whom God loves, which, of course, is everyone. By "faith" here, I mean both unreserved trust or confidence *in* God's love and unqualified loyalty or fidelity *to* God's love, or, as I like to say, to the *cause* of God's love, understanding by this simply the ever greater realization of God's glory in and through the ever greater, more inclusive fulfillment of all of God's creatures. By "love," then, whether our returning love for God or the love for all others as ourselves necessarily included in our love for God, I understand, first, acceptance of others as they really are; and then, second, action toward them informed and guided throughout by just such realistic acceptance. So, as I use terms, "love" is either simply another word for what I mean by "loyalty," or "fidelity," or

*Selected and Arranged for Various Occasions* (New York: Oxford University Press, 1960), 63.

it's the first all-inclusive fruit of faith in this, its second, relatively active aspect, trust or confidence being its first, relatively passive aspect. You'll understand, then, why I so appreciate Paul's formulation when he speaks of "faith active in love" (or, as we may also translate, "faith enacted by love"). I may also point out that Paul exactly parallels this formulation with two other phrases: "a new creation" and "keeping the commandments of God," thereby leaving little doubt about what he means by any of the three phrases (Gal 5:6; 6:15; 1 Cor 7:19).

But if the only faith that's Christian faith is faith active in love, I should also wish to insist that the only love that's Christian love is love incarnating itself in justice: in specific thoughts, words, and deeds whereby others, as ourselves, receive their due. Just as any self-understanding cannot but find expression in some way of leading one's life by all that one believes and does, so a Christian self-understanding in faith and love also inevitably finds expression in what I call a "Christian life-praxis," meaning by that a Christian way of leading one's life by believing and acting according to one's understanding of oneself decisively through Jesus Christ. Understood broadly, then, so as to include not only what it is but also what it necessarily involves, "Christian existence" includes just such a Christian life-praxis as well as the Christian self-understanding I've briefly characterized. Which brings us to the second basic concept and term that we need to clarify.

## Christian Witness

The most common way in which Christians have talked about what I call "Christian life praxis" is to speak, simply, of "Christian witness." By this they mean the testimony they're called to bear by all that they think, say, and do in leading their lives to the twofold assertion constituting all their beliefs and actions as Christians. I refer to their assertion that Jesus is the decisive revelation of the ultimate whole of reality by which they and all other things are encompassed, and that this ultimate whole of reality, which all human beings somehow understand in understanding themselves and others, and which at least some of them already understand and attest as God—that this ultimate whole of reality called "God" is nothing other or less than the "pure, unbounded love" that Jesus reveals it to be.

Several distinctions are commonly made in talking further about Christian witness so understood. One is that between the *direct* witness of Christian proclamation, in the two forms represented by preaching the word and administering the sacraments, and the *indirect* witness of Christian teaching. Whereas proclamation in either of its forms directly calls persons to obedient faith and all that it involves, teaching issues this call to faith only indirectly by spelling out the meaning of faith fully enough so that the decision either to accept the call or to reject it can be conscientiously made. A second common distinction is that between—in my terms—*explicit* witness and *implicit* witness. Explicit witness is the witness Christians bear through the special cultural forms of religion, commonly called *sacred* concepts and symbols, whereas implicit witness is the witness they bear through the so-called *secular* concepts and symbols of the other forms of culture and life-praxis. A third distinction also worth noting is that between the *constitutive* Christian witness, by which the visible church is constituted as such, and thus the witness proper to each and every one of us a Christian; and the *representative* Christian witness whose forms are such things as preaching the word, administering the sacraments, and special ministry, which are ordinarily entrusted, not to all Christians, but only to some. We must always remember, however, that there are representative forms of *implicit* Christian witness, too, as is evident from the visible church's having been represented historically not only by Christian places of worship and schools of theology, but also by such things as Christian hospitals and universities.

Whatever its kind or form, all Christian witness, by its very nature, makes or implies claims to validity. Precisely because their witness is authorized, Christians are not free to think, say, and do anything they please, but are bound to lead their lives so as to bear a witness that is valid, in that it is both adequate to a certain content and fitting to the situation in and for which it is borne. Just insofar as they're conscientious, then, they can't bear the witness they're called to bear without making or implying at least two claims for its validity: for its *adequacy* in expressing the content it's supposed to bear, and for its *fittingness* to the situation in and for which they bear it. Of course, in this as in any comparable case, it's one thing thus to *claim* validity for one's witness, something else again, to *be justified* in doing so. And with this we come to our third basic concept and term.

4

## Christian Theology

Simply put, Christian theology is the ways and means by which Christians accept full responsibility for the claims they make or imply for the validity of their witness, i.e., for both its adequacy to its content and its fittingness to its situation. Here again, as in any comparable case, to accept full responsibility for one's claims to validity is to be willing to validate them critically whenever they become sufficiently problematic to require such validation. Much of the time, the things we think, say, and do in attempting to bear a valid Christian witness may not seem, or even be, all that problematic. But whenever we find ourselves with others who think, say, and do different, not to say contrary, things, the while making or implying the very same claims to validity that we make, we have a problem. Either we simply break off communication with them altogether, and resort to merely strategic action of one sort or another, treating them simply as means to our ends rather than as also ends in themselves; or else we allow our communication with them to rise to the higher level of proper critical reflection. At this level, we each have to take responsibility for giving reasons for our claims and counterclaims in a completely free and open discussion, in which the only constraints are the weightier evidence and the sounder arguments. The name for this higher level of critical reflection when the question to be settled is the real meaning and validity of Christian witness is "Christian theology."

I include asking about "the real *meaning*" of Christian witness as an essential part of this theological question, because it's never proper to ask about the validity of something unless and until you have first understood what it really means. And this explains why, among the three disciplines into which the one field of critical reflection called "Christian theology" naturally breaks down, the first logically is what is usually called "historical theology," "biblical theology" being its first essential part. The distinctive task of historical theology is critically interpreting the real meaning of Christian witness. This is the indispensable first step before critically validating the adequacy of witness to its content and its fittingness to its situation, these being the distinctive tasks of the other two disciplines of "systematic theology" and "practical theology" respectively.

I won't go into any more detail about Christian theology here beyond observing that our discussion in this course is not only to be, as I said in the course statement, "an introductory *theological* discussion," but also, more exactly, an introductory exercise in doing *systematic* theology.

This means that our guiding concern throughout is not to be either simply critically interpreting the meaning of Christian witness or critically validating its claim to be fitting to its situation, but rather critically validating its claim to be adequate to its content. Thus we're to seek an answer to our main question about the authority of scripture for Christian existence today that will be both appropriate to Jesus Christ and credible to human existence—where "appropriate to Jesus Christ" means, "in substantial agreement with or representative of him," and "credible to human existence" means, "worthy of being believed or accepted as true by any and every human being simply as such." In other words, the adequacy to the content of Christian witness that we're to look for in our answer requires that we seek *both* appropriateness *and* credibility in these senses of the words.

## What Is Authority?

### Authority formally defined

Authority is ordinarily a certain kind of relationship between persons. But it's never an egalitarian personal relationship, because it's always between unequals, whether parent and child, master and apprentice, superior and subordinate, or leader and follower. Such inequality is nowhere more obvious than in the authority that has its reason in knowledge. It's simply a fact of life that some of us know more than others, in knowing *how* as well as in knowing *that*. This is why it's often rational for us to defer to the judgment of those who know more than we do, and irrational for us to prefer our own judgment to theirs. Indeed, complying with authority in many matters is usually the easiest way, and sometimes the only way, to make up for our own ignorance and ineptitude.

Upon closer analysis, however, the authority relation proves to be not merely two-termed, but four-termed. It's essentially a relation between, not only (1) a *bearer* and (2) a *subject*, but also (3) a *field*, and (4) a *reason*. Thus we may say, purely formally, "Bearer *A* is an authority for subject *B* in field *C* by reason of *D*." *Example:* "Master mechanic Tom is an authority for apprentice mechanics Dick and Harry in the field of auto repairs by reason of Tom's indefinitely greater knowledge and skill and more extensive experience in repairing automobiles."

*Authority in fact (de facto) and authority by right (de jure)*

With this brief definition in hand, we may turn to the first of three distinctions commonly made with respect to authority that we'll do well to keep in mind throughout our discussion. This is the distinction between authority *in fact* (*de facto*) and authority *by right* (*de jure*). The point of this distinction can be brought out by observing that making or implying a claim to authority is one thing, while doing so validly, because one's claim is justified, is something else. We've already learned from our purely formal definition of authority that A can be an authority for B in field C only for some reason D. But neither A's claim to authority nor B's acceptance of it is valid unless the reason D for A's authority in field C is both relevant and sound. Example: We've all heard of cases which someone impersonates a law-enforcement official in order to obtain favors or to extract money from unwitting victims. But, of course, the authority that such a person claims in fact is not at all authority by right, but is entirely spurious. Nor does the fact that the victims may comply with it make it anything else. To be sure, this is an extreme case, but the difference is not all that great between someone's simply impersonating a public authority for private gain and someone else's accepting appointment to a public office for essentially the same reason without in the least possessing the real competence and commitment necessary to performing its duties. In both cases, the authority in fact is not an authority by right but is either a spurious authority or else an abuse of authority. And in either case, even the most wholehearted compliance with the authority by those purportedly subject to it can do nothing to make it otherwise.

*Causative (or motivating) authority
and normative (or canonical) authority*

A second distinction has been of particular importance in traditional theological discussions of the authority of scripture. This is the distinction between so-called *causative* (or *motivating*) authority and *normative* (or *canonical*) authority. An important implication of this distinction is that one and the same person may function, directly or indirectly, through some agent or instrument, as the bearer of two different kinds of authority. Thus A may directly or indirectly authorize, and so motivate, B to understand her- or himself, or to lead her or his life, in a certain way, thereby exercising the causative or motivating kind of authority.

And *A* may also function, directly or indirectly, as a norm or canon for determining whether *B*'s self-understanding or life-praxis is or is not appropriate—this being an exercise of the normative or canonical kind of authority.

In more recent Protestant theology, this same distinction has sometimes been made simply by distinguishing between the authority of *A* as a *source* and *A*'s authority as a *norm*. But, whatever terms we use to make the distinction, it's important to make it and keep it in mind throughout our inquiry and discussion, since it's arguable that scripture properly exercises both kinds of authority over Christian existence, and so over our own existence as Christians today.

Having yet again used the verb "to authorize," I should briefly explain what I mean by it. I mean both of two things: to entitle, so as to give the *title* or the *right*; and to empower (or enable), so as to give the *power* or the *ability*. On my analysis, entitling and empowering are both present as essential aspects or moments of any authority. But whereas in one kind of authority entitling may be, as it were, dominant, while empowering is recessive, the reverse may be the case in another kind. This difference seems to me to be evident in the two kinds of authority just distinguished: whereas the dominant moment in causative or motivating authority is empowering, entitling being recessive, the reverse is the case in normative or canonical authority, where entitling is the dominant moment, empowering, the recessive.

## Executive authority and nonexecutive authority

The third—and, for our purposes here, final—distinction has been formulated in different terms by different analysts. Without making or implying any claims for its superiority to other formulations, I shall speak simply of *executive* authority, on the one hand, and *nonexecutive* authority, on the other. Probably the easiest way to understand the point of this distinction is to learn from logicians when they distinguish, as they commonly do, between what they call *propositions*, *instructions*, and *performatives*. Roughly speaking, propositions provide the logical contents of indicative sentences, which is to say, sentences to the effect that such and such is the case. Instructions, by contrast, provide the logical contents of imperative sentences instructing or commanding that such and such be done. Performatives, then, provide the contents of sentences that themselves, simply by being uttered, perform or enact what they mean, as when a minister, say, pronounces the absolution of sins: "In Jesus Christ, your sins are forgiven." Again, speaking roughly, instructions and performatives provide the conceptual ways and means for executive authority, while propositions provide such ways and means for nonexecutive authority. *Example*: In the well-known passage in 2 Corinthians 5:17–20, Paul begins as a Christian teacher exercising the nonexecutive authority proper to that office and therefore speaks in indicative sentences expressing propositions: "So if anyone is in Christ, there is a new creation: everything old has passed away; see, everything has become new! All this is from God, who reconciled us to himself through Christ, and has given us the ministry of reconciliation; that is, in Christ God was reconciling the world to himself, not counting their trespasses against them, and entrusting the message of reconciliation to us. So we are ambassadors for Christ, since God is making his appeal through us."

But, then, Paul concludes the passage by shifting abruptly into exercising the executive authority of the Christian preacher by means of an imperative command issuing an instruction: "We entreat you in Christ's stead," he writes, "Be reconciled to God!"

Sometimes theologians have made this distinction between nonexecutive or teaching authority, on the one hand, and executive or proclaiming authority, on the other, by distinguishing between two kinds of personal address: *indirect* and *direct* address respectively. You would be right to infer from what I said earlier that this is only another, verbally different, way of distinguishing between indirect and direct witness. Thus, whereas the address proper to teaching more or less fully spells out the meaning of faith, calling for a decision of faith only indirectly, the address of proclamation or preaching issues the call for a decision of faith directly, as Paul does when he commands, "Be reconciled to God!" But, once again, the terms we use to make the distinction are not all that important as long as we understand and appreciate it sufficiently to be able to use it ourselves whenever it becomes necessary or important to do so.

## The limits of authority

There's one more thing to be said about the meaning of authority whose importance for our purposes would be hard to exaggerate. I refer to what I call, simply, "the limits of authority." Two of these limits will already have become apparent from our very first point, when we defined the authority relation as having not only two terms but four: not only a bearer and a subject, but also a field and a reason. Because any authority is always *in a certain field* and *for a certain reason*, it is never global and unrestricted but always focal and restricted. So the fact that bearer *A* has a sound reason to be accepted as an authority by subject *B* in one field in no way means that *A* has an equally sound reason to claim authority over *B* in some other more or less different field. *Example*: Albert Einstein was a great physicist, and there are reasons both relevant and sound for his high authority in physics as well as in natural science generally. But it in no way follows that there are comparably good reasons for the high authority in matters religious or philosophical with which some of his admirers have endowed him.

There's still another, even more important limit on all authority that we especially need to acknowledge. In the very logic of the case, no appeal to authority, however high, can ever settle such questions as, "Is it really true?" and "Is it really right?" To be sure, appeal to a command issued by a competent official duly appointed to her or his office by law may very well settle the question of whether something is *legally* right within some particular legal system. But the question of whether it is also *morally* right, or even legally right beyond that particular system, remains completely unsettled by any such appeal. Likewise, appeal to the dogmas of a particular religious community may indeed settle the question of whether something is doctrinally true or right within that community as judged by its formal standards of doctrine. But, again, the question of whether it is really true or right, or true or right just for those who acknowledge the authority of these particular standards, remains completely open. In short, saying something's so can never make it true, any more than commanding something to be done can ever make it right. And yet, by its very logic, not even the highest authority can ever do more than say it's so, or command it to be done, leaving questions of truth or right to be answered in some way or ways other than by appeal to authority.

The significance of this for our inquiry here—to put it now in the terms I clarified earlier—is that the normative or canonical authority of even the most authoritative Christian witness can extend at most only to determining the appropriateness of our Christian witness today, never also to determining its credibility. Whether or not our witness is appropriate to Jesus Christ very well can and should be determined by appeal to authoritative Christian witness. But whether or not our witness is credible to human existence, practically as well as theoretically, is not a question that any appeal to authority can ever possibly answer.

## What Is Authoritative Christian Witness?

### Appropriateness and authoritativeness

You'll recall my arguing that all Christian witness, being borne under authority, makes or implies claims to be valid. Just insofar as they're conscientious, Christians can't bear the witness they're called to bear without making or implying at least two claims for its validity: for its *adequacy* in expressing the content it's supposed to bear, and for its *fittingness* to the situation in and for which they bear it. Of course, in this as in any comparable case, it's one thing for Christians to *claim* validity, something else again, for them to *be justified* in claiming it. Which explains, as we've seen, why bearing witness, by its very nature, anticipates also doing theology, insofar as the claims to validity that bearing witness makes or implies become problematic enough to require the critical validation that doing theology alone is able to provide.

Because of our purposes in this course, however, we need to be particularly clear about the first of the two claims to validity. I argued that, in claiming to be adequate to its own content, witness actually makes two claims: both to be *appropriate* to Jesus Christ and to be *credible* to human existence. Here "appropriate to Jesus Christ" means, I said, "in substantial agreement with or faithfully representative of him," while "credible to human existence" means "worthy of being believed or accepted as true by any and every human being simply as such." You may remember that it was just this distinction between appropriateness and credibility that then figured importantly in what I had to say about the limits of authority in concluding my remarks on that topic. The authority of even the most authoritative Christian witness, I said, can extend no further than to determining whether another witness is appropriate, never also to determining whether it is credible.

But because the appropriateness of our witness, even if not its credibility, can be determined only by its authoritativeness, the question of just what authoritative Christian witness is is precisely the question we now have to ask—and, so far as possible, answer.

11

### Substantially authoritative and formally authoritative

The first thing to be said in response to this question is that any Christian witness that's valid in the sense of being appropriate to Jesus Christ is *eo ipso* authoritative. It has the power as well as the right to cause or motivate Christian existence and all that it involves; and it has the right as well as the power to norm or determine whether other Christian faith and witness is appropriate. But there's a distinction to be made between a Christian witness's being *substantially* authoritative, as no witness that is appropriate to Jesus Christ can fail to be, and its also being *formally* authoritative. Any witness that agrees in substance with any other appropriate witness is itself, for that reason, substantially authoritative. But in order to be formally authoritative as well, a witness must be (or be part of) *the* witness, the *one* Christian witness with which any and all other witnesses have to agree in substance in order to be authoritative Christian witness.

Therefore, the question we have to pursue now, in this part of the course, is about the identity of *formally* authoritative Christian witness. And, unfortunately, it's a very real, not to say an intractable, question because there's no consensus in the Christian community, in either witness or theology, about how it's to be answered. As a matter of fact, there's no longer any agreement even about the principle by which formally authoritative Christian witness is to be determined.

### The classical principle of apostolicity

Of course, it's well known to anyone at all acquainted with the history of the scriptural canon that there never has been complete consensus among Christians about just which writings were to be accepted as formally authoritative in fact. Writings long respected and used in certain Christian churches were not used, and were even deemed unusable, in others. So it was well into the fourth century CE before there was a "canon," or official list, of formally authoritative writings that would correspond to what we find in the table of contents of our own New Testaments today. Moreover, as I'm sure all of you know, the main Christian confessions have never been able to reach agreement about just which writings critically appropriated by Christians from Judaism are to be acknowledged as formally authoritative. Whereas Roman Catholics and Orthodox have accepted the larger number of Jewish writings translated into Greek in the so-called Septuagint (LXX), which was the "scripture" used and referred to by most early Christian communities, Protestants, following the Reformers, have acknowledged only the smaller number of writings eventually included in the Jewish canon, thereby excluding those commonly called "the Apocrypha."

But, for all this long-continuing disagreement about which writings are to be accepted as formally authoritative in fact, there's also been widespread agreement from at least the second century about which of them ought to be accepted in principle. The principle, in a word, is *apostolicity*, in the sense that the Christian witness that is formally authoritative is the apostolic witness in the strict meaning of the words, which is to say, the original and originating and therefore constitutive witness of the Christian community. And yet, even where this apostolic principle has been accepted, just what apostolicity is to mean has been profoundly controversial. Although Protestants, Roman Catholics, and Orthodox have all classically accepted apostolicity, they've also understood it in sharply different ways.

To understand this, it will be helpful to recall one of the most important developments in early church history. From roughly the middle of the second century on, many Christian churches increasingly agreed in recognizing three supposedly apostolic authorities: apostolic *canon*, in the sense of an official list of formally authoritative writings; apostolic *tradition*, especially as expressed in creed and in liturgy; and apostolic *ministry*, meaning by this the threefold ministry of bishop, priest, and deacon. Despite this growing agreement, however, there increasingly proved to be very different ways of understanding these three authorities, or, if you will, this threefold structure of authority. Thus, since the Reformation, Protestants have classically affirmed that canon alone is apostolic in principle, in that both tradition in the form of creed and liturgy and a ministry comprising three distinct offices can have only such authority as the canon alone authorizes them to have—hence their motto, "scripture *alone*" (*sola scriptura*). Roman Catholics and Orthodox, on the other hand, have each continued to affirm, or have reaffirmed, their own alternative understandings of "scripture *and* tradition," this being the counterpart motto expressing their different positions on the real meaning of apostolicity. Thus what is apostolic in principle for Roman Catholics classically is canon and tradition as authorized by ministry, specifically, the unique, because supposedly infallible ministry of the Bishop of Rome (i.e., the Pope). For classical Orthodox, on the contrary, who reject papal claims to universal jurisdiction and infallibility in favor of national churches each having its own autonomous head, what is deemed apostolic in principle is canon and ministry as authorized by tradition.

## *The revisionary principle of the historical Jesus*

Nor is this anything like a complete account of the lack of Christian consensus about what is to count as authoritative Christian witness, even in principle. In the modern period, since roughly the late seventeenth and early eighteenth centuries, the classical principle of apostolicity, however understood, has been abandoned altogether, tacitly if not openly, by many Christians, in favor of the very different principle of the historical Jesus. For all who hold this modern revisionary position, it is not the witness of the apostles to Jesus as the Christ, but rather Jesus' own witness to the coming kingdom of God that is accepted as the real original and originating, and therefore constitutive, witness of the Christian community, and, for this reason, the real principle of formal authoritativeness. On this view, in other words, we're Christians, if we are so, not because we believe with the apostles in the significance of Jesus as God's decisive self-revelation, but because we believe with Jesus himself in God's inbreaking reign or rule, Christianity being properly, as they say, the religion *of* Jesus, not the religion *about* Jesus.

## *Ongoing developments in modern*
## *historical-critical study and their impact*

But now ongoing developments in historical-critical study of the Christian past, including, not least, intensive study of the New Testament writings, have raised profound questions about all classical understandings of apostolicity, on the one hand, and all modern revisionary appeals to the so-called historical Jesus, on the other. One after another, all three of the classical apostolic authorities of tradition, ministry, and canon have been shown to be nothing of the kind, because each is demonstrably a *post*apostolic—at the earliest, second-century—development.

Thus, for example, it's now widely accepted that the Apostles' Creed could not possibly have been composed, as pious legend long had it, by the apostles themselves, each contributing one of the articles before leaving on his respective apostolic mission. Nor was it at all possible to trace the classical threefold ministry of bishop, priest, and deacon in an unbroken succession all the way back to the apostles themselves. Indeed, before the middle of the eighteenth century, the chief teacher of my own denomination, John Wesley, had already concluded from the careful scholarship of certain Anglican historical theologians that, being, as he was, an ordained priest of the Church of England, he was already, as he put it, "a scriptural *episcopos*," "*episcopos*" being the Greek word we usually translate with our word "bishop." Why did Wesley conclude this? Well, simply because, in the New Testament writings, the word "*episcopos*" (or "bishop") does not really designate a distinct higher office or order of ministry, but is used there interchangeably with the word "*presbyteros*," which we generally render with "elder" or "priest." So to be a priest, as Wesley was, was already to be a bishop in the New Testament sense of the title.

But the story continues, and the plot thickens. For in the course of the twentieth century, with the still further development of source, form, and tradition criticism of the New Testament writings, we've come to know, if we know anything, that not a single New Testament writing could possibly be apostolic in the strict sense of being original and originating and therefore constitutive Christian witness. How do we know this? We know it simply by learning that there is no New Testament writing whose author does not make use of still earlier Christian witnesses, oral and/or written, as authoritative sources for her or his own formulation of the Christian witness. On the face of it, then, no New Testament writing could itself possibly be apostolic witness in the strict sense of original and originating Christian witness.

This means that the traditional distinction between scripture and tradition simply collapses, rendering both of the classical mottoes, "scripture alone" as well as "scripture and tradition," pointless. Why? Well, because "scripture," which is to say, the New Testament writings, have now, one and all, been shown to be themselves already tradition, even if relatively earlier stages thereof.

At the same time, and for the same reason, we've also learned that even the earliest sources that we're able to reconstruct from the New Testament writings as we now have them provide us neither with Jesus' own witness nor with properly historical reports about it, but with Christian witness of faith to Jesus as of decisive significance for human existence. Consequently, all the modern revisionary appeals to the historical Jesus himself as the alternative principle of formal authoritativeness are as futile and beside the point as all classical appeals to the apostolic canon of scripture. No matter how often and optimistically it may be undertaken, the modern quest of the historical Jesus is doomed to fail right from the start. The only thing our sources allow for is not a quest of the historical Jesus, but only something very different—namely, a historical quest for Jesus, the terminal point of which can never be, in the nature of the case, Jesus himself, but only Jesus as attested, in one way or another, by the earliest Christian witness.

### Either but not both: the demand for fundamental choice

The upshot of these important developments, of which I've given only the sparest account, is that anyone such as myself who stands in the tradition of the Protestant Reformation and is concerned to uphold its principles so far as they're still really tenable, is faced with a fundamental choice that's anything but easy to make. Either one decides for a traditional New Testament canon that one can no longer justify by the early church's own criterion of apostolicity; or else one decides for this same criterion of apostolicity, which now allows one to justify only some different, nontraditional canon.

The position to which I myself finally came is that the principle of apostolicity is as right now as it has been all along. What makes us Christians, if we are such, is not—as modern revisionary Christians would have it—that we believe with Jesus in God, but rather that we believe *in* God, decisively *through* Jesus and the Spirit, *with* the apostles—as well as, of course, with everyone else who has since believed with the apostles, on the basis of their original and originating and therefore constitutive witness to Jesus' decisive significance. But, given the best historical methods and knowledge now available to us, this apostolic principle points, not to scripture, or to the New Testament, but rather to the earliest stratum of Christian witness that can now be reconstructed as formally authoritative Christian witness and as therefore the real apostolic canon of the Christian community.

To be sure, even this earliest and therefore strictly apostolic witness derives its authority solely from a primal source beyond itself—namely, from Jesus Christ and the ultimate, all-encompassing whole of reality that he decisively re-presents as the God of boundless love. But it's equally true to say that it's this earliest Christian witness that is the sole primary authority through which we have anything at all to do, finally, with this sole primal source—with Jesus Christ and the God he re-presents. In other words, *sole primal source of authority*, on the one hand, and *sole primary authority*, on the other, are correlative concepts and terms that can be defined only in relation to one another.

## Neither the canon nor a canon within the canon, but a canon before the canon

Therefore, my own answer to our second question about authoritative Christian witness is that the formally authoritative witness by which all other witness requires to be authorized if it is to be appropriate is the unique, once for all witness of the apostles. But, then, given our best historical methods and knowledge, this means that it is neither the traditional canon of scripture or of the New Testament nor any so called canon *within* that canon but rather the canon *before* the canon constituted by the earliest Christian witness now accessible to us only by way of historical reconstruction. It is this earliest Christian witness that has now become, for us, the sole primary authority by which all other Christian witness, including that of the New Testament writings themselves, has to be authorized if it is to be accepted as appropriate Christian witness.

## What about the Old Testament?

There are two more points to be made about authoritative Christian witness. One has to do with the whole question of the Old Testament, which, as I'm sure you'll have noticed, I've all but completely ignored in our discussion up to this point. The main reason for this is simply that this question is by no means as easy and uncomplicated as many would have it—and that there are (already!) so many questions, and so little time. But I would feel irresponsible if I didn't say at least a few things by way of explaining how I think this question, too, should be clarified and answered, again, given our best historical methods and knowledge today.

The first thing I want to say is that the counterpart criterion to apostolicity that the early church employed in accepting the Hebrew scriptures as canonical was *prophecy*. From a very early time, Christians thought of themselves as belonging to a new community of the last days called out by God decisively through Jesus and built, as one of them put it, "upon the foundation of the apostles and prophets, with Christ Jesus himself as the cornerstone" (Eph 2:20). By "prophets" here, however, early Christians understood, not only the writings eventually included in the Jewish canon, alongside the Torah, or "the Law," as "the Prophets," but literally the whole of the Hebrew scriptures, all of which they read, in accordance with a more or less elaborate scheme of "prophecy and fulfillment," as really only so many prophecies of the coming of Jesus Christ. The big problem with this reading, of course, is that, in the light of what we today must judge to be responsible historical-critical scholarship, there's even less reason to think of any of the Hebrew scriptures as "prophecy" in this sense than there is to think that any of the New Testament writings is "apostolic" in the sense in which the church that canonized them took them all to be so.

This is closely related, then, to a second thing to be said about the Old Testament. It's one thing to accept a writing as itself formally authoritative, as the early church did in deeming certain writings "apostolic," and something very, very different to *use* a writing as authoritative only because, or insofar as, it has first been critically appropriated in the light of something else, oral and/or written, that is the *real* formal authority, not the writing itself. But this latter, of course, is exactly how Christians from the beginning have, for the most part, used the Hebrew scriptures in the light of their own witness to the decisive significance of Jesus Christ. Until the growing acceptance of modern historical-critical scholarship, they have all along used what they call—significantly!—"the *Old* Testament" in the same completely unhistorical way in which many of them have also used—and, I regret to add, continue to use!—the New Testament writings themselves—namely, not by accepting *them* as formally authoritative, but only in the light of the formal authority of *something else*: the traditions of their own churches. This was, as you know, precisely the charge brought by the Protestant Reformers against the traditional Roman Catholic and Orthodox ways of understanding the authority of the apostolic canon. But, as history has now made painfully clear, most Protestants themselves, most of the time, are guilty, in one way or another, of the very practice that their confessional writings so sharply condemn in others. What they read out as "scripture *alone*" is, in reality, "scripture *and tradition*," for it is simply what they themselves have already read into scripture on the authority of their own church traditions.

My point, however, is that it is in just such a thoroughly unhistorical way that Christians, by and large, have always used the Hebrew scriptures, as you'll learn ever so quickly if you ever compare exegetical notes with Jews reading the same writings. Their scriptures became our Old Testament, not by being accepted as formally authoritative in their own right, but only by first being used in the light of the other and very different formal authority of the Christian witness to Jesus as the Christ.

A third and, in this context, final thing to say about the Old Testament is that there's yet another, significantly different way of understanding and using it as authoritative, assuming the answer I've given to our question about formally authoritative Christian witness. This answer means, as I've explained, that the New Testament canon as such becomes, in effect, the primary historical source from which we today have to reconstruct the canon *before* the canon of the earliest Christian witness. But, in an analogous—partly similar, partly different—way, the Old Testament canon as such may be said to become, in effect, the primary historical source in the light of which we alone can understand the main religious and theological assumptions of that same earliest Christian witness.

To be sure, the more immediate historical source of what the earliest Christians assumed was not the Hebrew scriptures as such, but the Judaism contemporary with them: not only Pharisaic Judaism, but especially the so-called apocalyptic Judaism of the sort considerably illumined by the Dead Sea Scrolls discovered only in the last century. Nevertheless, the primary source to which one finally has to look in order to understand Judaism generally and Jewish apocalyptic in particular is precisely the Hebrew scriptures. So, in its own way, the Old Testament canon becomes—or remains—the primary historical source for understanding the assumptions of the earliest Christian witness, even as the New Testament canon, in its different way, is our primary source for historically reconstructing that earliest Christian witness itself.

I shouldn't wish to claim that the distinction I've made between "the assumptions of the earliest witness," on the one hand, and "the earliest witness itself," on the other, is only verbally different from the early church's distinction between "prophecy" and "fulfillment." But the two sets of distinctions are close enough in meaning in certain respects that it's hardly far-fetched to think of the first as perhaps a way given to us today to do at least some of the work that the second, in its time, allowed Christians before us to do.

### *The point of answering this question*
### *as well as the other questions of the course*

My other point may be made quite briefly. Although I have not hesitated to set forth my own answer to our second question about authoritative Christian witness, my purpose in doing so is not primarily to convince you to accept it. On the contrary, in this, as in everything else I shall have had to say in this course, my first concern is to clarify the question itself and to indicate the alternative ways in which it might possibly be answered more or less reasonably by Christians equally committed and sincere in their attempts to do theology and to preach and teach accordingly. Thus, in frankly stating my own answer and explaining, as best I can, why it seems to me preferable to any of the alternatives known to me, I've sought only to engage you in the kind of critical theological thinking for yourselves that you can no more avoid than I can, if you are to accept responsibility for making good on your claim to bear an appropriate Christian witness. It's simply a fact that there is not (and for the near future, at least) probably cannot be, any consensus among Christians about how it should be answered. But be assured that I'll be more than rewarded for my efforts toward initiating our discussion if each of you, for your part, more clearly understands the question itself and the possibilities for answering it, and is, to that extent, furthered in your own efforts to seek and find an answer that's at once adequate and your own.


## What Is the Authority of Scripture?

### *The authority of scripture as secondary to the*
### *primary authority of the apostolic witness*

The answer I shall now give to our central question about the authority of scripture should have been sufficiently well prepared by what I've already said that you will surely have anticipated it. Given our present historical methods and knowledge, as well as a concern to uphold, if tenable, the apostolic principle of the Protestant Reformers, the only conclusion I'm able to draw is that the authority of scripture is the secondary authority that the Reformers themselves assigned to tradition, as distinct from the primary authority they claimed solely for scripture. Not only the New Testament canon as such but all of its individual writings as well must now be said to be precisely tradition, even if relatively early tradition, because, as we've seen, they're not strictly apostolic but postapostolic developments. The writings, one and all, are already later interpretations and reformulations of the original and originating and therefore constitutive witness of the apostles. Far from being written by "disciples at first hand," as Søren Kierkegaard dubbed the apostles, they were all written by certain "disciples at second hand" out of later more or less different historical situations over the roughly eighty-year period from 50 to 130 CE. Therefore, they're themselves each subject to the same two critical questions that can and should be put to all Christian witness after the witness of the apostles and under its sole primary authority. Fully allowing for their different historical situations, and thus for their different concepts and terms and their different life circumstances, we must ask: (1) Are they nonetheless adequate to their content because they're both appropriate to Jesus in his meaning for us and credible to human existence? and (2) Are they fitting to their situation?

## The New Testament as primary historical source

There is, to be sure, the one important difference I acknowledged earlier between the writings of the New Testament and all other, later parts of the Christian tradition. With the exception of a few apocryphal or noncanonical writings roughly contemporary with them—such as the Gospel of Thomas and the Gospel of Philip, for instance—the New Testament writings are our only primary historical sources for reconstructing the earliest Christian witness that came before them and of which they are all more or less adequate and fitting interpretations and reformulations in later situations. The New Testament scholar Willi Marxsen puts this by saying—in my judgment aptly—that the New Testament, although not itself the canon, is the earliest extant volume of Christian sermons claiming to be authorized by the canon, which is to say, by the formally normative witness of the apostles. Of course, as we've seen, it's one thing to *claim* apostolic authorization, something else again to *be justified* in doing so. This is why any sermon claiming to be authorized, including those bound together in the New Testament, requires *to be* authorized, again and again, by the canon that came before it—no differently, in principle, from the way in which all of our own sermons today, and all of our other forms and kinds of witness, continually require to be authorized.

Anyhow, I should say, in somewhat the same way as Marxsen, that, although the New Testament is not itself the sole primary authority by which all Christian witness must be authorized, it nevertheless is, in another sense of the term, the primary *source*—i.e., the primary *historical* source—from which the earliest Christian witness that *is* formally authoritative now has to be reconstructed. I may also remind you of the analogous point I've made about the significance of the Old Testament. Just as the Old Testament writings provide the primary historical source, not for reconstructing, but for understanding the most fundamental religious and theological assumptions of the apostolic witness, so the New Testament writings provide the primary historical source for reconstructing the apostolic witness itself.

### Authorizing Christian witness today by the canon before the canon

Even so, the authority of scripture for Christian existence today is not primary but secondary, not original but derived—namely, from the original and originating and therefore constitutive witness of the apostles, which alone is formally authoritative Christian witness and therefore alone canonical. Consequently, to establish that a witness borne today may fairly claim the authority of scripture is not, in and of itself, sufficient to authorize the witness as appropriate. Further necessary to authorizing its appropriateness is establishing that the scriptural witness by whose authority it may fairly claim to be appropriate is itself authorized, in turn, by the witness of the apostles. How so? Well, because, being itself in substantial agreement with the apostolic witness, it is insofar appropriate to Jesus Christ, and so primally authorized through him and by the ultimate, all-encompassing whole of reality that he decisively re-presents as the God of boundless love.

### Following the trajectory of all historical-critical study of scripture

There are two other things I wish to do before concluding this third main part of our discussion. The first is to say at least a bit more about the process of historical reconstruction to which I've continually referred in what I've already said. From the seventeenth century on, when more and more students of the biblical writings began to apply to them the methods and knowledge of critical historical scholarship generally, the basic method they've followed is analysis of the whole into its ever smaller parts so as to reconstruct the history lying behind them as well as the history leading up to the whole itself. Thus the first important differentiation was of the New Testament from the Old. Then came analysis of the individual New Testament writings themselves, not only into their different literary types or genres—gospels, epistolary literature, and so on—but also as having been written at different times and in different places by different authors, over a fairly extensive period of, as I have said before, some eighty years. This was quickly followed, then, by source-critical study of the different individual writings, the results of which were to show, for instance, that the first three gospels are as closely related as they obviously are because the first and the third—Matthew and Luke—are extensively dependent, in different ways, on the same two written sources: both the second gospel, Mark, and yet another hypothetical source composed of sayings attributed to Jesus now known to scholars as Q (after the German word *Quelle*, meaning "source"). The next important breakthrough, then, was so-called form criticism, which, beginning with the insight that the still earlier sources behind even the written sources of the New Testament were oral, proceeded to apply to their analysis the methods and knowledge that scholars had already developed for studying folklore and oral traditions generally. Reversing this analytic process, then, scholars have been able to reconstruct the whole history prior to and ending in the New Testament writings as we now have them. Naturally, comments closely parallel to these could also be made about concurrent developments in the historical-critical study of the Old Testament writings.

I apologize for the roughness of this all-too-brief historical sketch. But I trust it will at least make clear how the whole development of modern historical-critical study of the New Testament, proceeding as it has by refinement after refinement of methods of analysis, has resulted in one, long and still ongoing process of historical reconstruction. So, in arguing, as I have, that, for us today, standing well along in this process, the real canon of the Christian community can be identified only as a canon *before* the scriptural canon that therefore requires to be historically reconstructed, I have in no way implied that we now have to proceed by some other, new, and different method, hitherto unknown. No, I've appealed only to the very same method of historical analysis and reconstruction already extensively developed and refined over the whole course of modern critical study of the New Testament.

I would recall in this connection the comments I made on the revisionary alternative of appealing to the witness of the historical Jesus himself, instead of to the witness of the apostles, as formally authoritative.

As scholars have known now for a century, the only sources available for Jesus' own witness are not primary but only secondary. We do not have a single line written by Jesus, and—for all we know to the contrary—not one of his own sayings, as distinct from sayings attributed to him by his followers at successive stages of the early church's witness. The result is that, if Jesus' own witness were to be the formal principle for determining the appropriateness of all other Christian witness, there would be no way of ever applying it, because his own witness as such would remain inaccessible. Or—to take the other horn of the dilemma now facing revisionary Christians—if it were to be held sufficient to appeal not to Jesus' own witness but simply to that borne to him by the earliest Christian community, then one would have given up the principle of the historical Jesus himself in everything but the name in favor of a position more or less like my own.

And yet, as true as this seems to me to be, I'm far from suggesting that there is no positive theological significance to the so-called quest of the historical Jesus, especially in its later, increasingly refined phases, such as are represented in our own country by the work of the so-called Jesus Seminar. Regardless of the self-understanding of the questers, who have refined the methods and produced the results of the quest, the fact remains that they have already been carrying out the very work of historical reconstruction on which all of us today have to depend if we're to appeal to the real Christian (because formally apostolic) canon. Precisely if one makes the decision I make to uphold the traditional principle of apostolicity, the first thing one has to do to apply this principle is to reconstruct by critical analysis and synthesis the history of tradition—oral as well as written—lying behind the New Testament writings. Only so can one establish the earliest and therefore formally apostolic stratum in this tradition. But this, of course, is exactly what one has to do insofar as one is to make any responsible historical judgments about Jesus himself. Therefore, even if one in no way shares the usual motives and objectives of the quest of the historical Jesus, one may gratefully appropriate its methods and results as the very things one needs in order to reconstruct the real canon *before* the canon: the apostolic witness.

At the very least, however, one is spared having to make the final inference that anyone engaged in the quest is obliged to make, but that our sources, by their very nature, preclude anyone's making successfully—namely, the inference from the earliest Christian witness that *can* be historically reconstructed to the witness of Jesus himself that *cannot*.

As surely as we can distinguish the two witnesses *theoretically*, they are—and, for all anyone can tell, will always remain—indistinguishable *operationally*, all the available evidence for either being the same as for the other.

To be sure, it lies in the nature of the case that the results of any historical reconstruction remain ever subject to criticism and that complete agreement among historians is hardly to be hoped for. But every possible answer to the main question before us in this course is bound to have its peculiar problems and difficulties, and, in any case, we simply have to accept the fact that any answer we ourselves give is not an answer for all situations but only for our own. At best, it will remain ever relative to the circumstances of our own situation today, with its particular problems and resources for solving them, and, even then, it'll be only one of the possible answers that equally sincere and responsible Christians and theologians may give to the question. But my point is that the answer I'm arguing for in no way departs from the now well-established tradition of modern biblical scholarship, but only follows its clear trajectory and requires no other methods than such as it has long since developed, refined, and applied.

### Applying Luther's "true test" of all "genuine sacred books"

The other thing I have to do is to point out yet another important respect in which the position I've argued for is not really as novel or unheard of as you might suppose. I refer to the clear precedent already set by none other than Martin Luther himself for asserting the authority of scripture to be in effect secondary to the sole primary authority of the apostolic witness. I say Luther asserts this "in effect," because he nowhere—to my knowledge—puts it as I have, in just so many words; and any careful reader can find him assuming, if not asserting, again and again, the generally accepted understanding of his time concerning the uniform authority and inspiration of scripture. Even so, there can be no mistaking his meaning when he says, "All the genuine sacred books agree in this, that they all preach and push Christ. And this is the true test by which to judge all books, when one sees whether they push Christ or not, since all scripture shows us Christ (Romans 3), and Paul will know nothing but Christ (1 Corinthians 2). What does not teach Christ is not apostolic, even though Peter or Paul teach it; again, what preaches Christ is apostolic even though Judas, Annas, Pilate, and Herod do it."

It was on the basis of just such reasoning, of course, that Luther voiced the deepest reservations about some of the New Testament writings, especially the Letter of James, dismissing it, in a well-known saying, as "an epistle of straw," fit only for lighting fires.

I can't go into any more detail concerning Luther's own, in its way, uncommonly critical understanding and use of scripture. Nor will I say anything more about an important difference between his use of the term "apostolic" in the passage cited and my own use of it in explaining my position. But, again, I trust I've said enough to make clear that even for the first among the Protestant Reformers, commitment to "scripture alone" in no way excluded judging the genuineness of "*all* books" by the "true test" of the apostolic witness.

## How Is Scripture to Be Interpreted in Order to Be Authoritative?

### *Summary of the argument to this point*

I proceed by first briefly summarizing the preceding argument. Essential to the answer I've given to our main question is the judgment that, since none of the usual ways of identifying formally authoritative Christian witness, whether classical or revisionary, is any longer tenable, there's nothing to be done except to find some other way. Thus, over against all classical positions, including the Protestant position of "scripture alone," I've argued that either one has to abandon the principle of apostolicity in order to continue to appeal to the three classical apostolic authorities of canon, tradition, and ministry in one combination or another; or else one opts to uphold the classical apostolic principle, but then can apply it to validate only another earlier, nonclassical authority as apostolic. Against revisionary positions, on the other hand, I've argued that either one continues to appeal to the alternative principle of the historical Jesus, even though one's appeal can never be carried out because, given our sources, the historical Jesus as such is inaccessible to us; or else one settles for the only thing that is historically accessible, namely, the earliest church's witness to Jesus, only thereby to give up the principle—in effect if not in so many words—that it is the historical Jesus himself who is formally authoritative.

My own position, then, as I have explained it, is a third, or, as it were, mean or median, position between the classical and the revisionary extremes. On the one hand, it agrees with classical positions in accepting the principle of apostolicity over against revisionary appeals to the principle of the historical Jesus. On the other hand, it insists that the only witness that can now be validated by the apostolic principle is not, as all classical positions hold, the canon of the New Testament, but rather a canon *before* the New Testament canon. This canon, however, is not the historical Jesus, as revisionary positions typically hold, but rather the earliest Christian witness or witnesses to Jesus that we now can and must reconstruct by applying our own historical-critical methods and knowledge.

The conclusion of my argument so far, then, is that the authority of scripture, and therefore its authority for Christian existence, is not original but derived, not primary but secondary. Contrary to the traditional claim that scripture is the authority that authorizes, but that itself is not authorized, scripture, also, is an *authorized* authority. This means that it itself is ever *to be authorized* by the sole primary authority of the apostolic witness, of which the New Testament writings themselves are one and all later interpretations and reformulations—each more or less adequate to its content and fitting to its situation in its other more or less different historical circumstances.

## *The question of interpretation (or hermeneutics)*

But now to know that the authority of scripture is not primary but secondary is to know only one of two things one has to know in order to comply with scripture's authority for Christian existence today. The other thing one has to know is how scripture is to be interpreted in order to function as the secondary authority it is. In the nature of the case, no authority can function as such unless it's understood, and this means, unless it's somehow interpreted, and—for us today, certainly—also reformulated in concepts and terms other than its own.

Allow me to dwell on this a moment, because it's an important point that's often forgotten or ignored. No doubt, because understanding one another is so vitally important to us as human beings that most of us become more or less adept at it at a fairly early age, we're usually unaware of the actual work of interpretation and reformulation that's already involved even in our ordinary day-to-day communications with one another. Thus we're apt to suppose, for example, that interpreting something said to us and putting it in other words is some wholly secondary, for the most part, unnecessary process that we have to resort to only in special circumstances, such as having to communicate it to a third party—to a child, say, or to someone else who, for some reason, has yet to attain mastery of the language. But this is to forget or ignore the considerable work of interpretation and even reformulation that has always already gone on, however spontaneously and rapidly, simply in our understanding what was said ourselves, never mind communicating it to anybody else. We can understand what we hear or read and make it really our own only by somehow interpreting it—and that always involves at least two things: (1) taking it as addressed to some question or other that we ourselves are asking, or are able to ask; and (2) grasping it in concepts and terms that are wholly our own, even as we may hope they are also appropriate to catching its meaning.

To recognize this is to understand that and why there's always more than one way of interpreting anything, depending both on the question we take it to address and on the concepts and terms in which we attempt to grasp its meaning. The question is unavoidable, then, how any authority is to be interpreted if it's to exercise its authorizing function, and scripture's no exception to the rule. In its case, also, we must ask how it is to be interpreted in order for it to be authoritative for our existence as Christians today. We may know, as I, for one, think I do, that, however it's interpreted, the results of any interpretation always have to be controlled or tested by the sole primary authority of the apostolic witness before they can be deemed appropriate Christian witness. But this only raises the further question of how the apostolic witness itself has to be interpreted in order to function as just such a primary control or test of appropriateness. In short, we simply have to ask the question of interpretation, or, to use the technical term that theologians and other specialists generally use, *the question of hermeneutics*—the word "hermeneutics" referring to both the practice (or, really, the art) *and* the theory of interpreting meaning somehow fixed in symbols, especially in writing.

### An answer to the question: existentialist interpretation

My own answer to this fourth—and, for our inquiry, final—question I shall put first summarily: If scripture is to be authoritative for our existence as Christians today, the interpretation called for, both of it and of the apostolic witness by which it is always to be authorized, is *existentialist interpretation.* I shall now proceed to unpack this summary statement, prefacing it with a brief definition of terms.

By "existentialist interpretation," I understand an interpretation (1) guided by our existential question about the meaning of our existence as human beings in its ultimate setting; and (2) formulated in concepts and terms appropriate to thinking and speaking about human existence (in other words, just such concepts and terms as I began the course by trying to clarify and have been using ever since: "existence," "self-understanding," "life-praxis," "self, others, and the whole," and so on).

The first thing I wish to say is that existentialist interpretation, like any other, necessarily presupposes, even as it also goes well beyond, both what is properly meant by "historical-critical interpretation" and what I shall call, for want of a better term, "literary-critical interpretation." Whatever the question a scriptural writing itself addresses, or that different interpreters, for their part, may have an interest in putting to it and so take it as addressing, it is given as such precisely as a writing, and as something, therefore, that, in different respects, is both historical and literary. This means, given the developed state of historical-critical interpretation today, that existentialist interpretation necessarily presupposes such things as text criticism and source criticism as well as form criticism and tradition or redaction criticism. But, then, it also presupposes literary-critical interpretation insofar as the text yielded by these several forms of historical-critical research is, in any case, a piece of literature as well as of history and therefore demands to be interpreted accordingly. This means that it is to be interpreted in accordance with its particular literary kind or genre as well as with the grammatical rules of the language in which it's written, its particular literary style, and the linguistic usage distinctive of its individual author as well as of her or his historical period and situation. But all this and several other things that could be said to belong to the necessary presuppositions of existentialist interpretation are only that—its *presuppositions*, not existentialist interpretation itself, properly as such.

It itself, as its name indicates and as I've already allowed, is an interpretation of a text guided or oriented by *the* existential question: the vital question that we human beings generally seem concerned to ask and answer about the meaning of our own lives in their ultimate context, and therefore about the meaning of ultimate reality for us and about how we both can and should understand ourselves in relation to it. Therefore, existentialist interpretation so interprets both the New Testament writings and the apostolic witness of which they are all later interpretations and reformulations as to make explicit the answer they give or imply to *this* existential question. This it does by explicating the faith or self-understanding of which these writings themselves, as precisely witnesses of faith, are all more or less adequate and fitting expressions. This means—to put it in the terms of our original definition of authority—that, for existentialist interpretation, the *field* in which both scripture and the apostolic witness are authoritative is the field defined by *the* existential question; and that the *reason* they're authoritative, insofar as they are so, is that the answer they express or imply to this basic human question is true. In other words, what is authoritative for existentialist interpretation in both the New Testament writings and the apostolic witness—and the *only* thing that's authoritative in them—is the self-understanding of faith out of which they all arose, and to the further actualization of which they are all directly or indirectly addressed. Being written from faith and for faith, it is matters of faith, and *only* such matters, about which they're authoritative—which means that they're authoritative concerning our self-understanding as human beings and the understanding of existence correlative with it. This includes, naturally, whatever is necessarily presupposed and implied by our self-understanding for our life-praxis, and thus for both our belief and our action—for the things that we are to believe (*credenda*) and for the things that we are to do (*agenda*).

This means, then, that existentialist interpretation can itself be held to be the appropriate way to interpret scripture as authoritative for Christian existence only to the extent that the scriptural writings and the apostolic witness by which they're primarily to be controlled or tested are themselves addressed precisely to the existential question about the meaning of human existence. The traditional way, in orthodox Protestant theology, of asserting that this is exactly what they are addressed to is disclosed by its discussions of "the attributes of scripture," one of which is its "perfection." Scripture is held to be perfect, not globally or in all respects, but rather focally or in one respect only. Its perfection, as it's put, is a *perfectio respectu finis*, literally a "perfection with respect to the end," this end being, of course, *the* end, the one *ultimate* end, of human salvation or authenticity.

I may add that exactly the same point is also made, in its different way, by the Collect for the Second Sunday in Advent in the old Book of Common Prayer with which I opened our course. What is the end for which God, according to this Collect, has caused all holy scriptures to be written but "our learning"; and to what end are we to "hear them, read, mark, learn, and inwardly digest them" but to "embrace, and ever hold fast, the blessed hope of everlasting life which [God] has given us in our Savior Jesus Christ"?

I do not hesitate to say, then, that, when it's viewed against the background of such traditional ways of putting the matter, my demand for existentialist interpretation may be seen to be simply a contemporary and somewhat more formal way of making substantially the same point about how scripture is to be interpreted and reformulated if it's to function authoritatively for our existence as Christians today.

## The approach of existentialist interpretation and its scope

I'm sure you'll have no trouble imagining that there's ever so much more that could and should be said not only about existentialist interpretation—about what it is and what it isn't—but also in order to illustrate just how it's to be carried out in interpreting specific texts. But I shall briefly make only two points before my closing comments.

The first has to do with how one is to approach any text in order to carry out a proper existentialist interpretation of it. Luther often quipped, "What good is it if there's a God if there isn't any God *for you*?"—or, as we'd need to translate to feel the full force of his German, "*for thee*"—in other words, not for you wholesale, or collectively, but *for you retail, or individually*. Just as each of us is, in Kierkegaard's phrase, "the single individual," who has to do her or his own living and dying, so each of us also has to do her or his own *faithing*, if I may coin a participle that doesn't exist in the English language. But, then, we must also each ask for ourselves and in our own individual way the existential question about the meaning of our lives: not as a question about the meaning of human life in general, such as philosophy might well be expected to ask, but as a question about the meaning of *my own* individual life in particular, here and now, in this concrete moment in which I've been given and called to live. Only by so asking can I approach any text in the way that existentialist interpretation of it requires, be it a text in the New Testament or a text that, having been historically reconstructed using the New Testament writings as sources, can be reasonably deemed to be (or to be a part of) the apostolic witness by which the appropriateness of the New Testament writings themselves is ever to be tested or controlled. But this necessary condition of existentialist interpretation is also its sufficient condition, assuming only that I'm at least able to understand what the text actually *says*; for to ask just this existential question as *my* question is the only other thing needed in order to hear what any text, either in the New Testament or as reconstructed from its writings, not only says, but *means*.

My second point has to do with just how utterly comprehensive the field of authority defined by the existential question really is. Critics of existentialist interpretation sometimes object that it's "too individualistic," being guided only by my own existential question and concerned only with how I'm given and called to understand myself and to lead my life as an individual if I'm to do so truly and authentically. But this objection is completely wide of the mark if existentialist interpretation is understood in the sense in which I'm calling for it here. Precisely in existing understandingly, as every human being does and must, she or he understands, in a certain way, or to a certain extent, everything: not only her- or himself, but also all others and, most important, the ultimate, all-encompassing whole of reality of which self and all others are parts. But, as we saw at the outset, in clarifying the term "Christian existence," to exist Christianly, as every Christian does and must, has exactly this same utterly comprehensive scope. Although it is mediated by specifically Christian witness, it, too, is an understanding of nothing less than everything—self, others, and the whole, only now disclosed decisively through Jesus Christ and the Holy Spirit as creature together with fellow creatures, all embraced by the boundless love of the Creator, of God the Father. Moreover, because, as we also saw right from the beginning, there's no Christian faith that's not a faith active in love, and no Christian love that's not a love incarnating itself in concrete words and deeds of justice, it should be clear to anyone who has eyes to see that Christian existence, understood for what it really is, in all its length and breadth, in all its presuppositions and implications, involves absolutely everything, from the most abstract truths of metaphysics to the most concrete demands of morality and politics. So don't ever underestimate just how comprehensive an existentialist interpretation of scripture really is, when it's as fully carried out as it can and should be.

*Concluding comments on the order of interpretation—*
*and by way of a final summary*

This brings me to some concluding comments. Scripture, I've argued, is to be interpreted in existentialist terms and therefore with reference, first of all, to its self-understanding of faith and then to all that it proclaims or teaches concerning belief and action, from—as I've just said—metaphysics to morality and politics. But the order of interpretation indicated here is, to my mind, of the utmost importance. The first and foremost thing about the authority of scripture, for us today as surely as for any other Christians who could ever possibly be subject to it, is the self-understanding of faith of which its several writings are one and all interpretations and formulations. On the other hand, all the particular beliefs expressed in scripture as well as all its specific teachings concerning action are authoritative for us today, as for any later generation, only insofar as they really do appropriately formulate the necessary presuppositions and implications of faith's self-understanding and are not simply the beliefs and teachings of another age whose assumptions were very different from our own. To the extent, however, that they're *not* thus appropriate to the self-understanding of faith, they have no authority for us today, beyond reminding us that faith, by its very nature, necessarily has just such presuppositions and implications for both belief and action: for what we're to believe about ultimate reality in its structure in itself and for how we're to act and what we're to do given all the vital interests affected by our action and the circumstances in which we have to act.

In the light of all that I've said, I don't have to explain, I think, that exactly the same must be true not only in interpreting scripture but also in interpreting the formally authoritative witness of the apostles themselves, by which, as I've argued, all other witness, including scripture's, always has to be authorized if it's to be appropriate to Jesus Christ and so itself substantially authoritative. Even here, the first and foremost thing to be interpreted is always the self-understanding of faith attested by the witness. Thereupon, one must go on and interpret the particular beliefs taken to be either presupposed or implied by this self-understanding as well as the specific consequences for action taken to follow from it. These are likewise authoritative for our existence as Christians today only because or insofar as it really does necessarily presuppose and imply them. To whatever extent, however, they're *not* thus presupposed and implied by faith itself, but are due simply to the assumptions that the first Christians perforce had to make in explicating their witness, or are the consequences they then drew in trying to apply it in their own lives, they have no more authority for us than the beliefs and teachings of the later New Testament writings or of any other still later stages of Christian tradition. Why not? Well, because what makes us Christians, insofar as we are such, is not that we share the assumptions made or the consequences drawn by any of our forebears in the faith, including the earliest Christians we call the apostles. Rather, it is that we share their self-understanding of faith and then, like them, seek to lead our lives accordingly, bearing witness to our faith by, among other things, explicating its necessary presuppositions and implications for both belief and action in the most appropriate and credible concepts and terms available to us in our situation—and, above all, so acting in our situation as to incarnate our love for others as ourselves concretely, in specific acts of justice.

In sum, the authority of scripture for Christian existence today is the authority it has as witness of faith authorized by the self-understanding of the formally authoritative witness of the apostles. Thus the New Testament writings are authoritative for us, for our own faith and witness, to the precise extent to which they appropriately interpret and reformulate the witness of the apostles and fittingly represent that witness in their own new and different situations, which are also different—in important respects, profoundly different—from our situation today. But if scripture is to function in this way as authoritative for our own faith and witness, both it and the apostolic witness by which it is always to be authorized require to be interpreted as precisely witness of faith. And this means that the interpretation called for can only be existentialist interpretation, so understood and practiced as to include interpretation not only of the self-understanding of faith but also of all that it presupposes and implies for our belief and action today, including, not least, our political action.

> O God, by whom the meek are guided in judgment and light rises up in darkness for those who seek it; grant us, in all our doubts and uncertainties, the grace ever to ask what you would have us believe and do, that the Spirit of wisdom may save us from all false choices, and that in your light we may see light, and in your straight path may not stumble; through Jesus Christ our Lord. Amen.[2]

2. Adapted by the author from ibid., 7.

# 2

# The Apostles' Creed: Is It Credible?

Christian faith, being trust in God and loyalty to God, is other and more than Christian belief. But faith would be groundless were the belief it necessarily implies not credible, not worthy of being believed. So there are good reasons why Christians have formulated their belief and handed it down in short summaries like the Apostles' Creed, and also why the question of the credibility of any such summary may always become a more or less urgent theological question. This is particularly true in our situation today when, for many persons within the church and without it, the apparent incredibility of many traditional Christian beliefs has become a stumbling block to wholeminded as well as wholehearted commitment to Jesus Christ. This seminar is designed to remove any false stumbling block that the Apostles' Creed may pose by taking a closer look at its proper use in the economy of the Christian life, the faith of which it is the symbol, and the belief it does and does not require of us.

> O God, we beseech you, make us honest money changers, so that in rendering your eternal gospel in currency of the present day, we may give full value for what we have received; through Jesus Christ our Lord. Amen.[1]

---

1. Adapted by the author from Robert N. Rodenmayer, *The Pastor's Prayerbook, Selected and Arranged for Various Occasions* (New York: Oxford University Press, 1960), 153.

# I Believe in . . .

## Introduction

What I propose to do in this seminar and why I want to do it is indicated in the course statement above. But I would like to say just a word more about the audience I've mainly had in mind in conceiving and planning it—and in writing my lectures. As in most of my work as a theologian and as a Christian teacher, I've been particularly mindful of two related but distinct groups of persons with whom I've become ever better acquainted in doing my job. In one group are those who would like to think of themselves as Christians, and who for the most part actually do, because they either accept or at least remain powerfully attracted by the offer of radical freedom that is decisively re-presented to them through Jesus and the church. At the same time, they are continually in doubt about whether they should really call themselves Christians after all; for even though they may be willing to entrust themselves unreservedly to the mysterious ultimate whole of reality encompassing them, and to love both themselves and all others in their unqualified loyalty to that same encompassing whole, they're still not able to accept honestly and with integrity at least some of the beliefs that appear to be set forth in the Apostles' Creed—and that ever so many of their fellow Christians are quick to assure them are "fundamentals" of the faith. In the other group are those who regard themselves as non-Christians, or no longer Christians, and who, whenever they hear of Christian faith, immediately think of the Apostles' Creed or some other creed and of the several beliefs that it appears to require of anyone who would affirm it. Because they're quite unable to come to terms with these beliefs (some of them, at any rate), they never get to the point of being confronted with the gift and demand of radical freedom that is decisively re-presented to them through Jesus as the church is called to bear witness to him.

I have no way of knowing how many of you here would count yourselves as belonging to one or the other of these groups. Nor do I have any way of telling the extent to which what I shall have to say, and what we shall then be saying in our discussions together, is likely to speak to the needs of persons in either group. But I'm quite clear that it's especially to them, whether they're within the church or outside it, that anything said today in response to our question needs to be addressed. And I shall feel more than rewarded for my part in our seminar if any of you who is sensible of having any such needs as your own finds something in it that helps you to meet them.

As for how I myself incline to answer our question, I will say at this point only this: Yes, the Apostles' Creed *is* credible—or, at any rate, cannot be easily dismissed as *in*credible—but only if we correctly understand its meaning, which is to say, its proper use in the whole economy of the Christian life and what it does, and does not, require of us if we are to make it our own and affirm it honestly and with integrity. Having said this, however, I hasten to add that it is not the purpose either of the seminar or of my lectures to argue for an affirmative answer to our question. Instead, the seminar is limited, and I shall limit myself throughout it, to the essential preliminary or preparatory work of achieving just such a correct understanding of the Creed's meaning, which is to say: of its proper use in living as a Christian and of what one does, and does not, commit oneself to in affirming it as one's own.

## Why is the Creed a problem for many of us?

This is obviously what a logician would call "a complex question." In much the same way as the well-known prosecutor's query, "When did you stop beating your wife?" it rests on the answer to another prior question whose validity can in principle be challenged. But that many of us today have a problem with the Creed—some of us, indeed, a very serious problem—seems to me in fact unchallengeable. So the pertinent question is not whether this is so, but only why. There are, in my judgment at least three reasons that are well worth thinking about.

First of all, the Creed is a problem for many of us *because or insofar as, being adult human beings living at this time and place in history, we are more likely than not to have acquired a differentiated consciousness.* This means that ours is likely to be a consciousness such as could hardly have belonged—and therefore may not be fairly attributed—to the early Christians to whom we owe all the classic formulations of the meaning of Christian faith. These include formulations both in the earlier Christian tradition usually called "scripture" and in the later tradition commonly distinguished from scripture as simply "tradition." And included in the latter are all the classic creeds of the church, foremost among which, for those of us in the West, is the Apostles' Creed.

Along with the gradual emergence of civilization in the proper sense has gone not only an ever-increasing division of labor, but also a further differentiation of consciousness. Just as many different jobs in society that were once done by a single person have increasingly come to be done by many persons, so concepts and terms that once served to perform many different tasks have come to be differentiated into their various different uses—or else to be supplemented by still other concepts and terms more apt for doing some of the jobs they once used to do. The result is that we're much more likely now to be aware of the important differences, say, between common sense and science, on the one hand, and religion (as well as theology and philosophy), on the other. Thus religious concepts and symbols, for many of us, are understood to have to do with something logically very different from what common sense and science are concerned with. Furthermore, we no longer think of them as having to do with some other world beyond the world in which we live, but rather with the ultimate reality and meaning of this our world itself. Instead of understanding them to refer merely to something *other*, some other item alongside the countless items that make up any world, we are disposed to take them as referring to something *more*, another aspect or dimension of our world that is therefore logically different from any and all of its items, whether actual or possible. So when we wish to express the unusual value or significance of some person or happening, say, we don't find ourselves doing what admirers of a folk hero like Davy Crockett once did with their legends and myths—assuring us that Davy is always there, every morning, helping the sun to come up on time. For us, an item is one thing, the value or significance of an item, something else: not just another item, however extraordinary, but something logically very different because, although always associated with items and even somehow dependent on them, it is logically something more than any item.

In other words, religion for us has to do, not with yet other exotic items alongside the ordinary items of our lives, but with the value or significance of *all* items: with our so understanding ourselves in relation to all of them as to be and become who we really are, instead of being and remaining lost in the profound self-*misunderstanding* of ordinary human existence as most of us try to live it most of the time. To the extent that this is true of us, however, the Creed cannot but be more or less a problem for us, and we can neither understand it nor make it our own except by critically appropriating it: by interpreting the concepts and symbols in which it is formulated into other concepts and terms more appropriate for expressing its religious meaning to persons like ourselves, given our more differentiated consciousness.

The Creed is a problem for us, secondly, however, *because or insofar as just what is properly meant by "Christian faith and belief" has long since become seriously confused in the churches as well as in secular culture generally.* "Faith," in its Christian sense, means primarily obedient *belief in* the One whom we have come to know as God through the event of Jesus Christ and the witness of the church. But from a very early time, as already attested by some of the New Testament writings themselves— notably, the Letter of James—faith, though primarily *belief in,* has been identified simply with *belief that* certain religious assertions are true. Thus what was originally understood (in much of the New Testament) to be, first of all, a matter of existential trust and loyalty has since come to be understood primarily, if not only, as a matter of intellectual assent and assertion. And this confusion has been the more difficult to overcome because Christian faith, as we shall see, is, in fact, both—both *belief in* and *belief that* or, better, it is *belief that* precisely because it is, in the first place, *belief in.* Because it is not just another human attitude or feeling, but the confidence in God and the fidelity to God called forth in a person by God Godself as revealed to us decisively through Jesus Christ and the church, faith, precisely in being *belief in,* is also, if only implicitly, *belief that*—namely, *belief that* the strictly ultimate mysterious reality called "God" really is the One who is revealed to us decisively through Jesus as attested by the church. This is the main reason, indeed, why, almost from the beginning, Christian faith has always found expression in certain *beliefs that* and that, eventually, the formal statements of belief that are the creeds—including the Apostles' Creed—came into being. Even so, these are not the only reasons such formulations of belief and creeds come to be, and, once they're on the scene, other reasons may make it all but inevitable that faith will again and again be misunderstood as primarily a matter of assent to certain religious assertions rather than confidence in God Godself and faithfulness to God as God is revealed to us through Jesus and the church's witness.

Of course, beginning with the Reformation, this traditional confusion was challenged, happily, by recovering the predominant New Testament meaning of "faith"; and subsequent developments having an especial effect on American Protestantism have made it harder, although hardly impossible, for many of us here, ever simply to identify faith with creedal belief. On the other hand, not the least fallout from the so-called modernist-fundamentalist controversy at the beginning of the last century has been the reinstatement of this traditional confusion. The so-called "fundamentals" that modernists were alleged to be denying and that fundamentalists, for their part, were bent on vigorously reasserting were certain religious assertions, assent to which and assertion of which in turn were held to be foundational for Christian existence. And so it is that, for many of us, living as we do in what has turned out to be really only a later phase of this same continuing controversy, creeds and other formal statements of belief have come to seem at best of decidedly secondary importance for Christian faith and life, and at worst to place demands on us that we cannot in conscience pretend to meet. In either case, the Apostles' Creed, along with other traditional formulations of Christian belief, has become a problem for us, and its credibility, as often as not, a serious question.

The Creed is also a problem for many of us, I think, for yet a third reason: *because or insofar as we have forgotten or ignored its proper use and, in particular, its ancient connection with baptism.* Speaking very generally, we may say that formulations of belief—including the creeds of the ancient church, of which the Apostles' Creed is almost certainly the best known to most of us—have served three main functions: (1) *liturgical*, as an integral component of the public worship of God; (2) *catechetical*, as a resource for instructing persons in Christian faith and belief; and (3) *polemical*, as a means of defining valid Christian faith and belief over against invalid, as well as against other forms of false religion. We also know, however, that what eventually became our Apostles' Creed was originally used as a baptismal symbol. The Greek word *"symbolon"* (Latin: *"symbolum"*), in this context, apparently meant a sign or signal of recognition by which human beings somehow identified themselves and one another—such as, e.g., a legitimation by which one could distinguish a friendly guest from a deceiver; a military password; a banner that was the sign of identity and recognition for a particular unit of troops; a passport that evidenced one's belonging to a particular people or city; a seal by which the authenticity of a letter or document was identified and recognized; a ring making such a seal; and, finally, a sign that one was justified in receiving something, such as the food stamps used in connection with the public meals well known in antiquity.

Therefore, when Christians in Rome already in the first half of the second century CE spoke of the confession of faith they made at baptism as a "symbol of faith" (*symbolum fidei*), they presumably understood it primarily as just such a sign of identity and recognition. To the candidate for baptism the symbol was communicated or handed over (*traditio symboli*), whereupon she or he then gave it back by reciting it at her or his own baptism (*redditio symboli*) thereby identifying her or himself and allowing others to recognize her or him as a member of the same community of faith. What further connotation, if any, this may have been understood to have we simply don't know—although we do know that Christians from an early time thought and spoke of themselves as "soldiers of Christ" (*milites Christi*) engaged in combat with a hostile world. Clear enough, in any case, is that what eventually became our Apostles' Creed was originally a liturgical-catechetical formula specifically associated with the sacrament of baptism. Quite possibly question-and-answer in its original form, it served as the basis for a suitable amount of teaching or instruction preparatory to a person's formally entering upon the Christian life and accepting her or his own responsibility as a member of the witnessing church.

But now, ask yourself, how many Christians today are really aware that this is the original use of the Creed in Christian life? Or, if we reckon ourselves to be Christians, how many of us have had the kind of experience in the church that would enable us to say, "Yes, that's right. That's the way I myself have used the Creed and also seen it used in my own life in the church"?

If we ask, then, how we can understand the Creed so as to deal with the problem it poses for many of us, I answer as follows: In addition to continuing to clarify and reclarify the ever-prevalent confusion of faith with belief, or, if you prefer, *belief in* with *belief that*; and then coming to terms with our own differentiated consciousness by finding more appropriate concepts and terms in which to interpret the Creed's intended existential meaning—in addition to doing both of these things, we need, not least, to take account of the Creed's proper context and use in the Christian life in connection with baptism and with an eye on just how it functions in this connection. And this brings me to the third and final part of this lecture.

### Baptism as a sign of grace and the Creed as a symbol of faith

What, I ask, is baptism? The summary answer is that baptism is the special revelation to an individual person by name of the great fact decisively

41

revealed through Jesus Christ to all humankind. "*Sarah Margaret*, I baptize you in the name of the Father, and of the Son, and of the Holy Spirit. Amen." The great fact thereby specially revealed to Sarah Margaret is that she, together with all the rest of us, not only righteous but also unrighteous, not only Jew but also gentile, not only male but also female, not only free but also slave—that all of us are, ever have been, and ever shall be the beloved children of God, notwithstanding our all having sinned and come short of God's glory.

It is this great fact that, together with every other human being, even I am God's dear child—it is this great fact that baptism reveals to me and that I am invited obediently to believe on a threefold ground composed of (1) the now-occurring witness of the church as it takes place through administering the sacrament of my baptism; (2) the decisive event of Jesus Christ, which is the abiding principle as well as the historical origin of the church's witness in general as of baptism in particular; and (3) the strictly ultimate reality of God Godself as the God of all humankind and as my God, to which reality both Jesus Christ and the church, in their different but related ways, bear witness. Thus the great fact of my being God's child is a fact twice over before I believe in it: not only in that God has by that time always already claimed me as God's child, together with all other human beings, but also in that this great fact has been decisively revealed to one and all through Jesus Christ before it's ever specially revealed to me through the church's witness in my own baptism. Consequently, my faith in response to my baptism in no way creates the great fact of my being God's child or of this being revealed to me through Jesus and the church; my faith only receives the fact by obediently accepting this revelation of it in confidence and faithfulness: this special revelation to me of God as *the* Father and as *my* Father through Jesus Christ, God's Son and our Lord, by God's own Holy Spirit through the witness of the church.

But now, let's unpack this summary answer a bit and look more closely at what it does and doesn't involve.

Contrary to a recurrent and widespread misunderstanding, my baptism makes me a child of God only in the sense of expressly revealing to me as an individual person what I, together with all of my fellow human beings, in fact always already am by reason of God's having created us and claimed us by God's love, decisively revealed to us through Jesus Christ as attested by the church. To suppose that the act of baptism itself in any way creates this great and final fact, instead of itself being entirely based on the fact and bearing witness to it, is not Christianity but magic.

But—and this is a much more controversial statement—it is just as mistaken, and just as magical, to suppose, as many Christians, unfortunately, have supposed and continue to suppose, that the event of Jesus Christ itself is somehow the ultimate ground of our and my filial relation to God. Although the event of Jesus Christ is, indeed, the decisive *revelation* of our common relation to God, it is not itself in any way the constitution of this relation. Children of God we all in fact are, ever were, and ever shall be, even apart from the event of Jesus Christ, although the decisive significance of Jesus, which Christians acknowledge by confessing him to be "the Christ," is that he is the revelation to all humankind of this great fact about each and every one of us.

In sum, baptism and the Christ-event alike are, in their different but closely related ways, authoritative symbols or signs of an *eternal* fact—baptism being the dependent sign of this fact addressed uniquely to each individual person, the Christ event being the primal sign of it addressed universally to all humankind. They are thus the revelation in time—in our common time as women and men, and in the particular time of *my own* individual life—of the great fact that is a fact from all eternity, before them and without them: the true constitution of all human beings and of each human being as both created by God and irrevocably claimed by God's love forever.

And this, of course, is why some—indeed, most—Christians have historically maintained that baptism is ordinarily performed not only properly but most appropriately as *infant* baptism. That I in fact am and, therefore, by right and responsibility ought to be God's own dear child does not in the least depend upon my own understanding or decision—although the whole end or purpose of baptism, naturally, is that I shall indeed come to understand who I in fact am and who it declares me to be, and so make the decisions that will alone enable me also to become exactly that as I lead my life as a human being.

This is to say, however, that baptism, rightly understood, is—in the phrase of my favorite Anglican theologian, Frederick Denison Maurice—"the sacrament of constant union." It is the authoritative sign of who, with all my fellow human beings, I really am, ever have been, and ever shall be, regardless of the extent to which I understand this, or fail to understand it, and in spite of my repeated failures, after as well as before, to live my life so as to become the child of God I really am. Far from being simply one particular act at the beginning of my life—or at the beginning of my fully conscious decision for Christian existence—my baptism is the ever-present reminder throughout my life of who I am and ever remain, whatever the twists and turns of my own individual destiny.

I always remember in this connection that the only thing Martin Luther ever found it helpful to remind himself of in face of the "temptations" (*tentationes, Anfechtungen*) that repeatedly assailed him throughout his life was, simply, "I am baptized." It is precisely because of my baptism that I know I always have the right to call upon God and to rely utterly on God's parental love—whatever may have been the lapses and failures of my sonship. More than that, my baptism is the reminder to me that the same is true of every human being, whether or not she or he has been baptized, and whatever may be her or his relation to Jesus Christ and the church. It is the reminder, as Maurice puts it, that "God has redeemed [hu]mankind, that [God] has chosen a family to be witnesses of that redemption, that we who are baptized into that family must claim for ourselves the title of sons [and daughters] of God, [and] must witness to others that they have a claim to it as well as we."[2]

I hope it will have become evident by now that the very event of baptism itself, thus understood, discloses the essentially triune or trinitarian structure of Christian faith and enables us to understand why the Apostles' Creed, with its declaration of just that faith, is the eminently appropriate counterpart of baptism. I do not mean by this merely that baptism historically takes place "in the name of the Father, and of the Son, and of the Holy Spirit," and that the Creed, correspondingly, is the symbol of our answering faith in this same threefold name. I also mean that the very *event* of baptism itself, understood as I've just interpreted it, involves the threefold, triune presence of God of which the trinitarian formulation of the Creed is the explication. The faith to which baptism is the invitation is grounded on (1) the event of baptism itself; (2) the event of Jesus Christ, on which baptism, like the church's witness otherwise, is in turn dependent and that it re-presents; and (3) the great fact of the strictly ultimate reality of God's parental love. But all three of these points are understood to be, or to involve, the act of God Godself. Although baptism is clearly a human act of the church, it is also understood to be the divine act of the Spirit of God, who alone accounts for the authority claimed by the church's witness, whether in this sacrament or in any other form its witness may take. And so, too, with the event of Jesus Christ, which is clearly a human event like any other in the context of

2. Frederick Maurice, ed., *The Life of Frederick Denison Maurice Chiefly Told in His Own Letters*, vol. 2 (New York: Scribner, 1884), 16.

our human history, and yet, as faith affirms, is also the divine event of God's own decisive self-disclosure to us through God's only Son. In short baptism simply as such is the revelation of the same triune God—Father, Son, and Holy Spirit—in whom each of us professes her or his faith by affirming the Creed.

The significance of all this, as I see it, is to remind us of the context in Christian life in which the Creed had its original—and, as I believe, still has its proper—use, and, in this way, to make us aware of just what it is that the Creed is really all about. Clearly, it is about the One whom Christians call God: Father, Son, and Holy Spirit. But the ultimate mystery that Christians name by the name "God" is the mystery whose meaning for us they believe to be disclosed to them decisively in and through their experience in the church, as those who gather as a community in the name of Jesus Christ and so also of the triune God. The crucial moment in this Christian experience, since it in fact signifies the beginning of all such experience, is the moment of baptism. Therefore—and this is my main point in this first lecture—if we would understand the Creed, not only what it affirms but also how it properly functions in the lives of Christians, we must understand this experience of which it is the expression, and, hence, above all, the event of baptism that signifies the first crucial moment in this Christian experience.

This is not in the least to imply, however, that administering the sacrament of baptism is the only occasion in the liturgical life of Christians in which the Creed has a proper place. Just as and because baptism, as I've said, is rightly taken to be "the sacrament of *constant* union," of an *indissoluble* relation to God through Jesus Christ, the Creed, in one way or another, has a proper place in every part of the Christian liturgy—be it the order of morning worship in which Christians again and again re-enact the whole drama of Christian existence, or, most especially, every celebration of the Eucharist or Holy Communion, in which they gather at the table of their Lord. My point, however, is that we will not understand the Creed in such a way as to be able to join in its affirmation in any of these liturgical contexts unless and until we understand its proper use therein. Far from being only or even primarily a summary of beliefs that we are expected to assent to and then join in asserting, it is, in fact, the symbol of Christian faith that corresponds to the authoritative sign of grace in which that faith is founded: the sacrament of baptism.

I close with yet another, more extended word from Maurice, which says far more eloquently than I can all that I have so far intended to say:

The Creed is evidently an act of allegiance or affiance [sc. trust, or entrustment, as well as loyalty]; and since it has ever been connected with Baptism, one must suppose that from Baptism it derives its interpretation. If by that act we are acknowledged as spiritual creatures, united to a spiritual Being, by this act we claim our spiritual position, we assert our union with that Being. The name into which we are adopted there, is the name we confess here. Those acts which, having been done for all [hu]-mankind, were the warrant for our particular admission to the covenant, are the acts which we here proclaim to be the warrant for our faith and fellowship. . . . [T]he primary postulate of [Christ's] kingdom [is] a condescension of God to [woman and] man, a cognizance taken of the creature by the Creator; the second [postulate of Christ's kingdom is] an apprehension of God by [women and] men, a recognition of the Creator by the creature. By *grace* are ye saved; by *faith* are ye saved. The position is freely given; a position of union and fellowship with another, a position of self-renunciation; [and] the power is given wherewith to claim it: then comes the claim itself. Such seems to be the testimony of Scripture; and the relation in which the Creed stands to Baptism, and their common relation to that name and that kingdom which Scripture is revealing, surely expounds, in a remarkable way, that testimony.[3]

## God the Father Almighty

### Summary of the argument to this point

The Creed, properly understood, I've argued, is the symbol of faith that corresponds or answers to the sign of grace that is baptism. Thus, although it consists in certain beliefs that are formulated in terms that are likely to be more or less problematic for anyone with a relatively more differentiated human consciousness such as our own, we have every right so to interpret it as to penetrate behind its formulations and even its particular beliefs to the faith of which it is the symbol and to the threefold reality that is the ground and object of this faith. Summarily put, this reality is (1) the mysterious encompassing whole of our existence as this whole is revealed through (2) Jesus Christ, which is to say, the event of Jesus experienced and understood as the decisive revelation of this mysterious

3. Frederick Denison Maurice, *The Kingdom of Christ*, vol. 2 (London: James Clarke, 1959), 5.

whole as God, and (3) the witness of the church, which is founded on the Christ-event as thus decisively revelatory. Correspondingly, the faith that answers to this threefold reality is obedient trust in and loyalty to this ultimate mystery as the triune God: Father, Son, and Holy Spirit. My thesis, then, is that, by understanding the Apostles' Creed as a symbol of this faith, we will be better able both to understand and critically appropriate the beliefs that the Creed expresses and to come to terms with the problems posed for us by its particular formulations of these beliefs.

## Presuppositions of understanding the first article

Before commenting on the first article and on what is, and is not, required of us today to affirm it honestly and with integrity, I want to try to clarify—all too briefly, I fear—certain presuppositions necessary to my understanding both of it and of the Creed as a whole.

I presuppose, first, that our common experience simply as human beings has two distinguishable, if also inseparable, aspects or dimensions. It is not only or primarily what I call our *empirical* experience, our experience in the horizontal dimension, as it were, of the variable items of our existence in its immediate setting in the world around us. It is also, and first of all, what I distinguish as our *existential* experience, our experience in the vertical dimension, so to speak, of our own existence in its ultimate setting as invariably an existence together with others—other persons and other things—all parts of the mysterious whole of reality encompassing us. It may also be helpful to recall here the distinction I made in the first lecture between being something *other* and being something *more*: something that is merely one other item among items and something that is more than any item and all items. In any case, my first presupposition is that our common human experience is not merely empirical, but also, and primarily, existential: our existential experience of the threefold ultimate reality of ourselves, others, and the whole.

I then presuppose, second, that insofar as our experience as human beings is precisely that—*human* experience—it is also *understanding* experience. To live humanly, at the distinctively human level, is to live, not only feelingly, as other animals do, but also understandingly. And this, of course, is why we do not, and cannot, simply live our lives as they do, but rather (as we say, revealingly) *lead* them: each of us as a single individual, freely and responsibly, if also always within the limits of her or his own unique destiny in the world.

For us to live thus understandingly as mere parts of reality, however—and this is my third presupposition—is also for us to live *questioningly*, by not only asking, but also *having* to ask, all sorts of vital questions about ourselves in both the immediate and the ultimate settings of our lives. Although we never fail to experience and understand ourselves somehow in both of these settings, we always experience and understand only partially or fragmentarily, and so always with questions as yet unanswered about all that we do not understand.

Included among these vital questions that we find ourselves asking and trying to answer simply because we're human is what I, following others before me, call *the* existential question. By this I mean what I take to be the most vital of all our vital questions, including any of the other questions that are or may become of existential concern to us. This is our question about the meaning of our existence in its ultimate setting as a part, together with others, of the all-encompassing whole of reality. So my fourth presupposition is that as soon and as long as any of us is a human being at all, she or he is engaged somehow, if only implicitly, in asking this existential question about the meaning of ultimate reality for us: for how we are to understand ourselves, others, and the whole if we are do so truly and authentically and are then to lead our own individual lives accordingly.

Once, however, this existential question becomes explicit, by being asked and answered in certain particular concepts and symbols, it may well be called the *religious* question. The reason for this, my fifth presupposition, is what I understand to be properly meant by "religion." In a completely generic, purely formal sense applicable to any of the specific religions, "religion" refers to the primary form of culture, the concepts and symbols—and so, in Clifford Geertz's term, "the cultural system"—in which individuals living in a given society and culture ordinarily ask and answer *the* existential question about the meaning of ultimate reality for them.

My sixth presupposition, then, is that among the different main types of religion so understood is what may be called "*theistic* religion" or simply "theism." By this, I understand the way of explicitly asking and answering *the* existential question for which the constitutive concept/symbol in Greek is "*theos*," and in English, "God." Insofar, then, as such theistic religion develops historically to the point of what is usually distinguished as monotheism, or what I distinguish, more exactly, as radical monotheism, the concept or symbol "God" is used to refer to nothing other or less than reality as such. God is thus implicitly, if not also explicitly, understood to be the one all-encompassing whole of reality of which we ourselves and everything else are but parts and that all of us, insofar as we are human beings at all somehow experience and understand in experiencing and understanding anything.

My seventh and—for our purposes—final presupposition is that this point of religious development had already been reached, in their different ways, in the societies and cultures in whose concepts and symbols the first article of the Apostles' Creed, and the Creed as a whole, was formulated. Both among Jews, particularly Jews of the diaspora, and also among many enlightened gentiles, the term "God" had come to be used in the radically monotheistic sense to designate, not one being among many, not even the highest or the greatest, but *the* being—the one being that is in effect all being because it is the unique, all-encompassing whole of reality of which all beings as such are parts or fragments and in which each being has both its primal source and its final end. Thus, when Paul, for one, speaks of God in 1 Corinthians 8:6, he speaks of "one God the Father, from whom are all things and for whom we exist," "we" here referring, I take it, to human beings generally as well as to Christians in particular. Or, again, in Romans 11:36, Paul presupposes that the God who is to be glorified forever is the One *from* whom and *through* whom and *for* whom are all things. I don't know about you, but, so far as I'm concerned, if Paul's formulations don't add up to as good a definition of the one all-encompassing whole of reality as you're likely to find, they'll certainly do until such a definition comes along.

So much for some of the necessary presuppositions with which I now turn to comments on the first article.

### God Father Almighty, Creator of heaven and earth

It is significant that the order of the Creed reverses the order of Christian experience. It thereby makes clear that the only *ultimate* ground and object of Christian faith is precisely the mysterious, all-encompassing whole of reality that, in radically monotheistic religious traditions, is named "God." Whatever else it is, then, Christian faith is faith in God in this radically monotheistic sense of the term—from which it immediately follows that, from the Creed's standpoint, any notion of a Christian faith without God, or of what some have called a Christian atheism, is logically an absurdity.

But if the very order of the Creed indicates that *belief in* God and the *belief that* God that it necessarily implies are foundational for Christian existence, it is still true that the *belief in* God and the *belief that* God expressed by the first article are formulated in the particular, historically conditioned forms of those who formulated them, as distinct from the no less particular, historically conditioned forms in which you and I today normally think and speak. Therefore, if we are to understand the first article so as to make it our own, we must penetrate behind its formulations to the *belief that* which they serve to formulate, and even behind this *belief that* to the faith, or *belief in*, which necessarily implies it and which its explication in the Apostles' Creed formulates only more or less adequately. My contention is that when we proceed in this way, we learn that, in affirming the first article, and thus in affirming one's own belief in God, one is in reality expressing a certain self-understanding, or understanding of oneself as a human being in the ultimate setting of one's life: the setting in which we experience and somehow understand ourselves as invariably parts, together with others, of the one, all-encompassing whole of reality itself. One thereby expresses the understanding according to which the bottomless depth of this encompassing mystery is truly, if only symbolically, said to be the boundless and almighty love from which all things come, and for which Christians as well as human beings generally have all been given and called, in one way or another, to exist.

It is equally significant, however, that Paul makes clear in the very same passage in 1 Corinthians that I've just cited that Christians as such have been given and called to exist for God in this sense through a correspondingly unique means—namely, through the Lord Jesus Christ, "*through* whom," as he puts it, "are all things and *through* whom we [as Christians] exist." If we recognize this and take it seriously, we avoid yet another common misunderstanding of the Creed.

It is now generally thought by close students of the matter that the Creed as we know it gradually developed out of the so-called Old Roman Symbol (*R*, for short, both because of Roman and because it is, in fact, a historical reconstruction from the Creed itself, somewhat in the way in which—as you may remember if you've studied the Synoptic Gospels closely—the sayings source that scholars call Q is their historical reconstruction from Matthew and Luke). Presumably, then, the Roman

Christians of the second century CE, to whom we owe R (and, to that extent, also the Creed) understood the first article to set forth a belief in God as the ultimate, all-ruling ground or creator of all things, the term "Father" being commonly used by them as well as by both Jews and many enlightened pagans to refer to God in just this capacity.

Even so, for them as Christians, the term "Father" had another distinctive, if largely implicit, meaning, because they believed that the One quite generally acknowledged by radical monotheists as the eternal Father of all things was none other than the Father of Jesus Christ and then, by their adoption through Christ and the Holy Spirit, also their own Father. So even in its earliest form in R, the first article was already understood, arguably, not just in itself, but only in relation to the second and the third articles.

It is not at all surprising, then, that the favorite lines of interpreting the first article that began to emerge in the third century CE took the affirmation of belief in God the Father to have to do not so much with God's being the one ultimate creative ground and sovereign ruler of all things as with God's being the all-loving Father of Jesus Christ and, through adoption, our own Father, too. Such interpretation became so common, in fact, that the original reference of the first article to God as creator and ruler of the universe, having now become in effect merely implicit, eventually needed to be made explicit again by adding the phrase, "Creator of heaven and earth." In any case, you'll see if you consult the Appendix that this is the only addition made to the first article, as it presumably existed already in R.

Let me say, parenthetically, that there cannot be anything like certainty as to just what the motives were that led to the expansion of the original Old Roman Symbol into what we find in our own Apostles' Creed. Probably the most common interpretation of this addition holds that it reflects a specifically polemical motive over against the denial by various heretical views of a Gnostic or, at any rate, dualistic sort, that earth as much as heaven was created by the one sovereign God. On such heretical views, the maker of earth and flesh was some merely subordinate, quasi-evil deity, who was to be distinguished from the highest God who had made the heavens and spirits alone and had then subsequently redeemed women and men from the earthly and fleshly bondage into which they had fallen by sending his Son. But, plausible as this common interpretation may be, I incline to regard it, like similar interpretations of other parts of the Creed, as an overinterpretation. I find it sufficient to hold, as I've just explained, that what was originally only implied in the first article by virtue of its context along with the second and third articles eventually came to be understood as its primary meaning, at which point what it had originally meant needed to be restated explicitly by means of the additional phrase.

Be this as it may, there cannot be any doubt about the essential point. The only *ultimate* ground and object of Christian faith and belief is the mysterious ultimate whole of reality encompassing our existence and all existence, which Christians, in union with other radical monotheists, name by the name "God." And yet it is just as true that the only *immediate* ground and object of Christian faith, on the basis of which Christians understand everything, including most especially the more exact meaning of the name "God," is the Christian witness of faith, of which the event of Jesus Christ is at once its historical origin and its abiding principle, and so its explicit primal authorizing source. God the Father Almighty—or, in a more exact rendering of the Latin original, which has no definite article, God Father Almighty—is none other than the all-loving Father of Jesus Christ.

Of the many other things that might be said about the meaning of the first article for the early church in which it was originally formulated and interpreted I shall mention only one—namely, how we're properly to take the term "Father." Gendered as it certainly is, with all that this has fatefully meant, and continues to mean, for Christian history as well as Western history generally, this term, as it is actually used in the first article, clearly seems to function less as a description than as a name or title. This means, above all, that it is properly used to identify God (i.e., the one mysterious ultimate whole of reality encompassing us and everyone and everything else) in a distinctive way: as the all-loving One to whose domain or rule Jesus himself bears witness and whom the early Christian community, decisively through Jesus, understood to be the primal source of all things and the sovereign power with which not only they but all women and men have to do. In other words, the point of the term "Father" as it is used in the first article is to identify the ultimate mystery of the whole, not so much as *paternal* love as, rather, *parental* love—that itself being but in turn a symbol for the unconditional love from which all things come and for which not only Christians but all women and men are irrevocably called to exist.

*Faith in God as existence in and for radical freedom*

But now what does it mean for us today to affirm this historic Christian belief in the God of Jesus Christ, and thus in the ultimate reality of pa rental, unconditional love, as the primal source or origin of all things, of earth as well as heaven, and as the sovereign power by which the course of all things and their final meaning is determined? To get at this, I shall ask and answer three further questions.

1. *What kind of a commitment do we make when we affirm this belief as our own?*—As is abundantly clear from the first article itself, the kind of commitment we make when we affirm it is primarily *existential*: a commitment of entrustment and fidelity to God Godself, not a merely *intellectual* commitment to the truth of a certain assertion or assertions about God —not even the assertions in which the first article itself consists. In other words, the first article, like the Creed as a whole, is properly understood, first and last, as *symbolum fidei*, symbol of faith, and so the belief it expresses is primarily *belief in*, as distinct from *belief that*.

However, precisely because it is primarily an existential commitment that is required of us in affirming the first article, also required of us, if only implicitly, is an intellectual commitment—a *belief that* as well as a *belief in*, or, really, as necessarily included in or implied by our *belief in*. Thus, even though Christian faith itself and as such is different from a so-called worldview, it nevertheless necessarily presupposes and implies a worldview, but for the truth of which Christian faith itself could not be the appropriate and so authorized response to the way things really are that it understands itself to be. This explains why the *belief that* that the first article calls for has to be expressed somehow by all Christian witness and theology if they're to make good on their claims to be *Christian* witness and theology just because they are appropriate to Jesus Christ. Even so, the only ultimate object as well as the only ultimate ground of Christian faith is God Godself, to whom one rightly commits oneself only by what Paul calls "the obedience of faith," i.e., by unreservedly entrusting one's life solely to God's sovereign, unconditional love and by then living in unqualified loyalty to that same love as the only cause that can and should finally claim all of us and all of our powers.

2. *On what basis does this commitment rest?*—The commitment we make rests essentially or substantially, of course, on God Godself, i.e., the mysterious all-encompassing whole of reality as such, construed in the light of Jesus Christ as all-sovereign, unconditional love. Just as God

Godself is the only ultimate *object* of the faith expressed in the first article, that *in* which we believe—in whom we trust and to whom we are
loyal—so God Godself is also the only ultimate *ground* of this faith, that
*because of* which, *by virtue of* which, *by the power of* which, we believe.
But there remains the question: How does one ever come so to experience God that God Godself thus becomes the ground as well as the object
of one's faith?

Considering all that I have said, I trust it will seem only natural if
I respond to this question by saying, first of all, that the basis of one's
commitment experientially is precisely one's Christian experience. We
have seen that the faith in God affirmed by the first article is not merely
radically monotheistic faith in general, but faith in *the* God, the one and
only God, decisively revealed through the event and the community with
which the second and the third articles of the Creed respectively have to
do. But this means that for us, too, if we're Christians, the basis on which
our commitment to God the Father Almighty rests in the experiential
sense can only be our own experience of the witness of the church and
of the event of Jesus Christ that ever continues to take place anew in and
through the church's witness.

True and important as this is, however, it is not, I think, a sufficient
answer to the question. It remains to ask whether the witness with which
the church confronts us is, in fact, true or credible, as it claims to be.
Are we really the children of God that the church through our baptism
declares us to be on the authority of Jesus' decisive re-presentation to this
effect? And are these events—the event of his decisive re-presentation
and the event of the church's special re-presentation of this event through
one's own baptism—themselves the very presence and power of God's
love confronting us with who we really are by freeing us from the deep
self-*misunderstanding* of our ordinary existence in sin? So far as I can
see, there's no way of satisfactorily answering such questions as these
except by appealing beyond all specifically Christian experience also to
our common human experience in general or simply as such. If anyone
is to affirm understandingly and honestly that God is indeed her or his
almighty Father, this can only be because such an affirmation, both as
existential commitment and as the intellectual assertion that any such
commitment necessarily implies, is the only way, finally, that one can
make sense of *all* of her or his experience as a human being who has also
been called to be a Christian. Put differently, one must be able to affirm
that the commitment to God Godself that one is called to make through

Jesus Christ and the church is but the full and adequate explication in particular concepts and symbols of the commitment that one is always already at least implicitly called to make simply by existing as a human being, through literally every thing and every one that one happens to experience.

In sum, the only basis on which our commitment can rest experientially is the *double* basis of our specifically Christian experience of Jesus Christ in and through the church, *and* our common human experience simply as women and men, each of the two kinds of experience confirming and being confirmed by the other.

3. *What difference does it make in our actual lives if we in fact make this commitment?*—One difference it makes, obviously, is that we then have certain beliefs, implicitly if not explicitly, about ourselves and reality generally that are more or less different from other such comprehensive beliefs that human beings may have. Although the understanding of reality, or worldview, to which our Christian faith thus commits us intellectually may remain to some extent merely implied, it's important, for others as well as ourselves, that we do our best to make it explicit both adequately and fittingly. Only so can we play our part in bearing the church's witness to Jesus Christ and to the God who sends him, and so really live out the commitment we make in affirming the Creed. And this, of course, explains, in turn, why each of us as a Christian has to be and become at least a lay theologian as well as a lay minister if she or he is to make good on the commitment that the first article requires of us.

But important as this is, it's neither the only nor the most fundamental difference that the commitment of faith makes in our actual lives insofar as we make it. This commitment, as we've seen, is primarily an existential, not a merely intellectual, commitment. It is a commitment of obedient trust and loyalty: of unreserved trust in the one mysterious all-encompassing whole of reality as sovereign, unconditional love; and of unqualified loyalty to the cause of that love, and thus to all to whom it is loyal, as the only cause for which we are finally to live and die. But what difference, really, does this kind of existential commitment make in one's actual life?

The difference it makes, I answer, is that one's life thereupon becomes a life lived in and for a radical, paradoxical freedom, by which I mean, both a freedom *from* all things, whether ourselves or others in the world in which we live, and a freedom *for* all things, ourselves and all our fellow creatures, nonhuman as well as human. If it is the sovereign, unconditional love of God alone that is the primal source and the final end of all things, and if we ourselves really believe this by entrusting ourselves to this love without reservation and being faithful to its cause without qualification, then nothing else whatever can finally claim us or in any way become essential to the final meaning of our lives. Whatever is owes both its being and its meaning, finally, solely to God's almighty love for it, and so, but for this great fact of God's love, would be nothing at all. But really to believe in this love is to be done with the arrogant pride that imagines it is somehow we ourselves who are the source and end of our existence, as though all that we are or can ever become were not entirely the gift of God. Likewise, it is to be freed from our bondage to other things—as though any of them was more than a mere creature as absolutely dependent on God's love for all that it is and means as we are ourselves.

I fear we only too often overlook this negative or critical meaning of faith in God Father Almighty. Instead of reminding us of our absolute dependence, and of the absolute dependence of all things, upon God, the doctrine of creation is taken to imply their own quasi-divinity as creatures—as though, once having been created and found good by God, they somehow become sufficient in and of themselves, or good in their own right. In reality, however, the doctrine of creation implied by the first article is by way of negating any such claim that human beings and the world are in some way independent and self-sufficient. Because their only source and end, finally, is God's love for them, they are absolutely dependent on this love for both their being and their meaning.

And yet, just because it's solely God's sovereign, unconditional love on which all things absolutely depend, trust in this love and loyalty to it means that we are also free *for* all things, ourselves and all others, as pre-cisely God's good creation. So, if arrogant pride no longer has any place in our lives, it's far otherwise with the confident self-affirmation with which we venture to realize our own deepest possibilities as creatures. Because we believe that what is finally sovereign over all things is nothing other or less than the parental, unconditional love of God, we have the courage and the freedom to love ourselves, as well as to love all others beyond all the limits of custom and convention by which our love for them is otherwise restricted.

It is just this radical, paradoxical freedom both from and for our own existence with others in the world that seems to me to be the existential meaning of faith in God Father Almighty, Creator of heaven and earth.

So, if the Creed, as I have argued, is rightly understood to be precisely "symbol of faith," the first article makes clear that the faith of which it is the symbol is the faith whose existential meaning is existence in perfect freedom in and under God's love: both the freedom *from* ourselves and the world and the freedom *for* them that is love—which in the case of all of our fellow human beings can only be the freedom for them, too, to be free and, above all, to exist in the same radical freedom of faith in God's love.

## Jesus Christ, His Only Son, Our Lord

### Preliminary remarks

I noted in the preceding lecture that the order of the Creed, beginning, as it does, with God Father Almighty, reverses the order of our actual Christian experience, which begins with our own individual encounter with, and experience of, the church and its witness of faith. But it's just as evident that central to both orders alike—to that of the Creed, even as to that of our experience as Christians—is the subject of the second article, Jesus Christ. The Creed thus reminds us, in its way, that, as theocentric as Christian faith certainly is, it is also, and no less certainly, christocentric.

There's simply too much contained in the second article, however, to do anything like justice to it in a single lecture, especially to the history of its emergence and interpretation. All I can hope to do, in fact, are three things: (1) to suggest a key to interpreting it; (2) to comment very briefly on its distinctive structure; and (3) making use of the interpretive key, to offer a single illustration of what all of its several different assertions are rightly taken to mean.

### A key to interpretation

I would ask you to recall three points from the preceding lectures. The first is what I've called my thesis—namely, that the Apostles' Creed is historically and properly understood as symbol of faith, and thus as something like the colors of the army of Christ, or the church militant, in the world. It is the sign of recognition by which Christians have historically identified themselves and recognized one another, and thus the historic emblem of their unity as a community of faith and witness. Therefore, the Creed is both historically and properly intimately connected with the sacrament of baptism, understood as the primary sign of grace, and thus as the special revelation to each individual person by name of the great fact decisively revealed to all humankind through Jesus Christ: that each of us and all of us, gentiles as well as Jews, unrighteous as well as righteous, slave as well as free, female as well as male, are, ever have been, and ever shall be beloved children of God. So the several beliefs expressed in the Creed are all by way of explicating and asserting the special, decisive revelation of God made to each of us in our baptism. In this sense, the Creed is based on and gives expression to our specifically Christian experience, understood—as I stressed last time—as both confirming and being confirmed by our common human experience more generally simply as women and men.

The second point I would ask you to recall is my suggestion, in the concluding part of the last lecture, about the existential meaning of the faith in God required by the first article. Since the term "God" stands for the one mysterious ultimate whole encompassing our existence; and since "Father Almighty" interprets this whole Christianly as nothing but sovereign, unconditional love, the difference made to our actual lives by our existential commitment of faith in this whole—of obedient trust in and loyalty to it alone—is that we're thereby enabled to lead lives of radical, paradoxical freedom: both freedom *from* all things, ourselves and the world, and freedom *for* them.

The third point I ask you to recall, also from my last lecture, is that since this kind of faith or *belief in* God is not simply a generally monotheistic, even radically monotheistic, faith, but is the quite specific faith that we are explicitly, indeed decisively, called to share through Jesus Christ—since this is so, Christian faith in God, by its very nature, is itself, at least implicitly, faith in Christ and the church, even as Christian faith in Christ and the church is by its very nature faith in God. This being so, however, the essential existential meaning of the second article, and also that of the third, cannot be really different from the meaning that we've already found in the first article. I'm not saying by this, of course, that there aren't different *beliefs that* expressed in the second and third articles from those expressed in the first. Clearly, there are real, and, at their own level, important differences in specific beliefs; and these differences reflect the peculiar complexity of the distinctive ground and object of Christian faith. Although its only *ultimate* ground and object, as we've seen, is the one mysterious whole of reality encompassing our existence, its *immediate* ground and object is the specifically Christian witness of faith re-presented decisively through Jesus Christ and then specially re-presented through the church. And this goes to explain why the historic formulation of Christian faith in God is not mere monotheism, even radical monotheism, but rather trinitarianism.

Even so, Christian trinitarianism is not tritheism, nor are the real and important differences between specific Christian *beliefs that* differences entirely lacking in an underlying unity. In and through all the differences reflected in the Creed in both Christian experience and Christian *belief that,* there is expressed but one faith or *belief in*: one trust in and loyalty to the all-encompassing mystery as sovereign, unconditional love. And there is even, in a way, but one *belief that,* however complex and many-sided that one *belief that* is and has to be. Accordingly, the existentialist interpretation I've already given of faith in the first article could only be repeated in the cases of both the second and the third articles—the while taking fully into account the very real and important differences between the specific *beliefs that* that each of the three articles expresses.

For reasons of time, however, I shall not, in fact, repeat that inter-pretation in either this lecture or the next, beyond what I've already said in briefly summarizing it and asking you to recall it as my second point. The thing to keep in mind is really only this: all the assertions of the second article, whose immediate object is Jesus Christ, God's only Son, our Lord, are also by way of expressing the one faith that the mysteri-ous ultimate whole encompassing our existence is just as Jesus decisively reveals it to be. It is neither a mere indifference to our lives nor an un-reconciled enmity toward them, but—in Luther's phrase—"sheer love": nothing other than their boundless and unconditional acceptance, which liberates anyone accepting it through faith both from and for oneself and all of one's fellow creatures, to lead the life that Paul characterizes as "faith active in love" (Gal 5:6).

With these three points firmly in mind, it remains only to draw the obvious implication for what I've called "a key to interpretation," mean-ing by that a key to interpreting all the clauses in the second article. That key, I think, is this: all that's said in the second article of the Creed is by way of making one underlying assertion: that the historical person or event generally referred to as Jesus, or Jesus of Nazareth, is the decisive revelation of the encompassing mystery of our existence that human be-ings not uncommonly call by the name "God." Just as this God is the One whose meaning for us is decisively re-presented through Jesus, so Jesus is the one through whom this God decisively reveals Godself as the gift and demand of boundless, unconditional love. But, then, just as the first theological assertion about God expresses the whole point of the first article, so the whole point of the second article is expressed by the second christological assertion about Jesus. It is the one assertion expressed, in so many different ways, by saying that Jesus is God's only Son, our Lord; that he was conceived by the Holy Spirit and born of the Virgin Mary; that he suffered under Pontius Pilate, was crucified, died, and was buried; that he descended into hell; that on the third day he was raised from the dead; that he ascended into heaven; and that he is seated at the right hand of the Father, whence he shall come to judge the living and the dead.

This is to say, of course, that what makes anyone a Christian insofar as one is such is the experience of Jesus himself—mediately, if not immediately—as of decisive significance for human existence and, therefore, also for one's own existence as the single individual one is. It is precisely their shared experience of Jesus as thus decisive that somehow comes to expression through everything that Christians think, say, and do. But they express their experience of him explicitly as such by what I call "the constitutive christological assertion"—by which I mean the one assertion of which I have just been speaking: the one assertion that they all make or imply, in so many different concepts and symbols, that Jesus is of just such decisive significance, because, through him, our existential question as human beings receives its decisive answer—a decisive answer being simply *the* answer, the *true* answer by which the truth, if any, in any and all other possible answers can and should be decided.

The thing to note, however, is that it is through Jesus himself as a person, or through the actual event of his living and dying, that Christians believe that the decisive answer to our existential question is received. *Through Jesus himself*, not simply through his teachings and example, the encompassing mystery of our existence is decisively revealed in its meaning for us as the gift and demand of sovereign, unconditional love. *Through Jesus himself*, we are called to respond to this revelation through our own obedient faith, our own unreserved trust in God's love and our own unqualified loyalty to its cause, thereby existing in just that existence of radical, paradoxical freedom that I talked about last time. In this way, Jesus himself, or, if you will, the event of Jesus precisely as a historical event as real as any other, is the decisive re-presentation of a wholly other event—namely, the *transcendent* event, or, as I've also referred to it, "the great fact," of God's love: of God's ever new acceptance from and to all eternity of all creaturely lives into God's own. By the same token, the one and only point of the christological assertion, however it happens to be formulated, is to assert that just this is the case: that the person or event of Jesus, without prejudice to its being every bit as historical as any other, is of decisive significance for human existence.

So much, then, for what I mean by a key to interpretation. I turn now to

## The structure of the second article

And I want to begin with a few words about the changes made in the second article of the earlier Roman baptismal symbol (R) in order to yield what we now have in the traditional version of the Apostles' Creed. Of the eleven such changes made in R, only one was made in the first article—namely, the addition, as we saw last time, of "Creator of heaven and earth"—and only three changes were made in the third article, of which more in the concluding lecture. The remaining seven changes were all made in the second article, although with one exception—the disputed clause "he descended into hell"—the doctrinal changes they involve are all really quite minor. Even so, it may be helpful briefly to note them.

1. The original word order in the later form of R, "Christ Jesus," is reversed, in keeping with the tendency prevalent in gentile churches to treat what was originally applied to Jesus as a title as though it were simply part of his proper name. "Jesus the Christ," or "Christ Jesus" thus becomes "Jesus Christ"—the title Christ, which derives, of course, from the Greek translation of the Hebrew term "Messiah," having little or no significance except for Jews or those otherwise knowledgeable about Jewish religious beliefs.

2. The original assertion of R, "born of the Holy Spirit and the Virgin Mary," is rendered more precise by the formulation, "conceived *by* the Holy Spirit and born *from* (or *of*) the Virgin Mary." Beyond its use of these two different prepositions, this formulation adds the new participle "conceived." Just what lies behind this change is not easy to say, although it is at least questionable, in my judgment, whether the motives behind it were polemical or antiheretical, even if the change certainly does evidence a concern to formulate a doctrinal nuance and, perhaps, to rule out a possible misunderstanding. What is

certain is that the formula eventually became a powerful weapon in the arsenal of orthodox opponents of adoptionism—which, roughly speaking, is the christological position that Jesus *was* not God's Son already at or even before the beginning of his life, but only *became* God's Son somewhere in the course of his career, by being adopted by God, whether by his resurrection from the dead or, still earlier in his life, at the beginning of his public ministry, by his baptism at the hands of John the Baptist. I shall be returning to this point presently.

3. and 4. The Creed inserts the participles "suffered" before "under Pontius Pilate" and "dead" before "buried." There is hardly any doctrinal significance to these insertions beyond saying still more emphatically that Jesus' crucifixion and burial involved real human suffering and death. We do know that some of the church fathers preferred "suffered" to "crucified" in speaking of his death.

5. The Creed expands *R*'s "at the right hand of the Father" to "at the right hand of God Father Almighty," the reasons for this presumably being mainly, if not entirely, stylistic.

6. The Creed changes "whence" to "thence" to yield "from thence he shall come to judge," which appears to have no doctrinal significance whatever.

7. The Creed includes the phrase "descended into hell," although nowadays this clause is omitted from the Creed as used in certain churches (including my own United Methodist Church). Being the latest addition to the Creed—first appearing only at the beginning of the fifth century CE—it has been the most vulnerable to objections. And in modern times it has sometimes been made optional or eliminated altogether. Beyond this, I need say only two things: (1) since the idea of Christ's descent figures in early Eastern materials, it was probably admitted into the Apostles' Creed, often referred to as "the Western Creed," under Eastern influence; and (2) the assertion may very well retain a certain significance symbolically in its reminder of the full scope of Christ's redemption. By decisively revealing the truth about human existence, Jesus explicitly vindicates the rights of every woman and man, dead or alive, as a beloved child of God, over against all the worldly powers that would deceive human beings as to their rights, tempting them to doubt that they even have any. This is just the truth, of course, often powerfully expressed in Christian graphic art, with its

portrayals of Christ's descent into hell as his triumph over Satan and his release of those who have already died from Satan's power.

These, then, are the seven changes. As for the structure of the article, even in its original form in R, without the changes, it is evidently a composition of two quite different strands of christological tradition. As you can confirm by consulting the Appendix, the earlier form of the second article in R itself probably consisted simply in the one phrase, "And in Jesus Christ, his only begotten Son, our Lord." But it was not too long, apparently, before this original core of the article, as it has been called, was combined with the so-called Christ-story of Christ's origin and destiny, as expressed in the extended relative clause, "who was born of the Holy Spirit and the Virgin Mary, crucified under Pontius Pilate and buried," and so on. This twofold structure of the second article, already in the later form of R, has long been recognized, and the usual explanation of it has been that the Christ-story was added to the original core about Jesus' person in order to combat the Gnostic heresy called Docetism, according to which his was not a fully real human life after all, but, at most, the semblance of such (hence the name Docetism, which derives from the Greek infinitive meaning "to seem," or "to appear"). But plausible as this interpretation may be, it's hardly necessary. The anti-Docetism of the Christ-story is not pronounced, and, in fact, it's notably lacking in the emphatic adverbs familiar to us from the anti-Gnostic writings of the church fathers—as in the formulation, e.g., "was *truly* born." So, even if the Christ-story could have well served an anti-Gnostic purpose, the more likely explanation for its addition to the core is simpler.

We know that the events of Jesus' life and his origin and destiny had long been stock themes of the catechetical instruction preliminary to baptism, even as the Christ-story had from very early times been one important way of formulating Jesus' decisive significance as faith understands and bears witness to it. Consequently, there's every reason to suppose that as the answers to the questions put to candidates for baptism more and more tended to become summaries of the whole course of their preparatory instruction, there was more than sufficient motive to combine the original core with the extended relative clause provided by the Christ-story. In this way, two originally independent but logically interrelated ways of formulating Jesus' decisive significance were combined.

And this simpler explanation becomes the more plausible, I think, when we remember that, beginning already in New Testament times,

Christians tended to formulate their faith in Jesus as God's decisive self-revelation in both of these different but interrelated ways: both by entitling him with such honorific designations as "Christ," "Lord," "Son of God," and the like; and by telling the story of what happened to him, particularly of what happened after his death—with his resurrection or exaltation, and then later with his baptism, and, still later, with his birth, and, finally, even with his preexistence before his appearance on earth. In any case, the important thing to keep in mind is that in both parts of the article—in the Christ-story as well as in the core with its different honorific titles—one and the same thing is going on: the church is formulating its symbols of faith in Jesus' decisive significance for human existence.

## What is and is not fundamental

If time allowed, I should now like to take up each of the clauses in the second article in turn, in the light of these brief comments on its structure, so as to make use of what I have suggested is a key to interpreting their meaning. But I must be content with a more modest undertaking, which can at most serve to illustrate what only an extended discussion could achieve. Specifically, I want to comment briefly on the phrase "born of the Holy Spirit and the Virgin Mary," or, in its more precise form in the Creed itself, "conceived by the Holy Spirit and born from (or of) the Virgin Mary." I choose this particular clause because it is so often regarded as fundamental to the faith of which the Creed is the symbol—no less by those who scruple to affirm it than by those who affirm it without hesitation.

In the more fully developed formulation of the second article eventually worked out by Christian orthodoxy, there is included an affirmation of Christ's preexistence and incarnation, which is to say, an affirmation to the effect that, before Jesus' earthly life began, the divine revealer whom we encounter decisively through him already existed with God, indeed, was God (cf. John 1:1–2). Thus, as the Nicene Creed has it, "I believe in one Lord Jesus Christ, the only begotten Son of God; begotten of the Father before all worlds, God of God, Light of Light, very God of very God, begotten, not made, being of one substance with the Father, through whom all things were made." Although it would be anachronistic to hold that those who first developed the Roman baptismal symbol, or even the Apostles' Creed itself, already intended this later affirmation, it's significant that certain tendencies in this direction are already evident. There is, for example, the word "only" in "his only Son our Lord," whose sole authorization in the New Testament is in the Johannine writings, where it clearly means divine preexistence (cf John 1:14, 18; 3:16, 18; 1 John 4:9). And then there are those precisions we noted in the phrase "conceived by the Holy Spirit and born from (or of) the Virgin Mary."

My point, in any case, is that the idea of Christ's preexistence and incarnation, which is at least adumbrated by the formulations of the Apostles' Creed, is, by clear implication, contrary to, or contradictory of, the idea originally involved in the New Testament assertions of Jesus' virgin birth. As anyone can readily see by consulting the version of this assertion in the Gospel of Luke, which is almost certainly older than Matthew's, its original intention was to explain the designation of Jesus as Son of God. Recall what the angel in Luke's story is made to say to Mary: "The Holy Spirit will come upon you, and the power of the Most High will overshadow you; therefore, the child to be born will be called holy, the Son of God" (Luke 1:35). In other words, given Christian belief in Jesus as God's Son, which was itself by way of expressing faith in him as God's decisive self-revelation, the story of Jesus' virgin birth developed in order to provide an explanation of *why* he's God's Son.

But that it was only *one* such explanation is clear, not only from the fact that, except for Matthew's Gospel, the virgin birth is otherwise undocumented by the New Testament writings, but also from the fact that the New Testament writings offer clear documentation of other, contrary explanations. Thus in Romans 1:4–5, for example, Paul affirms (apparently citing an already traditional formula) that Jesus was "declared to be Son of God with power according to the spirit of holiness by resurrection from the dead." So there is considerable agreement among New Testament scholars today that the earliest explicit christology was not incarnationist but adoptionist, in that it understood Jesus' resurrection as the moment of his adoption by God as God's Son. Quite soon, however, the intention behind this understanding led to viewing the still earlier event of Jesus' baptism by John as already the moment in which God had adopted him (cf., e.g., Mark 1:11; Matt 3:17), only to lead then to the still different view that he was already God's Son at the very beginning of his life because of his miraculous conception and birth. But this very same process of christological development—backwards, as it were—continued on to the affirmation that the Christ who is to be encountered through Jesus was already God's Son even before his earthly life began, because that life was in reality the incarnate life of a preexistent divine being who was God's Son, not by God's adopting him at some moment in time, but by his very nature, being begotten of God from all eternity. And this, of course, is why the two kinds of belief are, strictly speaking, contrary or contradictory. If the divine revealer whom we encounter decisively through Jesus already eternally *preexisted* as God's Son, then he neither did nor could have first *become* God's Son at the time of his conception and birth, to say nothing of his baptism or his resurrection from the dead.

In short, the affirmation of Jesus' virgin birth in its original New Testament meaning was but one way, and that a way destined to be superseded, of asserting what the later affirmation of Christ's preexistence was also intended to assert.

So what the phrase concerning Jesus' virgin birth was originally intended to affirm, and in the Creed still does affirm—however contradictorily with what else is affirmed or implied there, if it, too, is taken in its original meaning—is simply what every other phrase in the second article is also by way of affirming: that Jesus himself as a historical person, or in the actual event of his living and dying as a human being, is the decisive self-revelation of God, whose primal source and final end, therefore, are nothing in the world, but are nothing other or less than God Godself. To understand this, however, is to realize why any who would make the affirmation of Jesus' virgin birth a so-called fundamental, and as such a litmus test of valid Christian belief, simply don't know what they're doing. Like resurrections and ascensions and comings again, not to mention preexistences, virgin births are, so to speak, a dime a dozen in the history of religions, especially some of the religions in whose context the Christian religious tradition took shape. As with all the other things affirmed about Jesus in the second article, whether by designating him with honorific titles or by telling the Christ-story (more exactly, the Christ-myth) of his divine origin and destiny, what's significant christologically is not that someone is said to have been miraculously conceived and born of a virgin but that this familiar claim to decisive significance is made about *Jesus*.

Accordingly, to believe this claim in the only sense in which it was originally intended and still is properly intended is to believe in the one of whose decisive significance it is no more than one formulation among many others, all of which are interchangeable and, therefore, reducible or dispensable. And to believe in this one is not primarily to *believe that* something is true about Jesus, whether this ancient belief or the modern belief by which I've been trying to interpret and reformulate it; it is quite simply to *believe in* Jesus—in the word that he himself not only speaks but is—as God's own word of grace and judgment that sets us free *from* ourselves and all others, and free *for* them, to love and to serve them to their good and to God's glory.

Contrary, then, to what is only too often supposed, the several different *beliefs that* that the second article generally has been and certainly still may be taken to summarize are not one and all irreducible Christian beliefs. On the contrary, they're all, in their ways, reducible, being simply so many different, interchangeable, and therefore dispensable ways of formulating one and the same *belief that*, which alone is properly irreducible, or fundamental, although any formulation of it—whether its formulations in the Creed or the contemporary formulation I've offered in interpreting them—can and should be criticized theologically with respect to their appropriateness to Jesus Christ as well as their credibility to human existence.

Thus, just as the faith or *belief in* of which the first article is the symbol implies the irreducible, or fundamental, *belief that* the one mysterious ultimate whole of reality encompassing our existence and all existence is nothing other or less than the sovereign, unconditional love that it is decisively re-presented to be through Jesus, so the faith or *belief in* that Christians pledge symbolically by means of the second article implies the irreducible, or fundamental *belief that* Jesus himself is nothing other or less than the decisive re-presentation of the mystery encompassing both us and everything else.

In its way, then, the second article, like the Apostles' Creed as a whole, is there to remind us that to be a Christian is to believe *in* God *through* Jesus, *with* the apostles. Through the church's ever-renewed bearing of the apostles' witness, Christians believe in God decisively through Jesus, whom they therefore call the Christ. Consequently, they cannot but affirm their belief that God, which is to say, the one mysterious whole of reality encompassing us and all things, is the all-loving Father, to faith in whom they're decisively brought through Jesus (first article) *and* that Jesus, for his part, is the one decisively through whom they are again and again brought to faith in this God as nothing but sovereign, unconditional love (second article).

## The Holy Spirit

### Preliminary remark

By this time, my approach to interpreting the Creed and what I've called my thesis should have become clear enough to obviate my summarizing them yet again. This is just as well, because the third article, in some ways even more than the second, is so rich in content as to claim every minute I can give to it in this one remaining lecture. So I turn at once to analysis and interpretation, by first taking up the question whether the third article is the mere miscellany of *beliefs that* that it's often taken to be.

### A mere miscellany of beliefs that?

I begin by recalling my statement in interpreting the first article that the only ultimate ground of Christian faith in God, even as its only ultimate object, is God Godself. I recall this statement because, in my judgment, the first and most important thing to say about the term "the Holy Spirit" is that it designates the active presence and power of God Godself as the sole ultimate ground both of our being and of all being, and also of our new being as authentically human. God alone primordially creates all things, giving all living things their life; and then, in the case of those of us who are not only living and feeling, but also understanding creatures who can think and speak, also authorizes each of us to understand her- or himself authentically as God's own beloved child. This means that God alone at once entitles us, or gives us the *right*, so to understand ourselves, *and* enables us, or gives us the *power*, to do so. It is precisely this moment of power, or enablement, that belongs to the active presence of God in our lives that is singled out by trinitarian talk of God the Holy Spirit, even as it is the other moment of right, or entitlement, that is lifted up in talk about God the Son, whom we as Christians encounter decisively through Jesus Christ as the vindicator of our rights as beloved children of God. Thus it is entirely apt that, in the other great creed of the church, the so-called Nicene Creed, the Holy Spirit is identified as "the Lord and giver of life," which is to say, the vivifier, the One who is the very breath by which all creatures live and, if I may put it so, also the *re*-vivifier, the One who is the only ultimate ground of genuinely new life, of the true and authentic understanding of ourselves lived out in obedience to God as unreserved trust in God's love and as unqualified loyalty to God's cause.

I would suggest that this way of thinking and speaking about the Holy Spirit may make more sense to you if you simply reflect a moment on how it is that you ever in fact come to trust in someone in your ordinary day-to-day life with other persons. I submit that wherever our trust in another is real, we always realize, once we think about it, that it's nothing we owe to ourselves, but rather something grounded in the other, literally created in us by the other's disclosing her- or himself as loyal to us and as such worthy of our trust. So even in our interpersonal relationships, our trust in another—and much the same may be said, I think, of our loyalty to another or our love for another—is entirely a gift that we owe solely to the other's own presence and power in our lives. It is analogous, then, with our trust in God and our loyalty to God: they too are sheer gift, the gift of God's own presence and power, which alone can enable or empower us to either.

But if this is what is properly meant by speaking of the Holy Spirit, it should be becoming clear why, contrary to what the third article may at first glance appear to be, and is only too often mistaken to be, it is by no means simply a remainder of miscellaneous credenda not easily consigned to either of the other two articles. Far from being any such mere miscellany of other beliefs, the third article, in its way, and for essentially the same reasons, has every bit as much unity or integrity as either the first or the second. Just as the catholic or universal church is the one community of faith and witness that the Holy Spirit creates and sustains, and just as the *communio sanctorum* spoken of thereafter—however exactly this phrase is to be translated and interpreted—is also a matter of sharing in the same Holy Spirit, so the forgiveness of sins is that Spirit's gift as regards our past, even as the resurrection of the body (or, literally, of the *flesh*) and the life everlasting are the same Spirit's gift as regards our future.

So, at any rate, I shall now assume as I proceed to the second and principal part of my lecture by talking about what I call

## The structure and meaning of the third article

I begin with comments, mainly historical, on the several specific beliefs included in the article, as well as on the three additions made to its earlier version in *R*. You'll see from the Appendix that, in the later form of *R*, the article is composed of four phrases and reads, simply, "I believe in the Holy Spirit, the holy church, the forgiveness of sins, the resurrection of the flesh."

1. So far as the first phrase, *"the Holy Spirit,"* is concerned, suffice it to add to what I've already said only that in *R*, even as later in the Creed itself, the precise identity and activity of the Holy Spirit and its relation to the Father and the Son are not clarified, as they are in the Nicene Creed, in the passage I already cited. There the Holy Spirit, who is said to be "the Lord, the giver of life," is further said to proceed "from the Father" as the One "who together with the Father and the Son is worshipped and glorified, who spoke through the prophets." Already at the time of *R*, however (ca. 150 CE), the Holy Spirit was almost certainly understood (1) to sanctify or make holy both the community of the church and the individual believer; (2) to have been active already, before the coming of Christ and the church, through the prophets, which is to say, not only "the Prophets" strictly so called, but also the whole history of revelation documented by the Old Testament; and (3) to fill the church as its veritable esprit de corps and to be bestowed on each individual Christian through her or his baptism.

2. The term *"church"* (*ekklesia*) is borrowed from the Septuagint (LXX), the Greek translation of the Hebrew scriptures, where it translates the Hebrew term *"qahal,"* the title commonly given to Israel as the chosen people, called out by, and solemnly assembled before, God. As appropriated by Christians, *ecclesia* expressed their claim to be the new Israel. For Irenæus in the last half of the second century CE, the church was the so-called great church standing over against the sects of the heretics, filled with the Holy Spirit, and admitting God's people to all the blessings of God's kingdom. As for the other term, *"holy,"* it was becoming a stock description of the great church, so understood, even earlier. It, too, goes back to the LXX, where it could be applied to whatever concerned or belonged to God, especially God's people, Israel. But, like the term in the New Testament that we translate with "saints," meaning "holy persons," the connotation of "holy" was not, in the first instance, moral. The church described itself as holy because it was called out and chosen by God decisively through Jesus Christ for a glorious inheritance, and was indwelt by God Godself as, or in the person of, the Holy Spirit. By the middle of the second century, however, the doctrine of the church was assuming a much more distinctive role as the conflict intensified between "the great church" and

the sects. It's reasonable to infer, then, that the presence of this second phrase in R and in the Creed, although not only or directly polemical, is a by-product of the enhanced and more self-conscious emphasis on the church that was becoming increasingly characteristic of the orthodox teaching and theology of the second century.

3. *"The forgiveness of sins"* was ever closely associated with baptism, which was understood to wash away past sins and to open up a new life—hence the formulation in the Nicene Creed: "I acknowledge one baptism for the forgiveness of sins." In the course of the second century, however, there seems to have been a heightening of the emphasis placed on the release from the burden of sin that baptism brings about. Indeed, a close student of it has accurately characterized the whole elaborate catechetical preparation for baptism as one vast exorcism.

4. Belief in *"the resurrection of the flesh [or of the body]"* had been integral to Christianity from the beginning, having been taken over from Pharisaic Judaism, and also, presumably, from Jesus' own witness of faith. But by the middle of the second century there were groups of Christians, or pseudo-Christians (sc. Gnostics) who denied the resurrection, on the dualistic ground that because matter is essentially evil, salvation is of the soul or spirit alone, not also of the body or flesh. So this controversy may well lie somewhere in the background of this phrase and help to explain its provocative wording, "resurrection of the *flesh*," instead of the more common New Testament formula preserved in the Nicene Creed: "resurrection of [or from] the dead."

So much for the four clauses that were simply taken over from R. By the time the Creed assumed final shape, the third article was almost certainly understood in the light of the church's developing doctrine of the trinity. So "the Holy Spirit" at least tacitly named the third person of the Godhead, coeternal, coequal, and consubstantial with the Father and the Son. Also, the third phrase, concerning the forgiveness of sins, was explained after ca. 350 CE as including the forgiveness to be obtained not only through baptism but also through the additional, more recently developed, sacrament of penance, with its two principal elements of confessing sins committed after baptism and thereupon receiving priestly absolution. Beyond these differences due to later doctrine and theology, the third article has three differences from R, of which the most important is the phrase affirming belief in the *communio sanctorum*. But this phrase, as I've indicated, is also difficult to translate, because the plural noun "*sanctorum*" can be neuter as well as masculine in gender. Since the other two differences can be treated more easily, I'll deal with them first.

One is the qualification of the church as not only "holy" but also "catholic." The term "catholic" means, simply, "general," or "universal," and it was so understood in its original application to the church, where it served to distinguish the one universal church from all the local or regional churches in each of which it was believed to subsist. But after ca. 150 CE, "catholic" began to acquire the new connotation of designating "the great church," as I've called it, in contrast to what Christians belonging to it thought of as just so many heretical or schismatic sects. When, then, the term began to appear in Western creeds late in the fourth century, it no doubt also gave expression to the majority church's consciousness of its unique authority over against the dissident minority churches, which it distinguished from itself pejoratively—as precisely "sects."

The other difference is the addition of the phrase "and the life everlasting," which seems to have made its earliest appearance in African formularies. It is usually thought to have served as a reassurance to persons affirming the Creed at their baptism that their resurrection was to be continuing or permanent, like Jesus' own, rather than merely temporary, as was that of Lazarus whom Jesus, according to John 12, brought back from the dead only to face death again. Hence this wording was sometimes found: "I believe in the resurrection of the flesh *to* the life everlasting." Eventually, however, another independent, more positive meaning attached itself to the phrase. It was taken to mean something more than mere permanence or continuance of life beyond death—namely, what the church father Cyril of Jerusalem calls "the real, veritable life" that is God's own life as God. Some such notion is already to be found in the Johannine writings in the New Testament; and, according to Thomas Aquinas much later, the first truth about everlasting life is union with God, who is Godself the reward and end of all our labors and who crowns all our desires.

As for the remaining, more important but difficult difference—the phrase "*communio sanctorum*"—I shall add here only three brief comments to what I've already said about translating it. The first is simply that the phrase was probably Gallican in origin. The second is that the earlier and—between the fifth and the eighth centuries, at least—dominant interpretation of the phrase seems to have been "communion of (or fellowship with) holy *persons*" (in our term, "saints"), whereas the sacramental interpretation, "communion of (or sharing in) holy *things*," has all the air of being secondary. My third comment is that the fourth century CE witnessed an enormous expansion of the devotion that the church paid to its saints and martyrs as well as to its dead generally. Therefore, although the addition hardly seems to have been merely apologetic, in defense of this growing cult of the saints, it may very well have reflected an ever deepening sense of the fellowship that the militant church on earth is already privileged to enjoy with the triumphant church in heaven.

With this I must turn from analysis of the structure of the third article to some all too brief reflections on its meaning for us today. I shall touch on only certain, to my mind, high points, and I will risk re-expressing much of what I understand the article to affirm in first-person terms as what I myself understand and believe in affirming the Creed. I do this gladly because, like many, and perhaps most, of you, I'm not only a Christian theologian but also—and first of all—a member of the church who gratefully receives and uses the Creed as the symbol of my own faith and belief.

First of all, it should be clear from what I've said how I would interpret Paul's characteristic talk of "life according to the Spirit," as contrasted with what he calls "life according to the flesh." If the Holy Spirit, as I've argued, is the active presence and power of God Godself as the enabling, empowering ground of our own obedient faith, our unreserved trust in God's love and our unqualified loyalty to its cause, then life according to the Spirit is just that life of radical, paradoxical freedom that I spoke of already in interpreting the first article. I can thus live in freedom *from* all things, myself and all others, and in freedom *for* them just because I'm freed so to live by the Holy Spirit, by the active presence and power of God's love that sets me free in just this radical, paradoxical way.

As for affirming faith in *"the holy catholic church,"* I'm not in the least hesitant, as some seem to be, to acknowledge the church as the object of my faith. Unlike those who feel the need to exploit a verbal distinction between "I believe *in* the Holy Spirit" and "I believe the holy catholic church," I unhesitatingly pledge my obedience, and thus both my trust in, and my loyalty to, the holy catholic church. This I do because it is solely in and through this church with its Spirit-inspired witness that I'm enabled to trust in and be loyal to Jesus Christ and, decisively through him, God the Father. Of course, the holy catholic church that is the immediate object and ground of my faith is something other than, and distinct from, any and all of the various institutional churches; and this distinction would remain even were there to be, in some distant future, no longer many churches, but only one institutional church. Although I by no means take the term "the holy catholic church" to refer to anything other than the visible Christian church, I abide by the teaching of the Protestant Reformers, wittily expressed in the words of the Westminster Confession, that this one visible church "hath been sometimes more, sometimes less, visible"—namely, in all the many different institutional churches. The only holy catholic church is the church that subsists more or less visibly in the various institutional churches; and in expressing my trust in and loyalty to it, I am at the same time expressing an always only reserved trust in, and an always only qualified loyalty to, all churches as institutions, including, not least, my own, for whose witness and its validity—its adequacy to its content and its fittingness to its situation—I bear particular responsibility.

So far as "*the communion of saints*" is concerned, I must frankly admit that I'm no longer as sure as I once was how rightly to interpret it. Assuming, as I do, that it's not merely redundant, not just saying "the holy catholic church" all over again, I continue to waver between my earlier, rather confident interpretation of it as only verbally different from what the Reformers distinguished as "the invisible church," and another somewhat different interpretation. On it, I give more weight to what I referred to earlier as the traditional sacramental interpretation, on which the plural noun "*sanctorum*" is understood to be neuter rather than, or as well as, masculine, and so rendered in English as "of holy things," rather than, or as well as, "of holy persons," or "of saints." But, then, still assuming that the phrase is more than just a verbally different way of saying "holy catholic church," I take it to refer most reasonably to the wider community of all, non-Christians as well as Christians, who are explicitly religious, of which the visible Christian church is but a part, along with all of the other religions in which our existential question as human beings and the different answers to it somehow become explicit. I must say, however, that my uncertainty about which of these interpretations to favor doesn't bother me all that much as a Christian who gladly receives and makes use of the Creed as his own symbol of faith. On either interpretation, I should have no hesitation in affirming, "I believe in the *communio sanctorum*." Why not? Well, because I believe in *both*: both in the invisible church embracing all, but only, those Christians whose faith and life, although visible but to God, are authentic as well as true *and* in a wider, really "ecumenical" community not only of all Christians and churches, but also of all other religious believers and institutions.

Belief in "*the forgiveness of sins*," as I understand it, is nothing other than or additional to belief in God as decisively disclosed through Jesus and the church, but is one and the same with this very belief. The sin (singular) that is the taproot of all sins (plural) is nothing other than un-faith, or unbelief, in God: distrust in God's love and disloyalty to its cause. And it is just such distrust and disloyalty that Christian faith understands to be our most fundamental problem as human beings. To be sure, it also recognizes our fragmentariness and death and such experiences as doubt and meaninglessness to be fundamental human problems. But it locates the crux even of them, and thus of our human predicament, not in the fact that we have to die or that we can never be altogether certain whether our lives somehow make sense, but in the fact that we refuse to accept our death and the meaninglessness of our lives apart from God by looking solely to God's love as our true life. Belief in the forgiveness of sins, then, also always implies a definite belief about ourselves as human beings—namely, that we are, precisely, sinners. But it also means that God's acceptance of us is an acceptance "nevertheless," *in spite of* our sin and our sins. And so forgiveness, as Luther rightly stresses, is the whole of the Christian life—not just a onetime event at baptism, and so something requiring to be regularly supplemented by means of yet another sacra-ment of penance. Baptism is, indeed, a onetime event; and there is ever a place for continued confession and absolution in some form in every Christian life, my own very much included. But just as baptism bestows forgiveness only by re-presenting it, so penance, rightly understood, is solely by way of re-presenting the promise already made in baptism as, again, in Maurice's words, "the sacrament of constant union," which means not only onetime, but also *once-for-all-time*. I know that I can and do again and again fall from the grace of God's acceptance in the sense of not trusting in it without reservation and not being loyal to its cause without qualification. But I also believe that God's grace itself is never absent from my life, or any other human life, just as soon and as long as it is really a human life at all; and neither baptism nor penance in any form can ever be more—even if never less—than special, solemn declarations that this is so.

Finally, I believe in "*the resurrection of the flesh and the life everlast-ing*." And I understand my belief therein to be the strict counterpart of my belief in the creation of all things, of myself as well as of everything else, out of nothing by God. Just as God alone is the primal source of all things, so God is also their sole final end. This means that there is nothing whatever alongside God whose primal source and final end are in anything other than God's boundless, all-embracing love. Thus, far from pertaining only to the righteous, or even only to human persons and any other morally free and responsible beings, the resurrection of the flesh in which I believe pertains to all creatures. *All things*, being embraced by God's unbounded love, thereupon become part-constitutive of God's own unending life and, in that sense, are resurrected in God Godself. Indeed, it's possible to say that, in this sense, all things participate in the life everlasting, that being an exact description of God's own unbegun and unending life. As even some of the church fathers rightly realized, the only truly everlasting life is God's life, so that such everlasting life as I may claim for myself, or as may be claimed for anyone or anything else, is simply my, or their, participation in *God's* life—thanks solely to God's all-loving participation in their lives. We also do well to remember that "life everlasting" in the Creed is the very phrase we find in the Gospel of John—notably in 3:16: "For God so loved the world that he gave his only Son, that whoever believes in him should not perish but have everlasting life." From this witness I learn—and teach—how justified those church fathers were who saw the meaning of the phrase to lie not in quantity of life, but in its quality—a quality in which I as a person can and should already participate even now through obedient faith. "Truly, truly, I say to you, whoever hears my word and believes in him who sent me, has everlasting life and does not come into judgment but has passed from death to life" (John 5:24). And definitively: "And this is everlasting life, that they know you the only true God, and Jesus Christ whom you have sent" (John 17:3).

## Conclusion

I end my lectures as I began them, with the question of credibility guiding our whole inquiry in this seminar: Is the Apostles' Creed credible? My own inclination, now at the end of the seminar, is still to answer the question with a qualified affirmation: Yes, the Apostles' Creed *is* credible—or cannot be easily dismissed as *in*credible—although only provided it is correctly understood in its proper place in the Christian life as "symbol of faith," and, as an essential part of such understanding, provided we correctly understand what it therefore means, and does not mean, to make it our own. If you've followed what I've tried to say in all of my lectures and in our discussions afterwards, you will realize that my objective throughout has been to provide just such understanding of the proper use of the Creed and of what it does, and does not, require of us if we are to affirm it ourselves.

You should also be clear, however, why, as indispensable as such understanding is to any adequate answer to the question of the Creed's credibility, it is not sufficient thereto, because, as a question about what the Creed really means, it is still only preliminary or preparatory to giving a reasoned answer to the question itself. Whether or not the Creed, rightly understood, is really worth believing can be determined only through our own common human experience and by following procedures of validation and verification appropriate to determining the credibility of any comprehensive self-understanding and of the kinds of assertions about the way things really are that all such self-understandings necessarily make or imply. But actually following these procedures has not been the task of this seminar and remains to be taken up by each of us simply in our own further individual study and critical reflection, if not in some other course or courses. And this is so, even if, as we may all hope, the preparatory work necessary to any such further inquiry has been advanced to some extent by what we've managed to do in this seminar.

There's another question, however, closely related to that of the Creed's credibility, that what we've tried to do should be more than sufficient to answer. This is the question of what is, and what is not, the right test of anyone's being able to affirm the Creed as one's own, honestly and with integrity.

If my argument is sound and to the point, that test is *not* whether one formulates one's faith today in the same concepts and symbols, terms and categories, that the Creed itself employs in its several formulations. On the contrary, the only test is whether one's faith as a human being is the same faith, i.e., the same *belief in*, the same trust and loyalty, and so the same self-understanding, and therefore also the same *belief that*, the same understanding of existence, or the same worldview—however differently one may—even must—formulate this faith and belief if they are really to be one's own.

Of course, in saying that one's *belief that* as well as one's *belief in* has to be the same as that expressed by the Creed, I cannot mean, consistently with what I've just said, that one must simply accept the several *beliefs that* (in the plural) included in the Creed as one and all irreducible Christian beliefs, as distinct from being simply alternative, in fact interchangeable and therefore reducible, yes, dispensable, ways of expressing some still more fundamental—and alone irreducible—Christian *belief that*. Just as there is but one Christian faith in the primary sense of one Christian *belief in*, and therefore only one trust and one loyalty—in short, one Christian self-understanding—so there is also but one Christian *belief that* (in the singular), one Christian understanding of existence, one Christian worldview, one *truth of Christian faith*. And this is so even if this one Christian truth certainly may be expressed, and, as the Creed itself sufficiently shows, in fact has been expressed, only in the form of many different Christian truths.

As we learned at the very beginning of our inquiry, faith or belief, in the primary sense of *belief in*, is one thing, belief in the other sense of *belief that*, something else. But there is this further distinction I've also been concerned to make—and that, in my opinion, somehow has to be made by anyone seeking to think and speak clearly in these matters—and this is the distinction between both faith and belief, *belief in* and *belief that* (in the singular), on the one hand, and all the particular expressions or formulations of faith and belief, and so all particular *beliefs that* (in the plural), on the other hand. Because or insofar as one makes this further distinction, one may say, with good reason, that expressing or formulating one's faith and belief in the Creed's own terms may never be rightly made the test of whether one can affirm honestly and with integrity the faith and belief of which the Creed, rightly used and understood, is the symbol.

This, then, is the thought I would leave you with, although I've never found it better expressed than in yet another statement of Frederick Denison Maurice's, to whom I therefore want to give the last word.

> [The Creed] is a tradition—often it has been called *the* tradition of the Church. As such we receive it, and rejoice in it. But on this ground especially, that it is a continual protection against traditions, that when they try to force themselves upon us, we can always put this forward as a declaration that what we believe and trust in is not this or that notion, or theory, or scheme, or document; but that it is the Eternal Name into which we are baptized, and in which the whole Church and each member of the Church stands. As it has come down to us it must be a tradition. But it is a tradition which we cannot value for its own sake.

Not the utterance, but that which is uttered; not the form, but the substance which it sets forth is the object and ground of our belief.[4]

Look with favor, O God, on all our attempts to learn and to teach. Enable us, above all, both to speak and to listen to one another in love: to say what we mean and to mean what we say; and, not least, to hear what is meant, not just what is said; in Jesus' name. Amen.[5]

# Appendix

## 1. The Old Roman Symbol (R) (Reconstructed)[6]

### 1.1 Earlier Form

I believe in God, the Father, the Almighty
And in Jesus Christ, his only begotten Son, our Lord
And in the Holy Spirit, the holy church, the resurrection of the flesh

### 1.2 Later Form

I believe in God the Father, the Almighty
And in Christ Jesus, his only begotten Son, our Lord
who was born of the Holy Spirit and the Virgin Mary
crucified under Pontius Pilate and buried
the third day he rose from the dead
he ascended into heaven
he sits at the right hand of the Father
from whence he will come to judge the living and the dead
And in the Holy Spirit
the holy church
the forgiveness of sins
the resurrection of the flesh

---

4. Frederick Denison Maurice, *The Prayer Book: Considered Especially in Reference to the Romish System* (London: Parker, 1849), 161–62.

5. Composed by the author.

6. Translated by the author from Bernhard Lohse, *Epochen der Dogmengeschichte* (Stuttgart: Kreuz, 1963), 40. See also Bernhard Lohse, *A Short History of Christian Doctrine*, trans. F. Ernest Stoeffler (Philadelphia: Fortress, 1966), 32–36.

## 2. Traditional Version of the Apostles' Creed

I believe in God the Father Almighty
creator of heaven and earth
And in Jesus Christ, his only Son, our Lord
who was conceived by the Holy Spirit and born of the Virgin Mary
suffered under Pontius Pilate, was crucified, dead, and buried
he descended into hell
the third day he rose from the dead
he ascended into heaven
he sits at the right hand of God the Father Almighty
from thence he shall come to judge the living and the dead
I believe in the Holy Spirit
the holy catholic church
the communion of saints
the forgiveness of sins
the resurrection of the flesh
the life everlasting

# 3

# *Being a Christian Today*

Although the call to be a Christian is ever the same, it is also always different because of the life-situations of those to whom it comes. Not only must we reckon with the difference between our situation today and those of the witnesses through whom we have received our summons to faith, but we must also come to terms with new problems for whose solution we have no ready precedents. This seminar is designed to heighten our consciousness about how we are called to lead the Christian life today—what we are to believe and what we are to do—given our situation and its problems as well as its possibilities for solving them. Particular attention will be given to being a Christian in the USA today.

> Almighty God, our heavenly Father, who through our Lord Jesus Christ has established your church to be a sign of salvation for the whole world; give each of us in this community the courage and the understanding to do our part in being this sign, both by bearing witness and—in order to bear it validly—by doing theology; this we ask for Jesus' sake. Amen.[1]

## The Call to Be a Christian

### Introduction

What is it to be a Christian today? This is the very general but also fundamental question that constitutes and will guide our inquiry in this

1. Composed by the author.

seminar. In order to answer it, we will pursue several more specific questions, beginning in this lecture with, What is the call to be a Christian? I shall seek an answer in two steps, asking, in order, What is the original call to be a human being? And then, What is the decisive call to be a Christian? Why I find it necessary to proceed in this way will, I trust, become clear as I develop my argument.

### The original call to be a human being

It's evident simply from the Greek word that we commonly translate by our English word "church"—which is to say, the Greek word "*ekklesia*" that literally means "a calling out"—that Christians from the very beginning have understood themselves to be the called out. So, too, have they always understood Jesus Christ as the one through whom God has decisively called them out into the community of the church. But it is scarcely less clear that, from their standpoint as Christians, they're by no means alone in having been in some way called by God. On the contrary, they understand themselves even as the decisively called to belong to an indefinitely larger and more inclusive community of the called. This community comprises not merely the people of the old covenant, Israel, whom Christians believe to have been specially called by God, but all other peoples as well, because it includes literally every human being.

The reason for this is not far to seek. Being Christians, they, too, are "people of the book," bound in their own way to the Hebrew scriptures with their clear teaching of God's original covenant with the whole human race through the creation of Adam and Eve and of God's then renewing that covenant with Noah and his descendants after the all but universal destruction of the flood. Of course, we today have been given to recognize that the biblical stories that are the vehicles of this teaching (Gen 1–2, 9) are mythical, or mythological, in that they have the same literary form that is familiar to us from any number of other traditional accounts of the origin of all things and of the constitution of the human race. This means that we seriously misunderstand the stories, and so quite miss their point, if we take them to be reports of events of the more or less remote past occurring at or near the beginning of the whole course of events that has continued right up to and includes things happening today. Far from being reports of any such remote past events, they are, in fact, stories about *our own existence as human beings right here and now in the present*: about our own origin together with all of the other nonhuman creatures and about *our own constitution* (and primal reconstitution) together with all other women and men as members of one human family. In short, the stories are intended to teach us that, exactly like every other human being who has ever lived or ever will live, we've received any special, or even decisive, call of God that may have come to us only as those whom God has always already called just in creating us. Before we ever receive any special or decisive call through the events and experiences of our own individual lives, God originally calls each of us to become the human being we've been created to be, so as thereby to become the covenant partner of God as well as of each and every other human being, whom God likewise originally calls.

If we ask now just what it means to say this, and in what sense it's true, I think the essential things to bring to mind are these:

To be the human being that each of us is, is to be a distinctive kind of being. We don't simply exist, we *understand* that we exist, and do so at the high level exhibited behaviorally by our thinking and speaking and by our capacity more generally to make use of concepts and symbols in all the different ways we use them. This means that we cannot exist at all except through our own *self-understanding*—through somehow understanding ourselves and others and the all-encompassing whole of reality of which we and they are all parts—and then leading our lives accordingly. For this reason, we not only *are* human, but also continually have to *become* human—to become who we really are—in and through our own free and responsible decisions.

Thus to live understandingly and responsibly, however, is something we do not only on one level, as it were, but on two: not only on the primary level of self-understanding and life-praxis but also on the secondary level of critical reflection and proper theory. On the primary level of our interaction with one another, on which we each understand ourselves and lead our lives accordingly, we think, say, and do things that make or imply certain claims to validity: claims to understand ourselves authentically, to think and speak sincerely and truly, to act rightly, and so on. But simply to make or imply these claims may or may not be to do so validly and is therefore in no way sufficient to validate them. Whether or not they're really as valid as we claim they are may always be, or become, more or less problematic; and when they become problematic enough, the promise to others that we in effect hold out in making or implying them obliges us to move to the secondary level of living understandingly.

There we critically reflect on the validity of our claims by way of a full and free discourse with our partners in interaction. But, clearly, one can never fairly validate or invalidate what one has not really understood. So, just as the secondary level of living understandingly by way of discourse includes critically *validating* the claims that we make or imply by what we think, say, and do on the primary level, so living understandingly also includes, as a necessary presupposition of validating them, critically *interpreting* what we really mean and do not mean in thinking, speaking, and acting as we do.

Because, however, each of us as a human being can and should live thus understandingly, we may each be said to have been originally called so to live and therefore to be capable of also being specially and even decisively so called if and when such a special or decisive call may happen to come to us through the events and experiences of our own individual lives. Someone may call us up short, say, by challenging our take on certain things. By offering a different take on them, she or he, in effect, issues a special call to us to reconsider our position in the light of this alternative. In a particular case, then, such a special call may even prove to be a decisive call to us, because it turns out to provide us with a criterion by which we are enabled to decide for or against *any* other way of taking the same things, including the way we ourselves once took them. But neither such a decisive call nor even just a special call could ever be received by us at all did we not find ourselves always already called to understand ourselves and everything else realistically, in keeping with things as they really are, instead of unrealistically, at cross-purposes with them.

We're originally called, first of all, to understand ourselves and everything else truly and authentically: truly, because realistically in this sense, and authentically, because we ourselves, at the deepest level, always already understand things as they really are. This means that we are called to understand ourselves in accordance both with what we understand at least implicitly to be the meaning of ultimate reality for us and with the witness of anyone or anything explicitly re-presenting its meaning—in direct proportion to the validity of the "re-presentation." We're further called, then, to lead our whole lives as human beings according to our true and authentic self-understanding; and this means that whatever we think, say, or do is somehow to give expression to *this* understanding of ourselves instead of any other.

Then, as an essential part of this call to understand ourselves truly and authentically, and to lead our lives accordingly, we're also called, whenever it becomes necessary to do so, to reflect critically on all self-understanding and life-praxis, our own as well as all others', to see whether or not our self-understanding really is in accordance with things as they are, and as we ourselves at least implicitly understand them to be, and whether or not our life-praxis in all of its aspects and forms really does validly express what we most deeply understand to be the case.

But now Christian faith and witness understand all that I have thus expressed in purely formal—if you will, philosophical—terms to have a distinctive material meaning in the light of Jesus Christ. Specifically, the ultimate reality of human existence, understood formally or philosophically simply as self, others, and the whole, is understood Christianly to be the threefold reality of self and all others embraced within the all-encompassing love of God. I'm suggesting, in other words, that the term "God," as Christians use it, refers to the *strictly* ultimate reality of the whole, but for which none of the parts, neither the self nor anyone or anything else, would be so much as possible or have any lasting significance. So, in Christian terms, what I mean by our original call to be human beings, by understanding ourselves truly and authentically and leading our lives accordingly, is the call to understand ourselves and live our lives in keeping with the strictly ultimate reality of God's all-embracing love as the sole primal source and the sole final end of all things, ourselves very much included.

This is to say that the meaning of ultimate reality for us, as we see it as Christians, is the meaning of *this* ultimate reality for us—namely, that we each can and should entrust ourselves, finally, solely to God's love, confident of God's unconditional acceptance both of us and of all our fellow creatures, and then loyally live in returning love for God and for all whom God loves—which is to say, of course, everyone and everything, anyone and anything. But if it is thus that we and all other human beings are originally called to understand ourselves, we're also called to a life-praxis, a way of leading our lives, that is expressive of such trust in God's love and loyalty to its cause. In the terms that we as Christians are wont to use, we're called *to bear witness*: both *explicit* witness through the forms of religion, and *implicit* witness through all the other forms of culture, secular as well as religious. And, then, in order to bear a *valid* witness, all of us, just as and because we're human beings, are also called to reflect critically on our own self-understanding and life-praxis to see whether or not they really are what they're supposed to be and also claim to be: whether or not what really does claim our unreserved trust and our unqualified loyalty is God's all-encompassing love, and whether or not all that we then think, say, and do, be it religious or secular, really is expressive of just such trust in God's love and loyalty to its cause.

To sum up, the original call to be a human being is the call to understand oneself in a distinctive way and to lead one's life accordingly. In what way? Well, in Christian terms, in such a way as to entrust oneself without reservation to God's pure unbounded love and to serve it loyally without qualification, loving God and therefore also loving all the others whom God loves, to whom God is likewise ever loyal. To one's fellow human beings, all of whom, like oneself, are thus called to become who they really are, one can be loyal only insofar as one is willing, whenever necessary, to submit one's own self-understanding and life-praxis along with all others' to critical reflection, critically interpreting their meaning and critically validating their claims to validity. Thus, although one is indeed bound to accept any life-praxis whose claims are valid as either explicit or implicit witness, and so as expressing God's own special, even decisive, call to one, one is also bound—whenever it becomes necessary—to validate critically the claims of all life-praxis before making it one's own and handing it on to others as God's special, indeed, decisive, call also to them.

In short, the original call to be a human being, formulated in Christian terms, is the call to entrust oneself to God's love and then, on the basis of such entrustment, to live in loyalty to God and to all to whom God is loyal and, in this sense, to love God and all things in God. In order to exist in just such trust and loyalty, however, one is also called—as to a means thereto that may always become indispensable—to critical reflection on one's own self-understanding and life-praxis as well as on those of others.

### The decisive call to be a Christian

I trust it will now be clear why, in order to answer our question about the call to be a Christian, we first had to ask, What is the original call to be a human being? We had to ask and answer this question first because the call to be a Christian, like any other special call that comes, not to all human beings but only to some, necessarily presupposes the original call that comes to each and every human being and that alone makes possible their ever receiving any special or decisive calls—namely, the original call to be and to become a human being.

But now if the call to be a Christian, which we as Christians understand to be not only special but also decisive, necessarily presupposes the original call to be a human being, it itself is nonetheless a special call and as such distinctively different. It is a call above and beyond the original call that comes to all to—in Christian terms—exist in faith in God's prevenient love for us and in returning love for God and for all whom God loves, and then to enact such faith and love in the whole of one's life-praxis. To be sure, God's original call to each of us to become human is irrevocable, and so we as Christians, like everyone else, ever remain subject to it and can never be validly called to be or to do anything that doesn't somehow confirm it by authorizing—entitling and empowering—us to obey it. Even so, the call to be a Christian is distinctively different in that it is the call to accept Jesus as the Christ, by which I mean, to accept the historical person Jesus of Nazareth as the decisive re-presentation of the meaning of ultimate reality for us, and to understand oneself and lead one's life accordingly. Such leading of one's life—or life-praxis, as I also call it—involves both acknowledging the authority and making effective use of all valid Christian witness and means of transformation and then sharing in bearing this same witness and administering these same means to others. And it further involves, whenever it becomes necessary, critically reflecting on the validity claims expressed or implied in bearing Christian witness—one's own as well as that of other Christians. In this sense, or for this reason, to be called to be a Christian is to be called both to be a Christian *minister*, by sharing in bearing valid Christian witness and in validly administering specifically Christian means of transformation, and to be a Christian *theologian*, by critically interpreting the meaning of Christian witness and critically validating the claims to be valid that bearing it makes or implies.

Such, stated summarily, is my answer to our second question, What is the decisive call to be a Christian? I now want to unpack this summary answer, and this I shall do by speaking briefly on four main topics.

The first is what I shall call "*the other presuppositions*" *of the call to be a Christian*. I've already explained why the original and universal call to be a human being is necessarily presupposed by the decisive call to be a Christian. But this original and universal call to be human is not the only necessary presupposition of the distinctively Christian call. Also necessarily presupposed by it is that the call to be a human being, which is presented to each of us implicitly through all of our experience and is re-presented to us explicitly through the primary form of culture properly distinguished as "religion," also needs to be *decisively re-presented* to us. That is, the call to be human needs to be presented to us *again*, a *second* time, *explicitly*, and with such full, perfect, and sufficient adequacy and fittingness as allows us to *decide* between the Christian understanding of the meaning of ultimate reality and all the more or less inadequate and often conflicting re-presentations of its meaning for us.

Our original call to be human needs to be thus decisively re-presented for two reasons: not only because, without such a re-presentation, we can never be completely clear and certain about the meaning of ultimate reality for us, but also because each and every one of us has not only always already received the call to be human but has again and again disobeyed it. We have elected instead to understand ourselves and lead our lives falsely and inauthentically because unrealistically, not in accordance but at variance with ultimate reality as it really is and as we ourselves, at the deepest level, understand it to be. In other words, among the necessary presuppositions of the call to be a Christian is not only the original and universal call to be a human being, but also the two universal facts of human creatureliness and human sin. Because of our creatureliness, we need our original call to be human to be *decisively* re-presented to us, so that we no longer have to be in any way unclear and uncertain about the meaning of ultimate reality for us. But because of our sin, we need our call to be decisively *re-presented* to us, so that we once again have the possibility of obeying it, notwithstanding all of our previous failures to do so.

I may mention in this connection that, even as I was working on these lectures, I ran across a saying of C. S. Lewis that I had copied into my notebooks as a student only to have eventually quite forgotten. In it, he offers a succinct summary of his own understanding as a Christian whose bearing on what I'm calling the presuppositions of the decisive call to be a Christian could hardly be clearer. First, he says, "human beings, all over the earth, have this curious idea that they ought to behave in a certain way, and cannot really get rid of it. Secondly, . . . they do not in fact behave in that way. They know the Law of Nature; they break it. These two facts are the foundation of all clear thinking about ourselves and the universe we live in."

This brings me to the second topic: *the point of christology*. The call to be a Christian, I've indicated, is not merely a *theological* call but also a *christological* call. By this I mean that it not only summons us faithfully to accept God's unconditional love for us and then to love God in return by also loving our neighbors as ourselves, but also to accept Jesus as the

Christ—such acceptance and the christological assertion necessarily implied by it being constitutive of Christian faith and witness respectively. By speaking of the christological assertion as thus "constitutive," I mean simply that it is the assertion that—together with the constitutive *theo logical* assertion that Christians also make—constitutes Christian belief and witness explicitly as such. Actually, I should put this more carefully by distinguishing between the christological *assertion itself*, on the one hand, and its *classical formulation* in the words "Jesus is the Christ," on the other. This formulation is rightly said to be the classical formulation, not only because it is presumably the earliest such formulation, but also because it is from it that both the proper name "Jesus Christ" and the term "christology" and its cognates are derived. Even so, there are any number of other formulations, quite distinct from this classical one, through which the constitutive christological assertion can be and, in fact, has been made, beginning already with the many quite different christologies—and different types of christology—attested by the New Testament writings.

But, however the assertion is formulated, it is by way of asserting somehow, in some terms or other, that the human being Jesus is, without prejudice to his being really and truly human, the decisive re-presentation of the meaning of ultimate reality for us as human beings. Thus, so far as Christians are concerned, the decisive re-presentation of our call to be human, for which we have a need because of both our creatureliness and our sin, is not, in the first instance, some law or teaching, oracle or writing, as it is for many other communities of faith or religions, but rather a human person, every bit as human as ourselves, through whose life and death we are each decisively confirmed in our original call to be a human being precisely by being called to be a Christian. It is decisively in accordance with this human person, through whom the meaning of ultimate reality for us becomes explicit, that we are called to understand ourselves and to lead our lives insofar as we are called to be Christians. And it is just this—this call decisively to understand ourselves through Jesus and to lead our lives accordingly—that I mean by "the point of christology." I speak of it so because to respond to any formulation of the christological assertion so as really to get its point is to understand ourselves through Jesus to be a beloved child of God and then to love God and all whom God loves, ourselves and our neighbors, indeed, all our fellow creatures. And it is to do this, despite any unclarity and uncertainty we may have had previously about just how we are to live, and in spite of our having

89

always already failed so to live in the past, prior to our decisive encounter with Jesus.

But now to live in this way, understanding ourselves so and engaging in this kind of life-praxis, necessarily involves two things: what I call—and this is my third topic—*effective use and valid administration of specifically Christian means of transformation*. Of course, from a Christian standpoint, there's nothing whatever that doesn't bear at least implicit witness to the meaning of God for us, and is insofar capable of serving, in a very broad sense, as a means of transformation. It can be a means of so confronting us with the gift and demand of God's prevenient love for us as to open up the possibility of our own obedient faith and returning love for God and for all things in God—even after we've again and again fallen into sin and misled our lives accordingly. But there are certain things—things that we human beings think, say, and do, or things that serve as the media of our thinking, saying, and doing them—that are capable of being an *explicit* witness to the meaning of God for us, and so serve as means of transformation in the further sense of explicitly signifying the gift and demand of God's love, of which, like everything else, they are the bearers. Indeed, the whole reason for the existence of *religion* as a so-called sacred form of culture more or less distinct from all the other so-called secular forms is to bear just such explicit witness and so to serve as a means of transformation in this special sense. A religion, in other words, not only *provides* certain means of transformation, but itself as a religion, *is* just such a means. It is, in fact, the *primary* such means, while the various particular means that it may in turn provide are all secondary means relative to it. Prominent among such secondary means, of course, are a religion's representative means, such as, in the case of the Christian religion, preaching and teaching the word and administering the sacraments.

Any religion, however, can always fail to be the explicit witness and so the means of transformation that is its sole reason for being. Both our creatureliness and our sin as human beings have an impact on our religious praxis, on what we believe and do religiously, no less than on all the rest of our life-praxis and culture. So the explicit witness of this or that religion—or this or that part of its explicit witness—may not really be the valid witness it claims to be. Hence the need I referred to earlier for a *decisive* re-presentation of the meaning of ultimate reality for us and therefore also for an explicit witness or means of transformation authorized by this decisive re-presentation. For Christians, this need is met by the decisive re-presentation of the meaning of God for us through Jesus Christ, and by the explicit witness or means of transformation, both primary and secondary, that the event of Jesus Christ, as itself the *primal* such means, in turn authorizes—which is to say, the church itself and what it usually calls its "means of salvation." In this sense, then, to be called to be a Christian is to be called, both to make effective use of all such explicit witness and means of transformation to the extent to which they really are as valid as they claim to be, and then to share in the ministry of validly bearing this same witness and administering these same means to others.

By "effective use," I should explain, I mean simply responding to the witness and means of transformation through one's own obedient faith and witness, thereby understanding oneself as they explicitly give and call one to do and then leading the whole of one's life, or conducting all of one's life-praxis, accordingly, allowing them continually to discipline and reform one's own Christian witness. Here we may note the important distinction between the *effectiveness* of Christian witness or means of transformation, on the one hand, and their *validity*, on the other. They're valid, insofar as they are so, solely because they're adequate to their own content and fitting to their situation, their validity in neither respect depending in any way either on the faith of the persons bearing or administering them or on the faith of the persons receiving them. But even a valid witness or means of transformation can be effective only to the extent to which it meets with the obedient faith and witness of the persons receiving it. The effectiveness of such a witness or means, unlike its validity, in every way depends on *their* faith and witness, although even it in no way depends on the faith of the persons bearing it or administering it. Because, however, being called to be a Christian implies being called to bear a valid witness as well as to make effective use of the valid witness borne by others, the call to be a Christian is itself, as I said earlier, also the call to be a Christian minister—namely, by sharing, or playing one's part, in the church's ministry of bearing valid witness to Jesus Christ and validly administering the means of transformation that he authorizes as himself the primal such means. Paul puts it this way, in a well-known passage in 2 Corinthians:

> So if anyone is in Christ, there is a new creation: everything old has passed away; see, everything has become new! All this is from God, who reconciled us to himself through Christ, and has given us the ministry of reconciliation; that is, in Christ

God was reconciling the world to himself, not counting their trespasses against them, and entrusting the message of reconciliation to us. So we are ambassadors for Christ, since God is making his appeal through us; we entreat you in Christ's stead, Be reconciled to God (5:17–20).

Precisely as a call to Christian ministry, however, the call to be a Christian is also, as I've said, a call to do Christian theology, or, as I formulate this fourth and final topic, the call to *critical reflection on the meaning of Christian witness and its claims to validity*. Because the call to be a minister is the call to bear a *valid* Christian witness and to administer the specifically Christian means of transformation *validly*, it is, at one and the same time, the call to the critical reflection without which such validity cannot be secured except by a happy accident. Whether or not any Christian witness is really adequate to its own content and fitting to its situation, and in this sense is really valid Christian witness, is not something anyone can finally take responsibility for except by critically interpreting the meaning of the witness and critically validating its claims to be adequate and fitting. In this sense, the call to be a Christian is in itself and simply as such also the call to be a Christian theologian as well as a Christian minister.

This, then, is how I understand the call—the decisive call, as Christians affirm—to be a Christian. It necessarily presupposes the original call to every human being to be exactly that, but it itself makes this original call fully explicit, thereby *re*-presenting it in the literal sense of presenting it yet *again*, a *second* time, in *explicit* concepts and symbols. This, however, it does *decisively*, Christians maintain, because it re-presents our original and universal call to be human both adequately and fittingly, thereby sublating all other explicit or specifically religious calls by at once preserving everything valid and true in them, even while correcting all that is invalid and false. Of course, every other major religious tradition makes a more or less closely analogous claim to the same kind of decisive existential authority for its specific concepts and symbols and the explicit primal source authorizing them. And this is why, now that we can no longer conveniently ignore these other religions, one of the most important theological questions of our time is whether, from a Christian standpoint, their claims, also, to be the decisive call to human beings must be simply dismissed at the outset as not possibly valid, or whether Christians are, after all, in a position to allow that such other religious claims at least *could be* valid, whether or not they actually are.

But we will be in a better position to reflect further on this as well as on the other important questions we'll be pursuing in this seminar after we turn, in the next lecture, to look more closely at our situation today, in the sense of the situation in which you and I and our contemporaries in the United States must now receive our own call to be a Christian.

# Our Situation Today

## Introduction

Nothing is more obvious, if we think about it, than that no one can receive her or his call to be a Christian except in some particular situation: in a certain time and place in history, with its own possibilities and problems, and in its own forms of life and understanding. This means, among other things, that the distinction I've assumed in writing my first lecture and the present one—between the call to be a Christian, which is ever the same, and our situation today, which is not the same but different from those of other Christians, past, present, and future—can be subtly misleading. As much as what I wanted to talk about in my first lecture is itself indeed situation-invariant and the same for every Christian, the only way in which I or anyone else could ever possibly talk about it is in the situation-dependent terms of *some* particular situation—in my case, the terms of *my*, and, as I hope, at least to some extent, *our*, situation today. Even so, the distinction I've assumed remains valid and important, provided that we wish to avoid confusing what we want to think and talk *about* with the situation *in* which we perforce have to think and talk about it; and this is true, even when our topic, as in this second lecture, is precisely our situation itself.

Of course, we can't hope to think and talk about our situation within the limits of a single lecture except at a relatively high level of abstraction and in very general terms. The actual life-situation of any one of us is indefinitely more concrete and mysterious and bound to elude any attempt to capture it in such generalities, even if they could be far more finely tuned and nuanced than any lecture allows for. Moreover, the expertise required to understand our situation today as it really is is nothing any of us can claim simply as a Christian, not even as a Christian who also happens to be a professional, indeed, an academic, theologian. At this point, all of us, professional and lay theologians alike, are more or less amateurs, who have to depend on the knowledge and skill of others—especially social scientists and historians—whose business it is to throw light on where we are, by understanding the larger social and cultural forces that shape our lives, and by tracing the changes over time that have brought us there. But if we must be modest in our expectations for the lecture, the importance of trying to understand where we actually are today can hardly be exaggerated.

Christian faith claims, rightly or wrongly, that even the most ordinary decisions of our everyday lives finally depend on an understanding of ourselves in faith that only it, or some other religious or, possibly, philosophical faith comparably profound and true, can explicitly mediate. But Christian faith also claims—and just as insistently—that the self-understanding of faith can be authentic if, and only if, it ever continues to bear fruit in all our particular actions: in how we act in our interactions with one another and our world, and in what we do in face of the concrete claims that thereby encounter us. In this sense, the author of the Letter of James in the New Testament has it exactly right: "Faith by itself, if it has no works, is dead" (2:17, 26). But to determine just what works, or fruit, are called for in any concrete and particular situation, including our own, always waits on first understanding the situation itself, its needs and opportunities, its problems and possibilities. So, inadequate as it will surely be, we have no choice but to seek such understanding as we can get of our situation today, keeping in mind that complete consensus is not to be hoped for, and that there's plenty of room for honest disagreement even if we share something like the same understanding of our decisive call to be a Christian.

## *The changing face of controversy*

In keeping with the promise made in the course description for this seminar—that it would pay particular attention to being a Christian in the USA today—I want to begin with our immediate situation as Christians in the churches in this country.

The most obvious feature of American Christianity, no doubt, is still its extensive pluralization into any number of confessions, denominations, and sects. The Yellow Pages devoted to churches in any urban phone book are sufficient to show that, at the level of the institutional church, "Christian" is a term having many meanings, not one. There's nothing surprising about this, naturally, to historians of Christianity and of religion generally, or to other students of human society and culture.

94

Religion, no less than other social and cultural systems, actually exists only in plural forms, as *religions*—and this is typically so at several different levels. In the case of Christianity, it's now clear to any student of its history that from the New Testament period on, it has probably never existed in one form only but always only in more than one. Furthermore, the differences between these several forms with respect to what Christians are to believe and what they are to do have often been sufficiently great that there's been no possibility of composing them—hence the splits into the confessions, denominations, and sects attested by the Yellow Pages. In short, Christianity in particular, like religion in general, has proved to be genuinely controversial—at several different levels and more or less from its very beginning.

But if there's nothing new about controversy among Christians, the issues provoking it have not always been the same. On the contrary, the face of controversy, as I call it, has continually changed down through Christian history, to the point where the deeper issues between Christians today—in our country as well as elsewhere—are no longer reflected by the obvious differences between confessions, denominations, and sects. Here I draw especially on the work of the American sociologist of religion Robert Wuthnow, who argues resourcefully that perhaps the most important recent development in the history of religion in America is what he calls, in the titles of two of his books, "the restructuring of American religion" and "the struggle for America's soul."[2]

Since roughly World War II, the historical divisions in the United States between the several religions, confessions, denominations, and sects have all been increasingly relativized by another and very different type of religious division. Prepared for to some extent by the earlier split between fundamentalists and mainstream Christian believers, this more recent division is between conservatives, or, in the Protestant churches, evangelicals, on the one side, and liberals or progressives, on the other. Cutting across all traditional religious communities, it accounts for the fact experienced by so many of us that persons in one denomination or confession, or even religion, may find themselves closer in matters of belief and practice to certain persons in another such group than to many of the fellow members of their own. According to Wuthnow, a principal

2. Robert Wuthnow, *The Restructuring of American Religion: Society and Faith since World War II* (Princeton: Princeton University Press, 1988); and *The Struggle for America's Soul: Evangelicals, Liberals, and Secularism* (Grand Rapids: Eerdmans, 1989).

reason for this growing gap between different religious orientations within religious groups has been "rising levels of education." "The better educated typically adopted more liberal and relativist belief patterns and favored active engagement in social issues; the less well educated followed more traditional lines in belief and practice and came increasingly to focus on issues of personal morality."

This development, then, is what I mainly have in mind in speaking of "the changing face of controversy." To be called to be a Christian in our country today is to become immediately involved in *this* restructuring of American religion and *this* struggle for America's soul. Why? Well, because, as I've said, the call to be a Christian, by its very nature, is never merely abstract and general, but is always also concrete and particular, having to do with the most ordinary matters of everyday life-praxis: with how we're to lead our lives, and thus with what we're to believe and what we ought to do. To be sure, the most fundamental features of our call, which we were at pains to understand in the first lecture, are, in a way, abstract and general, in that they are, as I put it, situation-invariant, and so always the same in every situation—even if, as we saw, any attempt to think and talk about them is itself situation-dependent in that it has to be made in the concepts and terms of some situation, there being no other. But these most fundamental features—of trusting in the God whose all-embracing love Jesus decisively re-presents to us and then loyally serving this God by loving all things in God—these fundamental features of faith working through love can never exist simply in themselves but always have to become incarnate in words and deeds that are in no way abstract and general but are in every way concrete and particular. The problem facing us in our situation today, however, is that there's not just one, but rather two fundamentally different—indeed, in their clearer and more consistent forms, mutually exclusive—ways of concretizing and particularizing them. In this sense, to be called to be a Christian in our situation today is to have to take sides in this deeper controversy now dividing the Christian community, as well as—so Wuthnow and others teach us—other religious communities in our country.

## The controverted issues

If we ask now how this situation has come about, there are, as I see it, two factors that, above all, need to be taken into account. The first is indicated by Wuthnow when he observes that the present controversy was prepared for, to some extent, by the earlier split, especially marked in American Protestantism, between fundamentalists and mainstream Christians. Lying behind this split were all the complex changes that we've long been accustomed to summarize under the term "modernization." Thanks especially to the ever-increasing impact of modern science and a science-based technology, in their results as well as their procedures, the whole context of believing and acting Christianly radically changed. Many traditional Christian beliefs and practices were disclosed to be pre-scientific and questionably credible, with the result that more educated persons, especially, were increasingly confronted with the question of the truth of religious faith generally and of Christian faith in particular. Also important in bringing this about was the further breakdown in the West, with the Protestant Reformation and the Roman Catholic Counter-Reformation, of a single, more or less unified Christendom and the profound doubts raised at that point about all merely traditional religious authorities by the ensuing confessional wars. All appeals to mere authority were thereby exposed as at best insufficient, and, among persons seriously seeking enlightenment, and so freedom for themselves and others from error as well as ignorance, there was a widening appeal to what was ever more clearly seen to be the only truly ultimate authority—namely, that belonging to our common experience and reason as human beings. If the claim of Christian faith to be true is really valid, they concluded, this could only be insofar as the beliefs it necessarily presupposes and implies, practical as well as theoretical, can somehow be shown to be authorized by *this* sole ultimate authority.

The other factor, also connected in important ways with the first factor of modernization, I shall call "globalization." I realize that, in more recent discussion, this term has come to be commonly used more strictly, to refer to the accelerated growth of economic activity across national and regional boundaries, which involves such things as increased trans-national production of goods and services; increased international trade and investments; and increased movement of populations by relocation within nations as well as by migration, legal and also illegal, between them. But, as fundamental as such properly economic globalization certainly is, it is still only one facet of a much larger historical process: the multifaceted process by which the peoples of the world are becoming increasingly interconnected in all aspects of their lives—cultural and religious no less than economic and political. In any case, it is in this much broader sense that I am using the term here. But, once again, what lies behind this process of globalization is, above all, the development of modern science and a science-based technology, from which has resulted, not least, the continuing revolution in means of communication and transportation—to the point where our world today has been perceptively described as "a global village."

A main effect of all this is what I sometimes call "the emergence of plurality." Although human beings, so far as we know, have always lived, not in one society and culture, but only in many, they've also lived, to a great extent, in mutual social and cultural isolation. Only with the revolution in means made possible by modern technology has such isolation broken down to the point of allowing the plurality of ways of being human that has been there all along to emerge fully into the clear light of virtually everyone's experience. But now that we're becoming increasingly interconnected with peoples of all societies and cultures, including all religions and philosophies, all of us in our global village are faced with the full force of the challenge of emergent plurality.

For us, this means that doubts about mere tradition and authority in matters religious, which were raised for us in the West already with the rise of modernity and the wars between Christians after the Reformation and the Counter-Reformation, are now only intensified. It is simply a fact that if we are to obey our call to be Christians, to bear witness to the truth as it is in Jesus, we will have to do so in a situation in which the challenge of emergent plurality is unprecedented, other claims and counterclaims to truth now being known to be practically limitless. But how are we as Christians to face up to this challenge?

The deeper pathos of our situation, I believe, is that there's no single, generally agreed-upon answer to this question in the present Christian community. On the contrary, the answer to it is a matter of the profoundest controversy now dividing Christians between those who, as Wuthnow puts it, typically adopt more liberal and relativistic belief patterns and those who follow more traditional lines of belief. This is why, as I implied earlier, one can scarcely receive one's call to be a Christian in our situation before one has to take sides in this controversy. The theological question this raises, however, and so the question before us here, is which side one is to take, and, most important, for what reasons. What reasons, if any, do I have precisely as a Christian who would really obey my call to be such, to take one side instead of the other in the controversy now dividing Christians in our situation today?

Before we address ourselves to this question—in the third and fourth sessions of the seminar—I want to take account of yet another important aspect of our situation as well as of this deeply divisive controversy. And once again, I return to Wuthnow's point that the present controversy was prepared for, to some extent, by the earlier split, around the beginning of the last century, between Christian fundamentalists and so-called mainstream Christians. Actually, the original fundamentalist reaction was against what the fundamentalists themselves typically called "modernism." Important to the revisionary movement among Christians that they so designated was an openness to modern science and its revolutionary picture of the world as well as a more or less clear and consistent commitment to "the way of reason" generally, even in matters of religious faith. In other words, the revisionary Christians—commonly called "liberals"—whom fundamentalists charged with "modernism" positively appropriated the view of the modern Western Enlightenment that no mere authority, however venerable, is sufficient of itself to justify any claim to truth, whether secular or religious. The only ultimate authority by which all claims to truth must be adjudicated, they insisted, is our common experience simply as human beings together with relevant reasoned argumentation based thereon. But if the modernists in this way sharply raised the basic issue of the *truth* of traditional Christian belief, this was not the only basic issue they raised, nor was it the only reason for the intensity of the fundamentalist reaction against them.

To understand this we need to recognize that yet another important result of the process of modernization was what I call "the rise of historical consciousness." Together with the emergence of science and a science-based technology went the rapid social and cultural changes marked, first, by the industrial revolution and then by the successive revolutions ushering in what is now sometimes referred to as our postindustrial society and culture. But the ripe fruit of our modern experience of all such rapid social and cultural change is what I and others call "historical consciousness": the clear awareness of the thoroughgoing historicity of human existence and especially the realization that, far from being divinely ordained or naturally fixed, all structures of social and cultural order are, in reality, through and through historical, being the creations of human beings who continually create themselves in and through their creation of them. But, then, the scope of human power and responsibility is seen to include, not only moral action within such structures as may have already been created, but also properly political action directed toward maintaining and/or transforming these structures themselves.

Just this insight, together with a new vision of our fundamental equality as human beings, underlies not only our American Revolution but also subsequent revolutionary movements in the ongoing worldwide struggle for popular sovereignty and democratic institutions. Since governments are created and maintained by human beings, who are to be equally rulers as well as ruled, they also can and should be changed by human beings whenever they become obstructive of their proper ends as governments for the people as well as of and by them.

Given their resolve, then, not to ignore or to avoid, but to accept, such properly political responsibility, revisionary Christians and theologians also sharply raised the other basic issue of the *justice* of traditional Christian practice and institutions, along with those, of course, of secular society and culture. And they had all the more reason to focus on this basic issue because, for all of the changes that modernization had succeeded in bringing about, the historical inequality of all human cultures and societies known to us only too obviously persisted. At best, the old order's static inequalities in wealth and income had yielded only to the dynamic inequalities so apparent in the new technological civilization of modernity. Moreover, all the other inequalities of race, gender, and culture as well as class remained largely unchallenged in even the most advanced nations, to say nothing of the vast inequalities between the rich and the poor nations themselves.

You will have guessed by now, I suspect, that the name eventually given to this other aspect of the revisionary Christian movement was "the social gospel." And the sharp reaction of Christian fundamentalists against the whole movement was directed, not least, against precisely this aspect. Modernists, they charged, had abandoned the church's gospel of salvation through Jesus Christ for the world's gospel of self-salvation through social and cultural change toward ever-greater justice.

But if modernization is insofar a factor to reckon with in understanding this second aspect of our situation, the other factor of globalization, also, demands to be taken into account. In this respect, however, it is precisely globalization in the stricter sense of *economic* globalization that is relevant, especially if we're to understand the present controversy, and not simply the fundamentalist-modernist controversy that to some extent anticipated it.

Considered in itself, economic globalization, as I said, is just the accelerated growth of economic activity of all types across national and regional boundaries. But as the process of such growth has actually taken place, from the earlier periods of colonialism and imperialism to the new world economic order of today, evidence has continued to mount that it is, in fact, what its critics have called "globalization from above." Thus, although there is all but universal agreement that economic globalization, like globalization otherwise, is now an irreversible process, there's nothing like agreement that the same is true of the form it has taken up to now. Instead, there is growing awareness, confirmed by substantial evidence and argument, that this form can and should be reversed, because—as its critics charge—it is deeply unjust, environmentally unsustainable, and, worst of all, imposed by processes of decision making and institutional governance that are anything but participatory and democratic.

At once arising from this awareness and representing it is a worldwide movement of resistance unifying many older movements for social and cultural change and called by some "globalization from below"—in order to distinguish it both from the historical process of economic globalization as such and from its heretofore and still dominant form. Contrary to the promise held out by neoliberal proponents of this dominant form—that the rising tide of a global economy would "lift all boats"—its real outcome so far appears to be only an ever intensifying and now genuinely international "race to the bottom," whose effects are increasingly being suffered even in advanced countries such as ours as ever more jobs—including, increasingly, white-collar jobs—are outsourced in the worldwide competition to lower the costs of labor.

Thus, in a recent study asking for "a cause of worldwide rising inequality" in "the age of globalization," the economist, James K. Galbraith, summarizes his answer as follows:

> It is not increasing trade *as such* that we should fear. Nor is technology the culprit. To focus on 'globalization' as such misstates the issue. The problem is a process of integration carried out since at least 1980 under circumstances of unsustainable finance, in which wealth has flowed upwards from the poor countries to the rich, and mainly to the upper financial strata in the richest countries.
>
> In the course of these events, progress toward tolerable levels of inequality and sustainable development virtually stopped. Neocolonial patterns of center-periphery dependence, and of

debt peonage, were reestablished, but without the slightest assumption of responsibility by the rich countries for the fate of
the poor.

It has been, it would appear, a perfect crime. And while
statistical forensics can play a small role in pointing this out, no
mechanism to reverse the policy exists, still less any that might
repair the damage. The developed countries have abandoned
the pretense of attempting to foster development in the world at
large, preferring to substitute the rhetoric of ungoverned mar-
kets for the hard work of stabilizing regulation. The prognosis is
grim: a descent into apathy, despair, disease, ecological disaster,
and wars of separatism and survival in many of the poorest
parts of the world.[3]

I've cited this passage at length because it so effectively supports my
claim that yet another fundamental feature of our situation today is the
persistence of inequality—indeed, of abject poverty. I realize in doing so,
of course, that its reading of developments as well as its forecast of the
future is not the only view held even by experts in the field and that it
would, in any event, need to be continually confirmed by the ongoing
inquiries and forms of validation proper thereto. But I also have to say,
in all honesty, that I have every confidence that my claim is essentially
sound—one reason for this being that it is fully borne out by studies of
the state of things in our own country during roughly the same period.

Far from gradually closing, the inequality gap in income and wealth
between the richest and the poorest in the United States has only widened—to the point where it can be said to be, in the words of one student,
"unrivaled in the industrialized world." Thus one such study concludes
that our economy "has consistently produced the highest levels of economic inequality," and that inequality among us has shown a strong
tendency to rise, even as it was relatively stable or declining in most of
the rest of the OECD," i.e., the Organization for Economic Cooperation
and Development, founded in 1961 and comprising our own and some
twenty-eight other industrialized countries.

But now allowing, as I freely do, that this conclusion, also, can and
should be questioned, especially by any and all who are competent to
question it, I shall still proceed as though the essential soundness of my
claim is not in doubt. However differently further inquiry and discussion

3. James K. Galbraith, "A Perfect Crime: Inequality in the Age of Globalization,"
*Dædalus* 131/1 (Winter 2002) 25.

may require us to quantify it, there's no serious question about the persistence of inequality—in many places, indeed, of the direst poverty—in our situation today, here in the United States as well as elsewhere in the world. It's simply a fact that both in our own country and in other countries the benefits and burdens of our life together are still far from being distributed among us at an even tolerably unequal level. But here too the question, as I see it, is how we as Christians are to come to terms with this challenge of persistent inequality, given that the answer to it is so far from being agreed upon as to be the other basic issue now dividing the Christian community—here in the United States as well as elsewhere. On the one side of this aspect of the controversy are Christians who—in Wuthnow's words—typically favor engagement in social issues, whereas on the other side are Christians who follow traditional patterns of practice and therefore focus on issues of personal morality.

To be sure, this second aspect of current Christian controversy is not quite as simple as the first—not, at any rate, in the United States. Here, at least, it's complicated by the fact that so-called conservatives or evangelicals are not alone among Christians and churches whose moral concern is focused mainly, if not entirely, on issues of personal morality, as distinct from those calling for specifically social and political engagement. Despite the fact that the earlier social gospel has continued to bear fruit among mainstream Christians and churches, it's also true that it has always remained a minority tradition even there (African American Christians and churches aside), and that this has been particularly true during the last quarter century, even with such renewal of the tradition as may have taken place since the 1970s under the impact of various forms of liberation and political theology.

To understand fully why even mainstream Christians and churches have, for the most part, focused more on personal salvation and morality—even if they've interpreted them, in many cases, more in the psychological terms of self-realization and personal fulfillment than in properly theological terms—would require us to go into the powerful and persisting influence even on Christians and churches in our country of the political philosophies or ideologies that have risen to dominance in the course of our nation's history. I refer to the extreme individualism fostered both by liberalism in its two contrasting forms of libertarian and welfare liberalism and, especially, by more recent conservatism and neo-conservatism. But this is not the time to undertake such further analysis, important as it would almost surely be to our discussion. It must suffice to say simply that as much as mainstream Christians and churches may have found themselves—with whatever clarity and consistency—on one side of the current controversy on the basic issue of truth, they have only too often given support to the other side on the basic issue of justice. They too have failed, in their ways, to rise to the challenge of persistent inequality.

On the other side, one of the, to me, most encouraging recent developments among certain conservative or evangelical Christians and churches is an apparently growing concern to define a clear alternative to the "religious right." This, too, complicates the picture I've sketched insofar as there are at least more Christians and churches whose traditionalist position on the issue of truth is not keeping them from exploring possibilities of a more progressive or, at any rate, centrist position on the other issue of justice.

But be all this as it may, the question to which we've come is the same theological question we came to earlier, of how we—you and I—are to take sides in this current Christian controversy on both of the basic controverted issues of justice and also truth.

We must each ask, to repeat the question, To which side of this controversy ought I to give my support, and for what reasons? What reasons, if any, do I have precisely as a Christian who would really obey my call to be such, to take one side instead of the other? We can hardly hope to answer this question adequately in what remains of the seminar. But we can reasonably hope to make a beginning, and this we'll try to do in the two sessions still ahead of us.

## What We Are to Believe and What We Are to Do: In Principle

### Preliminary remarks

Before beginning the argument of this lecture, I have a couple of things I want to say.

First of all, I'd like to clarify a possible misunderstanding of my talk in the last lecture about "taking sides" in the controversy that, as I've argued, now divides the Christian community more fundamentally than any other. It's often the case that over time, religious and theological controversies—among Christians as well as others—become sharply polarized, even though the two sides may not, in point of fact, exhaust the positions that one might reasonably take on the controverted issues. The reason for this, to put it as a logician would, is that the polarized sides of the controversy are not proper contradictories, one of which must be true and the other false, but rather extreme contraries, only one of which can be true, although both can be false. This explains why the right response to make to many a polarized controversy is first to look for a mean between the two extremes, a possible third position that can justifiably claim to be their common contradictory. But unless I'm mistaken, this couldn't be the right response to make to the controversy mainly concerning us here. Its two sides, as I've characterized them, are precisely contradictories, so that if either is true the other has to be false. Either Christian claims to truth, as much as any other, require to be validated, finally, by common human experience and reason, or they don't. And so, too, either Christian moral responsibility requires a specifically political pursuit of justice, or it doesn't. In both cases, there's a clear-cut *either/or* that necessitates taking one side against the other. This is not to deny, of course, that either side may often be expressed so unclearly or inconsistently that the decision it calls for is obscured. But whether this is the case or not, in saying that we must each take sides in this controversy, I in no way mean that we must take one or the other of two extreme positions, both of which can be false even though only one can be true.

Second, you should know at the outset that, from this point on, I shall be explicitly taking sides in the controversy by developing and arguing for my own answer to the question that I've insisted each of us as a Christian today has to ask and answer. I put it this way purposely, because I couldn't honestly claim not to have been at least *implicitly* partisan— however unintentionally—even in what I've already had to say about our call to be a Christian and the situation in which we now find ourselves. As I've acknowledged before, there's no escaping our own historicity, not to mention our own creatureliness and sin, even when we try, as best we can, to formulate at least the question before Christians today in a nonpartisan, fair-minded way. But from now on, for sure, I shall be deliberately speaking from and for my own standpoint as a Christian so as to explain as simply and as succinctly as I can, why, precisely as and because this is my standpoint, I take one side in the controversy and not the other.

You may be sure that I take this side because I deeply believe it to be right. But in this I may be just as mistaken as anyone may be who sincerely thinks it's wrong. And yet, even if it is wrong, my main reason for proceeding in this way will not be in the least affected. Just because I want all of us as Christians to take only the right side, my deeper interest is in our all having good and sufficient reasons for taking whichever side we take. As I indicated earlier, I understand the question before us to be a genuinely *theological* question; and on my understanding, one thing necessary for any answer to it to be equally theological is that the reasons given for that answer can withstand even the most critical scrutiny and counterargument. So, if you'll accept a little advice, you'll benefit most from the example I hope to set by what follows if you each concern your-selves less with any conclusions I draw than with the reasons I give to support them—and then each go and do likewise as you continue to work out your own answer to the question now facing us.

As will be clear, I trust, from their titles, the question guiding this as well as the next lecture is essentially the same: What are we to believe, and what are we to do if we're to obey the call to be a Christian in our situation today? The one important difference is that, in this lecture, I shall pursue the question as *a question of principle*: By what principle (or principles) are we today to believe and act as Christians? In the last lecture, then, I shall continue to ask the same question, but as *a question of fact*: What are we actually to believe and do with respect to the basic issues of truth and justice, and in face of the two important challenges now put to us by our situation today?

### *What is presupposed and what is implied by the Christian call*

You'll agree with me, I think, that many, if not most, Christians today, as in the past, would very likely answer our question in this lecture by saying something like this: What we today are to believe and to do in principle is what Christians have historically believed and done in ac-cordance with scripture and tradition, including, not least, the beliefs and practices traditional in our own confession, denomination, or sect. Those who would give this answer would no doubt allow that there are, indeed, obvious and not unimportant differences between their own Christian group and others in the norms of belief and action that they uphold and therefore in the principles they enforce as binding in their churches. In fact, Protestants not uncommonly think of themselves as differing from Roman Catholics mainly because what they're to believe and to do in principle comprises significantly fewer beliefs and practices—completely excluding, for example, beliefs in papal infallibility or in the immaculate conception and bodily assumption of the Blessed Virgin Mary and such practices as receiving communion only after confirmation and having first gone to private confession and been granted priestly absolution. In a somewhat similar way, liberal or mainstream Protestants understand themselves to be different from conservatives or evangelicals, both in the relative fewness of the beliefs they are to believe, which no longer include even some that those on the other side reckon to be "fundamentals," and in no longer observing such practices as regularly attending Sunday evening as well as Sunday morning services or midweek Bible study groups. Even so, Christians of all groups by and large agree that if they're to be Christians at all, they're to believe and to do what Christians before them have historically believed and done in fidelity to scripture and to their own church tradition.

But now, as much as I think that this answer, in its way, makes the important point about what we as Christians are in principle to believe and to do, I cannot wholly concur in it. There are four main reasons for this, three of which I shall develop in this first part of the lecture, the fourth, in the second part.

First of all, the call to be a Christian as such is directly a call to faith and only indirectly a call to believe any particular belief or to perform any particular action. A difficulty, of course, in trying to make this distinction in English is that, although "believe" is a verb, "faith" is a noun, there being no verb cognate with it corresponding to the way in which "believe" is cognate with "belief." Therefore, I can only ask you to think of "to faith" in my phrase "call to faith" as if it were the infinitive form of a nonexistent English verb, "faith," analogous to the infinitive "to believe." And then I ask you to recall the argument of my first lecture, where I was careful to define faith primarily, in purely formal terms, not as belief, but as self-understanding—more exactly, as self-understanding involving the two moments of unreserved trust and unqualified loyalty. To be called "to faith," understood as an infinitive, then, is to be called, first of all, to trust and to be loyal: specifically—to put it now in the material terms of Christian faith and witness—to entrust oneself unreservedly to God's prevenient, all-embracing love and then to be unqualifiedly loyal to the cause of God's love by returning love for God and for all things in God.

To be sure, I also said that the call to be a Christian, and so to understand oneself in this way, is also the call to lead one's life accordingly, by a distinct kind of life-praxis that validly expresses one's self-understanding of faith, and thus one's trust in God and loyalty to God. In this way, the call to faith is indeed the call both to believe and to act, belief and action always being the two main aspects of any kind of life-praxis, be it Christian or any other. It is a call to believe and to do, namely, whatever is necessarily presupposed or implied by the call to be a Christian and therefore also by one's obedient faith in that call, which is to say, one's unreserved trust in God's love and unqualified loyalty to its cause. Obviously, a call to entrust oneself in a certain way necessarily presupposes that there's someone or something to trust in that way, so that a belief that this is the case has to be a true belief if the call is to be a valid call. And so, too, with a call to be loyal: unless there's someone or something to be loyal to, one's loyalty would be misplaced and any belief that one is to be loyal could only be false. In a similar way, the call to trust in or to be loyal to another necessarily implies acting in certain ways and doing certain things, depending on the concrete circumstances of the situation: the other's needs and interests and the possibilities and limits of alternative courses of action calculated to meet them. In this sense, there can be no question that any call to Christian faith is also a call both to Christian belief and to Christian action. But it is *not* a call, except indirectly, either to believe or to do *this, that, or the other particular thing*, not even something taken to be binding just because it was believed or done by the Christians through whose ministry one has received one's own call to be a Christian.

And this becomes all the clearer, I think, when we consider a second reason—namely, that any particular belief as well as any particular action must, in their different ways, always be situation-dependent. This means, in the case of any particular belief, that it always has to be formulated as such in the concepts and terms of some historical situation, there never being any other in which to formulate it. Here again I ask you to think back to my first lecture, where I corrected something I had said so as to distinguish clearly what I called "the constitutive christological assertion itself" from any and all of its particular formulations, even its classical formulation as "Jesus is the Christ." Given the concepts and terms available to the Palestinian Jews whom Jesus called out into what became the earliest Christian church, this formulation was no doubt an understandable way of expressing the christological assertion necessarily implied by their confession of faith in response to Jesus' call—as expressed, for example, in the words of Peter, in the familiar account in Matthew's Gospel: "You are the Christ, the Son of the living God" (16:15–16). But aside from the fact that the presence in this formulation of the other title, "the Son of God," already indicates that asserting Jesus to be "the Christ" was certainly not the only way early Christians expressed it—aside from this, we also know that, once the Christian witness was taken out of Palestine into the larger Hellenistic world, all such specifically Jewish titles ceased any longer to be adequate or fitting ways of formulating the christological assertion, anyhow. How do we know this? Well, by the twofold fact that the term "the Christ," which was originally a title, more and more became simply a part of the proper name "Jesus Christ"; and that earlier originally Jewish titles either came to be supplemented by such new characteristically Hellenistic titles as "the Lord" or else were used only with new and very different meanings—as in the case, for instance, of "the Son of God."

I cannot go any further into the history of christology. But I trust the point I'm making is clear: in being called to be a Christian, we're in no way called to believe, and so to think and speak, in the concepts and terms of any historical situation other than our own. On the contrary, we're called ever to trust and to be loyal, and then to formulate the beliefs necessarily presupposed and implied by our faith as validly as we can in the concepts and terms now available *to us* precisely in *our* situation.

And the same point is to be made—also making the necessary changes—in the case of any particular action. For the sake of time, however, I'll forego developing the argument, saying only that any particular action is also always situation-dependent in being relative to the circumstances in which it has to be performed. Thus, even allowing, for example, that what it means to be loyal to another is in one respect always the same—namely, first, to accept the other as other and then, second, to do what is necessary to realize the other's interests as fully as possible—still, what, in fact, *is* thus necessary will always be more or less different, given the circumstances of the different situations, in face of others having different needs and interests, and so on. So, in being called to be a Christian, and thus to be loyal both to God and to all others in God, one is in no way called to act in the circumstances of any historical situation other than one's own. On the contrary, one is called to trust and to be loyal and then to do what is necessarily presupposed and implied by one's faith, as well as one can, in the circumstances of *one's own* situation.

The third reason I can't simply agree with the usual answer to the question, What, in principle, are we to believe and to do? is even harder to develop in the limited time I now have to give to it. But it is this: what, on the usual answer, is typically appealed to as normative for Christian belief and action—namely, scripture and tradition—can no longer be validly so appealed to. I'm well aware that this is a highly controversial claim, and I cannot possibly argue for it here as I have elsewhere (cf., e.g., above, 1. "The Authority of Scripture for Christian Existence Today"). But despite the all but universal belief and practice to the contrary, one of the surest implications of historical-critical study of the Christian past is that the usual theological distinction between scripture and tradition completely breaks down—for the very good reason that scripture so called, or, more exactly, the part of scripture making up the New Testament canon, must now be said to be itself precisely "tradition" by the very criterion historically used to distinguish it from tradition. That criterion was "apostolicity," in the sense of the unique characteristic defining the witness of the apostles as the earliest, the original and originating, Christians: "disciples at first hand," in Søren Kierkegaard's phrase, as distinct from all other Christians, who can be only "disciples at second hand." So, by this criterion, to be validly included on the list, or "canon," of writings making up the New Testament required that a particular writing be rightly deemed "apostolic" because authored by one of the apostles. But the ongoing course of historical-critical study of the New Testament writings, including especially what are called "source criticism" and "form criticism," has established beyond serious question that not a single one of the New Testament writings qualifies as "apostolic" by that criterion. Why not? Well, because it has now been shown to have been authored by someone who in her or his writing made use of as sources (oral and/or written) other Christian witness or witnesses earlier than itself—from which the obvious inference is that it itself couldn't be formally "apostolic" in the sense of the earliest, original and originating Christian witness.

But if this inference effectively undermines all of the classical positions on the norms of Christian belief and action—whether Protestant, Roman Catholic, or Orthodox—yet another result of the same ongoing historical-critical study is that the alternative position typically held by many modern revisionary Christians is likewise indefensible. I refer to the position according to which the real norm for what we're to believe and to do as Christians is not the witness of the apostles and all subsequent witness substantially agreeing with theirs—in other words, scripture and tradition—but rather the witness of Jesus himself, the so-called historical Jesus, as he actually was prior to any and all interpretations of him by others. The insurmountable difficulty with this revisionary position is that there simply aren't any primary sources for Jesus' own witness: no sayings from his own mouth, no writings from his own hand, and so on. Even our earliest sources—those that can be historically reconstructed by working back from the Synoptic Gospels, on the one hand, and from the writings of Paul, on the other—are at best secondary, and are one and all witnesses of faith, and not historical reports in our usual modern sense of the term. Consequently, although we can indeed distinguish *theoreti cally* between the earliest Christian witness to Jesus and Jesus' own beliefs and actions, we're quite unable to distinguish them *operationally*, so as to identify in a non-question-begging way what Jesus himself believed and did prior to any and all interpretations of him by others: the others who responded to his call with obedient faith and then bore witness, in their ways, to his decisive significance for human existence. Thus, contrary to the reiterated claims of all those best known in our own country through the work of the "Jesus Seminar," any quest of the historical Jesus—old, new, or renewed—is really quite impossible. The only possibility allowed for by the very nature of our sources is something quite different: not a quest of the historical Jesus but a historical quest for Jesus, whose only attainable objective is the Jesus witnessed to by the earliest Christian witness now accessible to us.

My own position, then, on the formal norm, or first principle, of what we as Christians are to believe and to do is a third, or mean, position between the usual extremes of just the sort that I spoke about in my preliminary remarks. On the one hand, it agrees with the classical position in accepting the criterion of "apostolicity" as against the revisionary appeal to the historical Jesus. On the other hand, it insists that the only witness that can now be validated by this criterion as apostolic is not, as the classical position holds, the canon of the New Testament, but rather a canon *before* this canon, although not the historical Jesus, as revisionary Christians typically claim, but the earliest Christian witness or witnesses that we're now able to reconstruct, employing our own historical-critical methods and knowledge.

But if the three reasons I've given for not wholly concurring in the usual answer to our question are sound, what's the right answer? The right answer, I hold, is that what we as Christians are to believe and to do in principle is what is necessarily presupposed and implied by our call to be such, and thus also by our own obedient faith in response to this call. The sole formal norm, and in that sense the canon or first principle for determining this call as well as the validity of our own or of anyone else's witness of faith is the original and originating witness of the apostles. And for us today, this can be identified, not as the New Testament, but only as the earliest Christian witness now accessible to us by way of historical reconstruction, using the New Testament writings as our sources.

This is in no way to say, however, that what we are to believe and do is simply what the apostles themselves believed and did, as attested by this earliest witness. No, even their beliefs and actions as such, as much as any other, are relative to a particular historical situation—namely, the one in whose particular concepts and terms they perforce had to formulate their beliefs and in whose concrete circumstances they had to perform their actions. This means that all that can be normative in even their beliefs and actions for others like ourselves, who are given to live only in more or less different situations, is not their "what," if I may say so, but their "that": not *what* they believed and did, but *that* they believed and did it—that, on the basis of their faith and in the circumstances of their situation, they both believed and did what they judged to be presupposed and implied by their own call to be a Christian, and did so as adequately and fittingly as they knew to do. Therefore, what they or others who would follow in their succession have the right and the responsibility to expect from us today is not that we shall believe their beliefs or perform their actions, but only that we shall heed their example and believe and perform our own, taking care always both to formulate our beliefs and to perform our actions as validly as we can in the circumstances of our own historical situation.

## What is true and what is right

But now, as I said, there's yet another, fourth, reason why I cannot entirely agree with the usual answer to our question in this lecture. Not the least problem with this answer is its assumption that to believe and to act as Christians have historically believed and acted, in accordance with scripture and tradition, is not only to do so appropriately to Jesus Christ, as all Christians are called to believe and to act, but also to believe credibly and to act rightly, as all human beings are originally and irrevocably called to do just because they're human. Of course, there's a very good reason why Christians assume this. The whole point of their faith and of their constitutive christological assertion, that Jesus is the decisive re-presentation of the meaning of ultimate reality for us as human beings, is that to understand oneself as he decisively calls one to do is also to understand oneself truly and authentically because realistically, in keeping with things as they really are and as we ourselves, at the bottom of our experience and understanding, always already know them to be. And from this it immediately follows that to believe and to act according to this self-understanding is *eo ipso* to believe what is true and to do what is right, in the ordinary, straightforward senses in which "what is true" means what agrees with what is really the case, and "what is right," what agrees with what really ought to be done.

But, as clear and certain as all this is, the constitutive christological assertion is precisely that—an *assertion*, whose claim to be valid, exactly like any other, requires to be critically validated if and when it becomes sufficiently problematic. This means, so far as the christological assertion is concerned, that once this point is reached, whatever it necessarily presupposes and implies must be somehow verified as true, in the case of beliefs, or justified as right, in the case of actions. Nor is there any other way to do either, finally, than by appealing to our common human experience and our critical reflection thereon.

The usual objection to this position, especially (but not only!) by Christians on the other side of the current controversy, is that it simply adopts and applies the typical standards of the modern Western Enlightenment, instead of forthrightly recognizing the inappropriateness of these standards for Christian faith, witness, and theology, as well as indeed for religious beliefs and practices generally. Far from requiring verification or justification by common human experience and reason, Christian beliefs and actions, it is held, are always to be authorized solely and sufficiently by God's unique self-revelation in Jesus Christ. What this comes down to in practice, then, is either to appeal to scripture and tradition, on some understanding, as sufficient for establishing the truth of Christians' beliefs and the rightness of Christians' actions, or else simply to claim that, being authorized by divine revelation, their beliefs and actions are—as those who claim this like to say—"self-authenticating."

My reply to this objection can only be brief. I certainly do not question that my position is indeed closely convergent with that of at least many thinkers of the Enlightenment. But the inference made from the fact of this convergence, that I take the position I take only or primarily because I've accommodated my theology to the Enlightenment's alien claims, I judge to be as unwarranted as it is false—for reasons I shall return to momentarily. As for the alternative procedure that the objection proposes for verifying Christian beliefs and justifying Christian actions, I regard it as question begging on its face in both of the forms it takes in actual practice. Contrary to the assumption that appeals to divine revelation are an alternative, and also superior, way of verifying Christian beliefs and justifying Christian actions, the plain fact is that the assertion that something or other, whether scripture or tradition, is divinely revealed is simply one more assertion whose own claim to validity can be and in fact is disputed by others making or implying counterclaims for what they take to be revelation. And so, too, with any and all claims that this, that, or the other belief or action is "self-authenticating"; for such claims are just verbally different ways of repeating the identical claims to validity all over again, and so do absolutely nothing toward critically validating them.

But my biggest problem with the objection, as I've indicated, is its charge, made or implied, that I hold the position I hold only or primarily because, like earlier liberal or revisionary Christians, I've bought into—or sold out to—the alien "rationalism" of the Enlightenment. The truth in this charge is that I have, indeed, tried to learn from the Enlightenment and, in doing so, have become ever more firmly convinced that no appeal to mere authority, whether religious or secular, can ever be sufficient of itself, logically, to verify a belief or to justify an action. If the belief is true, or the action is right, it is so, not simply because someone says it is, but only because it agrees with what is really the case or with what really ought to be done, as these are disclosed to each of us through our common experience and critical reflection simply as human beings. Utterly false in the charge, however, is the entirely unwarranted inference that I hold this position, not as a Christian or as a Christian theologian, but only or primarily as a modern Western man who's still under the spell of the Enlightenment, having spurned the blessings of "postmodernism" when they were more recently offered to me. This inference is false, I maintain, because, in point of fact, I've long since found and argued that there are the very best of reasons why I can and should take this position *just because I am a Christian who is called to believe and to do what is necessarily presupposed and implied by my call to be such.*

Here, again, I ask you to recall the argument of my first lecture, where I sought to clarify what I called certain necessary presuppositions of the decisive call to be a Christian. One of these, I argued, is the original and universal call that is presented to each of us just as and because we're human beings. This call I defined, in purely formal terms, as the call to understand oneself truly and authentically because realistically, in accordance with things as they really are and also as one oneself most deeply understands them to be, and then to believe and to act accordingly, which can only mean, as we've seen, to believe what is true and to do what is right. But to be thus called to believe the truth and to do the right doesn't even make sense unless, on the sole basis of one's own experience and reason simply as a human being, one somehow understands the truth one is to believe and the right one is to do. No one can be validly called to believe anything unless one understands it to be true; and a corresponding condition requires that if one is to be validly called to do something, one must understand it to be right. If, then, our original call to be human is irrevocable, in the sense that, once issued, it can never be taken back but can only be confirmed by any valid special or decisive call that may ever come to us, to hold, as I do, that Christians, also, are called to believe only what is true and to do only what is right on the basis of their own experience and reason as human beings is only to make explicit what is necessarily implied by the Christian call itself.

The same conclusion follows just as rigorously, I think, from the other presupposition of this call that I also tried to clarify in that first lecture. I refer to the presupposition of the universal fact of human sin, understood as the disobedience of each one of us to the original and universal call to be a human being by electing to understand oneself falsely and inauthentically because unrealistically—not in accordance but at variance with ultimate reality as it really is and as one oneself deeply knows it to be. But, once again, sin in this sense presupposes that the sinner, which is to say, every one of us, must of necessity always already have understood what is true and what is right on the sole basis of her or his common human experience and reason. Why? Because otherwise her or his sin could not be the free and responsible act it has to be in order to be sin at all, as distinct from being merely ignorance or error. So to hold, as I do, that what Christians, also, are to believe and to do must be verified and justified, finally, by their own experience and understanding as human beings is, again, but to make fully explicit what the call to be a Christian itself necessarily presupposes.

I think I understand why many Christians are deeply disturbed by the full implications of this position. If any belief or action that the call to be a Christian necessarily presupposes or implies should prove to be false or wrong on the basis of one's own experience and critical reflection, the only conclusion one could draw is that this call itself must insofar be invalid. But disturbing as this may be, the fact remains that the only thing one could do in that event *consistently with the Christian call's own*

115

*necessary presuppositions* would be to draw precisely that conclusion and follow through accordingly. "What is truth?" Meister Eckhart asks—and answers: "Truth is something so noble that if God could turn aside from it, I could keep to the truth and let God go." And in any case, the price of trying to do anything else is simply too high. As Samuel Taylor Coleridge once put it, in one of my all-time favorite sayings, "He who begins by loving Christianity better than Truth, will proceed by loving his own sect or church better than Christianity, and end in loving himself better than all."

So much for what we're to believe and to do in principle. In the concluding lecture, we'll briefly consider at least some of the things that we're now called to believe and do in fact if we're to obey the call to be a Christian in our situation today.

## What We Are to Believe and What We Are to Do: In Fact

### *Preliminary remarks*

In turning now to our last question, What are we to believe and what are we to do in fact? I take for granted that only one answer is consistent with my argument to this point: we are to believe and to do in fact whatever is necessarily presupposed and implied by the call to be a Christian and is also true and right, given our situation with its particular concepts and terms and its particular concrete circumstances. But there's no question, obviously, of exhausting all that's covered by this answer in a single lecture—or in an indefinite number of lectures. As I've said, the actual life-situation of any of us is too concrete and particular ever to be thought and talked about adequately in the necessarily abstract and general concepts and terms on which any lecturer has to rely. Therefore, I shall focus on only two areas of Christian belief and action that I judge to be of basic importance in our situation today—the two, namely, that I highlighted in my second lecture and that are also indicated by the section titles of this one. In doing so, however, I'll try to keep in mind—and hope that each of you will, too—that there are any number of other areas that are also important in which we as Christians today are called to believe and to act and where what we believe and do can make a difference.

This leads to my other preliminary remark, which is also by way of underscoring something I've said before. As convinced as I am that the two areas I shall discuss are of fundamental importance and that the answer I shall give to our question is essentially correct, my main purpose here is not to solicit your agreement with my answer but to exemplify the kind of theological reasoning that any of us must pursue in order to obtain any answer worth having. This, to my mind, is what is most important if we're to attain the stated goal of the seminar: to heighten our consciousness about how we are called to lead the Christian life today.

## *The challenge of emergent plurality*

I ask you now to think back with me to my second lecture, where I tried to clarify the situation in which we now find ourselves by pointing up two fundamental challenges that it puts to each of us who is called to be a Christian. One of these I referred to as "the challenge of emergent plurality," meaning by this the gradual breakdown of the historic mutual isolation of human societies and cultures that has resulted from the processes of modernization and globalization, and, specifically, from the development by a science-based technology of radically new means of communication and transportation. The upshot of this revolutionary change is that the real plurality of social and cultural, including religious, forms in which human beings have always lived has now emerged out into the open, so that it is a patent fact in the ordinary everyday experiences of all of us. We've all been given to realize, whether we do so or not, that our particular way of being human—socially, culturally, and religiously—is so far from being the only such way as to be simply one of many, all of which make or imply the same claims to validity as ours does.

Prominent in all this, naturally, are the many different ways of being religious with their claims and counterclaims to truth—which is to say, claims not only to being *substantially* true by agreeing in substance with any and every thing else that is existentially true, but also to being *formally* true, by being the norm with which anything else has to agree in substance if its claim to be true is a valid claim. But for all of their prominence, the historic religions are not the only components of the now emergent plurality. Also included in it are all of the secular, nonreligious ways of asking and answering the same existential question that underlies and is somehow addressed by all of the historic religions, i.e., *the* existential question about the meaning of ultimate reality for us. In fact, even outright secularist ideologies and philosophies, revolutionary as well as evolutionary, are also to be reckoned with, although their ways of addressing the existential question may well prove to be either far less clear or else arguably inconsistent. The point, in any case, is that it is in the context of just such practically unlimited plurality that Christians, as much as everyone else, now have to make—and also make good on— their own claim to truth.

The challenge, then, is how this is to be done, and, as we know, there's no consensus about how to resolve the issue of the truth of Christian witness and theology. On the contrary, it's one of the two issues, justice being the other, that I identified as controverted in the most basic controversy now dividing the Christian community. Christians on one side of this controversy typically hold a strictly exclusivist position, according to which Christianity is the only possible formally true religion, and believing Christians alone have the possibility of salvation. For such Christian exclusivists, no change in Christian belief and action is either necessary or possible in order to meet the challenge. Those on the other side of the controversy are far less united on this issue, except in their common rejection of this one extreme of Christian exclusivism. Many of them—quite possibly a growing number—are attracted to the other, equally extreme position of Christian pluralism, so called, for which Christianity, far from being the only formally true religion, is, in fact, but one of many, all of which make the same claim with more or less equal validity. Others on this side of the controversy, who resist so radical a change in traditional Christian belief, are more inclined to what is, in a way, a mediating position, commonly referred to as Christian inclusivism. According to it, Christianity is indeed the only possible formally true religion, even though, thanks to God's saving grace in Jesus Christ being somehow made available to human beings universally, not only Christians but all other women and men also have a real possibility of being saved.

I can't go into this whole discussion any further, so I simply refer you to my book *Is There Only One True Religion or Are There Many?* It makes clear, I believe, that and why my own position, also, is a mediating one, although in the direction of a pluralistic inclusivism, as over against the usual monistic kind. In any case, the only point I want to make here has to do with the changes in at least many Christians' beliefs and actions that now seem to me to be necessary as well as possible if the challenge of emergent plurality is to be met as it should be.

The change in belief I mainly have in mind is the one I already argued for in the last part of the preceding lecture. Instead of believing, wrongly, that the Christian claim to truth can be sufficiently validated just by appealing in some way to scripture and tradition or to their own Christian faith, Christians are now called to believe what they always could and should have believed consistently with the necessary presuppositions of their own Christian call. They're called to believe, namely, that their claim can be validated only by verifying the truth of their assertions and the rightness of their actions by the same common human experience and reason required to validate any other assertion or action. Because all human beings, even as the sinners they are, are originally called to believe the truth presupposed and implied by their call to authentic self-understanding, Christians, also, are ever called to believe whatever they believe, finally, on the same basis: of their own experience and reflection in originally understanding themselves, others, and the whole simply as human beings.

But, then, the corresponding change in action now called for by the challenge of emergent plurality is simply to act consistently and resolutely on this belief. This requires, first of all, as I see it, a fundamental change in the way we as Christians express our beliefs in bearing witness and doing theology. For reasons connected historically with the mutual cultural isolation of which I've spoken, Christians in the past, like human beings in general, have typically expressed their beliefs in a dogmatic, unselfcritical way, without really taking account of the beliefs of other communities of faith—secular as well as religious. Confident of the truth of their own beliefs and, as I may add, the rightness of their own patterns of action, Christians have advanced the claim for the truth of their witness or theology without acknowledging the need to validate their claim over against the claims and counterclaims of others. In face of the challenge of emergent plurality, however, we as Christians today are called to adopt a new nondogmatic, self-critical way of expressing our beliefs, predicated on the frank acknowledgement that our disputed claim for the truth of what we believe *needs* to be critically validated, even as the counterclaims of others *deserve* such validation. This means, of course, that we must further acknowledge that the only way we can continue to be Christians at all is to accept the possibility and the risk of at some point ceasing to be such in face of experiences and arguments that on the whole tell against our Christian claim instead of for it.

But this is already to imply, if not to state, a second requirement: that we today must be willing to embark on the path of genuine dialogue, not only with all other religious believers, although most certainly with them, but also with anyone else whose claim to truth renders our own

Christian truth claim problematic, enough so, at any rate, to need critical validation. By "*genuine* dialogue" here I mean, first, a dialogue that is completely open and unconstrained: open in the sense of not closed to anyone seriously concerned to answer the same existential question about the meaning of ultimate reality for us; and unconstrained in the sense of constrained by nothing other than the force of the weightier evidence and the better argument. But I also mean, second, a dialogue that necessarily presupposes that everyone participating in it at least *could be* telling the truth: not only substantially, because it agrees in substance with every other truth of the same logical type, but even formally, because its claim to be the formal norm with which every other such truth must agree is likewise a valid claim.

I realize, of course, that insisting on this second condition of genuine dialogue may strike many as going too far. But if I'm right that the Christian call itself necessarily presupposes that not only Christians but all human beings always already understand the truth originally, if only implicitly, disclosed to each of us simply as a human being, then there can be no reason, in principle, why any particular religion, or any particular ideology or philosophy, for all that, couldn't, in its way, re-present this truth and do so decisively, even if not uniquely except for its own adherents.

Also worth remembering, I may add, is that to make any claim to truth is to hold out a promise: the promise, namely, to make good on one's claim whenever it becomes problematic enough to require one to do so. But, then, Christians precisely as Christians have yet a further reason to give themselves resolutely to just such genuine dialogue. For how else could they possibly be loyal to, or love, all others as themselves, if not by keeping their promise and making good on the claim that they make or imply in bearing Christian witness?

## *The challenge of persistent inequality*

Once again, I ask you to return in your minds to my second lecture, and specifically to my discussion of the other fundamental challenge to us as Christians in our situation today. Since I already gave attention there to characterizing this challenge, I shall limit myself here to reminding you of only the most important points I tried to make.

Foremost among them, certainly, is that, despite all the radical changes in human lives on this planet brought about by the complex processes of modernization and globalization, the historic inequality of most societies and cultures known to us has not diminished but persisted. The static inequalities in income and wealth of the agrarian past have given way only to the dynamic inequalities of the technological present. Moreover, there is, as I sought to show, disturbing evidence and argument that, during roughly the last quarter of the twentieth century, the inequality gap in our own country as well as in the world at large—between the rich countries such as ours in the North and the poor, undeveloped countries of the South—has actually widened, dashing any hope that the rising tide of a new global economy would, as its advocates promised, "lift all boats." The darkest side of all this, however, is that not only inequality but poverty, also—in the United States as well as elsewhere—appears only to have widened and also deepened, with a poverty rate in our own country approaching 20 percent, and with as many as 40 percent of the poor living below half the poverty line.

But if the rapid social change characterizing the modern world has not led to diminishing inequality and poverty, it has resulted in what I called "the rise of historical consciousness." By this, as I explained, I mean the growing awareness on the part of those undergoing such rapid change and at all thoughtful about it that structures of social and cultural order are not simply given, either by nature or by nature's God, but are the creations of human beings, who therefore bear responsibility, collectively and individually, for changing as well as maintaining them. Already by the eighteenth century, I said, this new awareness and sense of responsibility were shared widely enough to inform our own American Revolution and the other democratic revolutions following upon it. Then, by the end of the next century, they had sufficiently impacted the new revisionary movement among Christians and churches to give rise to the social gospel, which sharply raised the further basic issue not only of the truth of Christian beliefs but also of the rightness or justice of Christian actions, as well as, naturally, those of society and culture generally.

Even so—and this was a third point I made—the tradition of the social gospel, for all of its influence on mainstream Christians and churches, has for the most part remained a minority tradition even there, African American Christianity being the notable exception to the rule. Consequently, in our situation today, the persisting inequality in both the United States and the larger world is all the more urgently challenging because Christians on all sides seem to have become almost as ominously silent about it as politicians and civic leaders have been on both sides of the political divide—at any rate until quite recently.

But the point I want to make now, in these remaining moments of my lecture, is that the challenge of persistent inequality is precisely a *political* challenge, in the sense that it cannot be met solely by moral action in general but also demands specifically political action in particular. I use the term "political action" here deliberately in two distinct, if closely related, senses. Strictly used, it simply means what most of us ordinarily mean by it—namely, action pertaining to constituting and governing human communities at all levels, from local and regional to national and even international, insofar as there are, in fact, certain limited institutions of world government. But I also use the term more broadly to mean action directed toward creating, maintaining, and/or transforming social and cultural structures generally, including all other nongovernmental structures of social and cultural order as well. Thus the significant difference between political action in either sense and moral action in general is that the first is a special case of the second. Whereas moral action generally is doing what ought to be done, or what is right and just, specifically political action is doing what ought to be done to establish, maintain, and reestablish right or just structures, either, in the strict sense, for the constitution of a community and its governance by the state, or, in the broad sense, for the ordering of all communities and associations, including the state. My point, then, is that the challenge of persistent inequality calls for specifically political action in both of these senses of the term.

This is not to argue, however, that political action is a sufficient as well as a necessary condition of meeting the challenge. On the contrary, if we're ever to achieve greater equality, or, at least, the more realistic goal of a more tolerable level of inequality, moral action within existing structures is every bit as necessary as specifically political action to change these structures themselves. In point of fact, the only effective means of alleviating poverty in the short term—and where the direst poverty is concerned, that's the only term that counts—is precisely moral action within structures as they are, or, at most, the kind of broadly political action that I associate especially with agencies such as Freedom from Hunger and Oxfam America, which can effect minor but life-saving changes in the way some poor persons earn their livelihoods and feed their families. So there's not the least question in my mind that person-to-person acts of justice—commonly called "charity"—are as necessary now as they've always been and, from all indications, always will be. But, again, being a necessary condition of meeting a challenge is one thing, being a sufficient condition, something else; and my point is that persistent inequality has shown every sign of being the kind of challenge that cannot possibly be met without specifically political action to meet it: to change the structures, especially the economic and political structures, that make for its persistence.

The other clarification I may well add at this point is that the standard I'm applying in talking about inequality is nothing like complete equality of results. This is why, indeed, I've alluded more than once to the more relevant, more realistic goal as "a more tolerable level of inequality." Experience and wisdom make only too clear that real differences between human beings, natural as well as historical, allow them to make comparably different contributions to the common good. Moreover, given the powerful motivation of self-interest in all of us, there's a clear correlation between higher incentives and more effective performance that can be ignored only at the expense of the entire community. It's simply a fact that all of us are more likely to gain if relatively greater benefits accrue to those who are gifted and skilled and ambitious enough to provide the leadership needed for economic enterprise and political governance. And in any event, the interference with freedom of association, especially in the marketplace, that achieving anything approaching complete equality of results would require would be so egregious that justice itself would demand that it be resisted. So, no doubt about it, any just as well as realistic understanding of the problem will eschew any standard of complete equality of results in judging the inequality that persists all around us. But it is otherwise, I think, with the alternative standard of tolerable inequality, or, if you prefer, of equal opportunity, that I, like many others, would want to apply—namely, that inequality in economic benefits should extend no further than is needed to optimize the opportunity of *all* to contribute as much as possible to the good of the whole.

But now the usual reaction to the point I'm making by many Christians—not all of whom, by the way, are on the other side of the current controversy on the other basic issue of truth—is that Christians as such are not called to specifically political action. There are some who argue, for instance, that Christians can follow the social gospel in accepting a specifically political responsibility only by repeating the fateful mistake made when Christianity became the established religion of the Roman Empire under Constantine. For Christians to concern themselves with achieving greater social justice by acting politically to narrow the widening inequality gap only leads away from their proper mission to maintain the church as an alternative community of peace and virtue that is at once a sign and a foretaste of God's coming kingdom. But I will not further support my claim that many Christians, either do not recognize a summons to act politically even in face of so fundamental a human problem as persistent inequality and poverty, or else interpret such a summons as a temptation to be resisted if they're to obey their call to be a Christian.

I should not wish to deny that there are reasons why many Christians today continue to react in this way. It is undeniable that Christians have not always and everywhere acknowledged a call to specifically political action; and it's certainly true that their involvement in politics, when they've become so involved, has been at least as spotty and ambiguous as any other aspect of the history of their movement. But I should want to argue, along with others, that no such reasons outweigh the clear implication of the Christian call to us today, in our situation, as distinct from earlier situations in Christian history. Both historical consciousness and the specifically political sense of responsibility in which it results are distinctively modern, still relatively recent factors in ordinary Christian experience and reflection; and the same is true of any real possibility of Christians as citizens participating in self-government by means of democratic constitutions and the other institutions of governance they prescribe. But allow that these are all very much factors in our situation today, along with persistent inequality, and I don't see how anyone can either ignore or deny that Christians have a specifically political responsibility to work for greater equality of opportunity.

I can't develop the argument needed to make this point adequately in the time remaining. But its main steps right up to the last should already be familiar to you from what I've been saying all along. The call to be a Christian, I've argued, is the call both to trust unreservedly in God's prevenient love for oneself and all creatures, and to be unqualifiedly loyal in serving the cause of God's love by one's returning love for God and for all others as oneself in God. But, then, to be loyal to another and to love another finally come to the same thing. Both mean not only accepting the other as the other, in all her or his otherness, but then also acting concretely and particularly so as to take account of the other's real interests equally with one's own and to realize as many of them as possible. In other words, to be called to be loyal to God and to all others, or to love them, is to be called to do what is right, or just, in the precise classical sense of "justice" as giving each her or his own (*suum cuique*). Nothing is more surely someone's own than her or his real interests; and so, to accept anyone as loyalty and love alike demand and then to act accordingly by realizing her or his interests as fully as possible—consistently with one's always having to act on behalf of many neighbors, not just one or a few—is precisely to do what is right or to do justice. But if to be loyal and to love both thus entail acting morally in the completely general sense of doing what is right or doing justice, they also both entail acting to do justice in the specifically political sense *as soon as it becomes clear that one is fully authorized to create structures and to change them and that one also has the ways and means of doing so.*

It's this final step of the argument, naturally, that remains controversial. I submit to you, however, that it follows rigorously and conclusively given only conditions that are unquestionably satisfied by the circumstances of our situation today: not only the persistence of inequality, and poverty as well, but also our sense of responsibility for meeting their challenge by creating more just structures of social and cultural order, together with the availability of at least some democratic institutions at all levels for carrying out our responsibility.

Of course, such institutions are, for the most part, still to be created on the global level, and the few already there are like those at all levels in our own country in being themselves profoundly impacted by the persistence of economic inequality. The undue influence of large, transnational corporations and other moneyed interests on politics at all levels is obvious to all of us—scandalously so, sometimes—as are the apathy and indifference, not to say, cynicism of so many in lower-income brackets, who no longer trouble even to vote. But, thanks to the efforts of individuals and groups making up the encompassing movement of "globalization from below," some gains are being made toward democratizing existing international institutions; and steps here at home such as ongoing campaign-finance reform and voter registration and mobilization give at least some promise that ours can become a working democracy, not only formatively or constitutionally, but also substantively, at the level of actual day-to-day governance of our common life.

In any case, of one thing I have no doubt: Christians who really obey their call by what they believe and do have a distinctive contribution to make to the political debate in our own country on the just distribution of income and wealth as well as on any number of other important public issues. Why? Well, because the understanding of human community necessarily presupposed and implied by our Christian call is significantly different from the contrary understandings continually disseminated by the secular ideologies or philosophies that are so widely influential among us—including many of us in the churches who unquestionably want to believe and to act obediently to our call, only to be insufficiently critical of these ideologies. I allude here again to the highly individualistic ideologies of liberalism, on the one hand, with its understanding that the larger community exists so as to enable the individuals within it each the more effectively to pursue her or his own self-interest, and of conservatism, on the other hand, with its understanding that the larger community's proper purpose is to make possible each individual's successful cultivation of her or his own private virtue. Over against the extreme individualism of both of these contrary ideologies, the understanding of community presupposed and implied by the Christian call sees each individual precisely and only as an individual-in-community. As such, she or he is originally called simply as a human being to exist both *from* the community and *for* it, gratefully appropriating every opportunity it provides, not in order to pursue her or his own private self-interest or to cultivate her or his own private virtue, but in order to make the greatest possible contribution to the whole by increasing the opportunity of one and all to make their own unique contributions. By any measure, this understanding of human community, which I take to be necessarily presupposed and implied by the call to be a Christian, is sufficiently distinctive that Christians whose beliefs and actions are really and consistently informed by it cannot fail to make a contribution correspondingly distinctive to the democratic debate and decision making now called for in this country by the challenge of persistent inequality and poverty.

Admittedly, I haven't fully developed the argument for this contention, and I'm all too aware that ever so much more could and should be said to support even my basic point. But I hope I've given you at least some reason to think that with respect to the basic issue of justice, no less than that of truth, certain changes are now called for in what only too many of us as Christians still incline to believe and to do. If we are to obey the call to be a Christian in our situation today, we are first to believe that the justice that now ought to be done by us in face of persistent inequality necessarily includes our doing specifically political justice; and then we must act on this belief as resolutely and persistently as we can by doing our part in creating more equitable structures of social and cultural order both in our own country and in the world.

Having said as much as I have in this course about controversy among us as Christians, I want to conclude it by recalling an old rule that we all need to observe if we're to obey our common call. *In necessariis unitas, in dubiis libertas, in omnibus caritas*: in necessary things unity, in questionable things liberty, in all things charity. This rule seems to me to be as right and relevant now as it's always been. But, as with many other such rules, its interpretation and application have themselves been and still are controversial. For just what are the "necessary things," and what are the "questionable things," and how does one tell the difference? The suggestion I would make to you is simple, and with it I can summarize everything I'm able to say to our question, What is it to be a Christian today? The only strictly necessary things are the beliefs and actions necessarily presupposed and implied by God's gift and demand of boundless love in all things as this love is made known to us decisively through Jesus; literally everything else is and remains questionable.

> Be present with us, Lord Jesus, in all that we do both to bear witness and to do theology. Give us the courage to deal openly and honestly with our own real questions and with the real questions of others; and, above all, lead us ever to seek you where you are always to be found: in the faithful witness of your church; and in the neediest of our neighbors, in loving and serving whom as ourselves we love and serve you. Amen.[4]

---

4. Composed by the author.

# 4

# Questions and Answers
# about Faith and Practice

Bless, O God, all our attempts to learn and to teach, and enable
them to bear rich fruit in our lives. Help us, above all, both to
speak and to listen to one another in love: to say what we mean
and to mean what we say; and, not least, to hear what is meant,
not just what is said; in Jesus' name. Amen.[1]

## Session 1

*1. What is faith? How do we find it?*

The term "faith," like most of the other terms that are likely to figure
prominently in discussion among Christians, may be properly used in
different senses; and it may also be properly used to refer to different, if
also related things.

First of all, then, some of the different senses in which "faith" may
be used:

(1) "Faith," properly, has both an *objective* and a *subjective* sense, in that
it can refer equally well both to *what* one believes in believing and to
one's *act* of believing it.

1. Composed by the author.

(2) "Faith," properly, has both an *existential* sense and an *intellectual* sense, and, understood in either sense, is inseparable from "faith" understood in the other sense. Faith in its existential sense is a matter, subjectively, of self-understanding and objectively, of an understanding of existence—where by "existence" I mean not just the human self in isolation, but the self as it actually is, in its relations to others: to other selves as well as to other beings generally, and to the mysterious, all encompassing Other, the ultimate whole of reality, from which all things come and to which they all return. To exist as a self is to understand oneself somehow in relation to all these others, and what one understands in doing this is some understanding of existence. But if faith in its existential sense is thus a matter of actualizing some possibility of understanding oneself and leading one's life accordingly, it necessarily implies faith in the other intellectual sense of the term. To understand oneself and others in a certain way would really be to *misunderstand* them unless certain intellectual beliefs about them were true beliefs. Conversely, any such intellectual beliefs, for their part, necessarily imply that some existential faith is appropriate to, or authorized by, things as they really are in a way other contrary self-understandings and understandings of existence are not.

(3) "Faith" is properly used to refer to merely *implicit* faith as well as to faith that has become *explicit*. That a small child who has not yet learned how to express itself in relation to its parents and siblings is nonetheless guided by some self-understanding is clear enough simply from its behavior. And it is equally clear that the explicit beliefs that an adult sometimes professes—even sincerely professes—may or may not adequately express her or his actual beliefs, not to mention such other beliefs as they necessarily imply.

This brings us to some of the different things that "faith" may properly refer to. I shall limit myself to the two things that I take to be most important for the purposes of answering the question before us.

(1) The first thing "faith" may refer to is what I am accustomed to calling "*basic faith in the ultimate meaning of life*." On my analysis, to live humanly at all is to live out of a fundamental trust that to do so is finally worthwhile—somewhat as it also belongs to our life to believe that the course of events generally always has a certain order, warranting our expecting of the future, by and large, what we have experienced and

learned to expect in the past. For the most part, this basic existential faith is merely implicit in the various things that we think, say, and do in leading our lives; and the same is true of the intellectual beliefs that basic faith in turn implies. But even if it remains largely implied, and not explicit, it constitutes the fundamental presupposition of all our self-understanding and life-praxis, and thus also of all the forms of culture by which they're mediated, both secular and sacred. Thanks to this basic faith, we all believe (1) that there is a true and authentic, because realistic, way to understand ourselves and others as all parts of the encompassing whole; (2) that to understand ourselves in this way and to lead our lives accordingly is, like everything else, both really possible, in fact as well as in principle, and unconditionally meaningful or significant; and (3) that the structure of ultimate reality in itself is such as to explain its meaning for us, and thus to explain both why there is a true and authentic way to understand ourselves and why understanding ourselves in this way and conducting ourselves accordingly is really possible and also has the unconditional significance we believe it has.

(2) The other thing "faith" may refer to that is important for answering the question asked is any and all of *the several faiths, religious and also philosophical,* through which our basic faith in the ultimate meaning of life becomes explicit. Foremost here, obviously, are all the different religious faiths, properly so called. What I understand to be meant by "religion" is the primary form of culture, and thus the system of concepts and symbols, through which our basic faith in the meaning of life is not merely implied but also somehow made explicit. Actually, what any particular religious faith makes explicit is some answer to the *question* that our basic faith in the ultimate meaning of life makes it possible for us to ask—namely, what I'm used to calling "*the* existential question" of just how we're to understand the meaning of ultimate reality for us in which we cannot help but believe, and so how we're to exist truly and authentically, in accordance with that meaning, instead of falsely and inauthentically, at cross-purposes with it.

What makes this existential question urgent, however, is that the various conditions under which we're given and called to understand ourselves and to lead our lives often render our underlying faith in ultimate meaning somehow problematic—again, somewhat as a disappointed expectation of what is going to happen in the future may sometimes appear to pose a problem for our basic faith in the general order of things. But in the one case very much as in the other, we cope with our problem, not by abandoning our faith, which we couldn't do even if we tried, but by revising our expectations, or our understanding, as the case may be. And so it is that each religious faith, including the Christian faith, appears on the scene, making or implying a claim to provide the requisite revision: by decisively re-presenting the possibility of self-understanding, or understanding of existence, which, being the possibility originally authorized by ultimate reality itself, overcomes, at last, all uncertainty and misunderstanding.

Still other explications of our basic faith, however, are more properly said to be philosophical than religious. Because they're the result of more or less critical reflection on religion as well as on our life-praxis and culture otherwise, they form a secondary, not a primary, cultural system. Even so, they, too, at their reflective level, explicitly address the existential question and thus re-present our basic faith in life's meaning as well as an answer to our question that claims to be *the* answer to it.

Inadequate as it is, this will have to do for an answer to the first part of our two-part question, What is faith? I turn now to the second part: How do we find faith? If you've followed what I've said, you'll understand why, because of the two different, though closely related, things that "faith" may be used to refer to, there have to be two main parts to the answer.

If what we refer to by "faith" is what I have called our "basic faith in the ultimate meaning of life," then the only possible answer to the question is that we don't find faith at all, because we always already have it as something essential to our life—indeed as the necessary presupposition of literally everything that we think, say, and do. In the deepest sense of "our basic faith," we—all of us, simply as and because we're human beings—always already *live by faith*, and could not live humanly, which is to say, understandingly, at the high level of thinking and speaking in concepts and symbols, without it. To be sure, we may or may not be explicitly aware of this; and it seems clear that most of us, much of the time, may need to "find" faith, in the sense of somehow becoming aware explicitly of the basic faith in the meaning of life that we always have at least implicitly and without which we could not live as human beings at all. But "finding" faith in this first use of the term is always a matter of finding an understanding of it, an understanding of something we already have—and but for having which we could not think, say, or do anything whatever, including finding—indeed, even looking for!—faith as the referent of the other thing the term "faith" may be used to refer to.

As for how we find faith in this other way of referring to it—i.e., some one or the other of what I have called the several faiths, religious and also philosophical—there must also be two different but closely related answers.

(1) The first would be more accurately formulated, however, by saying, not that we find faith, but that *faith finds us*. That is, each of us is born into some human culture, one of the integral parts or aspects of which is some religion, in the sense of some way of explicitly asking and answering *the* existential question at the level of a primary cultural system. Depending, then, on the conditions of our individual rearing, each of us will normally be socialized and acculturated into our society and culture by somehow appropriating the answer to this question, and, in this sense, the faith, re-presented by our society and culture's religious concepts and symbols. I won't go into all the possible variations or permutations of this by taking into account the complexities of socialization and acculturation, given the familiar phenomena of subcultures, subsubcultures, and so on. The point is that we become human beings, in the sense of beings who somehow understand ourselves in relation to others and conduct our lives accordingly, only through the mediation of some human culture, and that any of the many cultures known to us includes, as an essential part or aspect of itself, what I have defined "religion" to designate. In this sense, each of us finds religion, first of all, because, or insofar as, religion, in some form, finds us and becomes more or less our own—in essentially the same way we are socialized and acculturated otherwise.

(2) But to be human is not only to be somehow socialized and acculturated, and, as an essential part of that process, somehow to appropriate the religion that is an integral part or aspect of any society and culture; to be human is also to undergo life experiences that more or less profoundly problematize one's cultural and religious inheritance, and yet, precisely by means of it, also to be capable of critically reflecting on it so as to cope somehow with its problems. For this reason, one may also be said to find faith in the sense that one discovers, or is discovered by, some particular religion, or philosophy, that more adequately addresses the problems that one has come to have in trying to answer one's own existential question. In other words, one finds faith, insofar

as one does so, by finding a religion, or, possibly a philosophy, that really answers, or seems really to answer, one's deepest question about the ultimate meaning of one's life as a human being. This implies—and I take this implication to be important—that one finds *Christian faith* if, and only if, one so experiences Jesus as he is re-presented by the church and its witness that he answers one's own existential question about the ultimate meaning of one's life as no one else, and no thing else, has ever answered it. And this implies, in turn, that one *continues* in Christian faith, once one has found it, as long, and only as long, as, through all of one's life experiences and encounters with all the other answers to the question, Jesus *continues* to be *the* answer: the *decisive* answer in the light of which such truth and falsity as there may be in any of the other answers can be responsibly decided. In sum, we find Christian faith by finding, or being found by, Jesus Christ—which is to say, Jesus in his decisive significance as the re-presentative of God, decisively through whom the ultimate meaning of our lives, in which we can never fail to believe, at last makes sense and can be understood—so far, at least, as we need to understand it in order to be and to become who we really are as human beings.

*2. Some people say different religions are simply different cultural expressions of one phenomenon—God, love, etc. Can you speak to that?*

Well, I hope I can—and that what I've already said about faith and religion, their relationship and their difference, will help to clarify at least some of the things necessary to an adequate answer.

You'll recall that, as I have defined it, religion—in the sense of any particular religion or religions—is the primary form of culture, or "cultural system," through which *the* existential question about the ultimate meaning of our existence is somehow asked and answered explicitly, in certain concepts and symbols. But this, clearly, is already to say that the different religions are indeed "cultural expressions"—if not, exactly, of "one phenomenon," then certainly of *one reality*. I have spoken of this one reality as "existence," explaining that what I mean by this is not just the human self taken by itself in abstraction from its relations to others, and to *the* Other encompassing all others as well as the self, but the human self precisely *in* these actual relations to others and to the whole. "Existence," in other words, is simply another term for "ultimate reality," in the sense of what all of us as selves somehow have to take account of,

no matter what else we may or may not need to take account of, insofar as we are human selves at all—which is to say, ourselves, others, and
the encompassing whole. But I have also made, or implied, a distinction
between existence, or ultimate reality, in its *structure in itself* and in its
*meaning for us*—when I argued, for example, that the *existential* sense of
"faith," although distinct from its *intellectual* sense, is nonetheless inseparable from it—and vice versa, that intellectual beliefs about the structure
of things in themselves necessarily imply, even as they're also implied by,
existential beliefs about the meaning of things for us. So, while I should
very much wish to hold that different religions are so many different expressions of the one reality of our own existence, or of ultimate reality, I
would also need to insist that they are existential in their proper meaning, not merely intellectual. That is, they express *the meaning of existence,
or of ultimate reality, for us*, for how we are to understand ourselves and
others and lead our lives accordingly, as distinct from merely describing
the structure of ultimate reality in itself—although, as I've just reiterated,
they necessarily *imply* that certain intellectual beliefs about that structure
also have to be true beliefs.

On this understanding, the terms "God," "love," and so on—at least
as they're ordinarily used in Christian witness and theology—are but the
way in which one religion—the Christian religion—thinks and speaks
about existence, or ultimate reality, in its meaning for us, for our understanding of ourselves and others as all parts of the encompassing whole,
and so for how we are to lead our lives, given this self-understanding. So
I would *not* wish to say simply and without some such qualification that
different religions are just different cultural expressions of the one reality of God and love, although the terms "God" and "love" are definitely
first and foremost among the terms expressing the concepts and symbols
through which I, *as a Christian*, think about the one reality of our existence, or, alternatively, the one ultimate reality with which all human
beings somehow have to do.

An observation that I have long found helpful in thinking about this
and other related questions is that of the cultural anthropologist, Clifford
Geertz. "What all sacred symbols assert," he says, "is that the good for
man is to live realistically; where they differ is in the vision of reality
they construct." In other words, while all religions are indeed about the
one reality of our existence in its meaning for us, and while each of them
summons us to live realistically, in accordance with that reality, instead of
at variance with it, just how each of them understands ultimate reality is

more or less different from the understandings of other religions. Nor do all of these differences appear to be merely verbal or conceptual, merely different ways of speaking or thinking about the same reality. Some of them, at least, seem to be real differences—such as for example, the difference between a theistic religion like Christianity, Judaism, or Islam and a nontheistic (some would say even, atheistic) religion like Theravada Buddhism or Zen. Subtle as they're likely to prove to be the more one carefully studies them, the differences between religions are hardly less striking than their similarities. Although they're all about the one ultimate reality of our existence, and are all addressed to one and the same existential question about it, they all also express more or less different understandings of its meaning for us: for how we are to understand ourselves in relation to it, and for how, in consequence, we are to lead our lives as human beings.

I should perhaps add that anyone seeking a more fully developed, and, I hope, proportionately more adequate, answer to this question may want to take a look at a little book of mine, Is There Only One True Religion or Are There Many?[2] There is also an essay-length answer to the same question under the same title in my book of essays called Doing Theology Today.[3]

3. How does one express [one's] faith to others when "Christian" has been kidnapped and now means a very narrow view?

I've taken the liberty of slightly reformulating this question, so as to make clearer what I take it to be asking. But if I'm mistaken in my interpretation, and the questioner would like to make the necessary corrections, I'll be more than happy to receive them—trusting everyone to understand that my prepared answer, in any case, has to be to the question as I've understood it, however the questioner asked it.

Here, too, I hope that what I've already said will be helpful toward answering the question. But let me say, first of all, that on my understanding of what it means to express one's faith as a Christian to others—or, as I'm accustomed to think and speak of it, to bear Christian witness, implicitly as well as explicitly, by what one does as well as by what one says— on my understanding of this, to express one's Christian faith is always to make or imply two claims to validity: that one's expression, or witness, is

2. Dallas: Southern Methodist University Press, 1992.
3. 1996; reprinted, Eugene: Wipf & Stock, 2006.

*adequate to its content*; and that it is *fitting to its situation*, which is to say, to the situation of the person or persons to whom it is expressed or borne. I also understand the first claim—to be adequate to the content of witness—to involve two further claims: to be *appropriate to Jesus Christ*—in the sense of expressing what *he* means for us instead of some other self-understanding—and to be *credible to human existence*—in the sense of being worthy of being believed by any woman or man simply as such as the truth about her or his own existence as a human being.

The second thing I would say is that just what expression of Christian faith, or Christian witness, satisfies, or fails to satisfy, the criteria implied by these claims is never settled, but must always be determined anew in each new situation in which faith is to be expressed or witness is to be borne. In other words, what Christians in the past have thought, said, and done in expressing Christian faith, or bearing Christian witness, in their earlier, more or less different situations, never closes this question. Given the incontrovertible fact of unceasing change from one historical situation to another, what may be adequate or fitting, appropriate or credible, in one situation may or may not be so in another. But although the forms of expression, or the formulations of witness, are therefore not constant but variable, the obligation to express Christian faith, or to bear Christian witness, remains ever the same, as does the obligation always to bear this witness validly, in accordance with the criteria implied by the claims that expressing Christian faith, or bearing Christian witness, itself necessarily makes or implies.

The third thing I would say is that from all we know from the long history of expressing Christian faith, or bearing Christian witness, there may never have been only one such expression, or only one such witness, but always only many—each making or implying the same claims to be adequate and fitting, appropriate and credible. In some cases, the differences between the several expressions, or witnesses, have been, if not merely verbal, then at most conceptual as well. But in other cases, the differences have proved to be more serious, because they're *real*, amounting in many cases, in fact, to outright contrarieties or contradictions. Still, those who have expressed the different expressions, or borne the different witnesses, have claimed, implicitly if not explicitly, to be doing what any expression, or any witness, of Christian faith, is obliged to do—and, in this sense, have laid claim to the label "Christian," even if they've not necessarily advanced an *exclusive* claim to it, which may be aptly described metaphorically as "kidnapping" the label. But that and why any such exclusive claim is, in the nature of the case, entirely out of place should be clear enough simply because, whether or not any expression, or witness, of Christian faith, is or is not valid in the several ways in which it claims, and is therefore obliged, to be so, is, as I've said, *never a closed question*, but *always* an open question. It is, to be exact, the properly *theological* question that Christian theology ever bears the responsibility of asking and answering as best it can in *its* historical situation, with its limits and its possibilities.

But now to come directly to the question: How does one express one's Christian faith to others when the term "Christian" is claimed exclusively for only one of many expressions, or witnesses, of Christian faith, and "a very narrow" one at that?

Among the considerations that, in my opinion, need to be kept in mind, having steadfastly forsworn from the outset any exclusive claims for the validity of one's own expression, or witness, of faith, the following seem to me the most important.

First of all—and that means, *above* all—one needs to remember that what one is obliged to express, or bear witness to, as a Christian is *Christian faith itself*—not what someone else, however sincerely, takes Christian faith to be or to mean. There is the most important distinction, in other words, between Christian faith itself and all the many formulations of it that have come down to us in Christian tradition from the original and originating witness of the apostles. To be sure, it is only by ever and again recurring to the apostles' witness, as it is attested in the New Testament writings and in the subsequent traditions of the church, that we can have any confidence that our own expression, or witness, of faith is, as it ought to be, appropriate to Jesus Christ. But the fact remains that the Christian faith itself is one thing, while all expressions, or witnesses, of it—including the constitutive, and therefore formally normative, witness of the apostles themselves—are something else. To the first—Christian faith itself—we as Christians are bound indissolubly, but from the second—all expressions or witnesses of it—we are free unqualifiedly: free to make use of any formulations insofar as they remain adequate and fitting also in our situation, but also free to set them aside in favor of more adequate expressions, or witnesses, given the possibilities and limits of our own situation today.

But, then, the second thing one must keep in mind, obviously, is that one must oneself—precisely as a Christian obliged to express Christian faith, or to bear Christian witness—be sufficiently engaged in critical theological reflection to be able to make this important distinction and to proceed accordingly. I do not mean by this, of course, that every Christian witness is *eo ipso* obliged to be a professional theologian, whether ecclesial or academic. No, I take for granted that not all, but only some Christians, are specially called to be theologians in this sense of the word. But all Christians *are* called, precisely in their call to be Christians, to be *lay* theologians, just as certainly as each of them is also called thereby to be a lay *minister*. Because one is called as a Christian to minister by bearing valid witness to Jesus Christ, one is therewith also called to do theology—in the very general sense of critically reflecting on one's own witness and the witness of one's church to test whether, or to what extent, it really is, or is not, valid in the several ways in which it itself claims to be so, i.e., adequate and fitting, appropriate and credible. So, in this sense, doing theology is a necessary condition of expressing Christian faith or bearing Christian witness. This is sufficiently evident, I take it, simply from realizing that, without doing theology, so understood, one could neither responsibly judge—as the questioner does—any other Christian view to be "a very narrow view" nor have even the least justified confidence that one's own view was anything other than that.

Third, one needs ever to keep in mind that the life-situation of particular individual others is never simply the same as that of persons generally who live in the same historical time and place. To do theology, as we have seen, is, among other things, to test the claim of witness to be fitting to its situation. But that is a task that can be reasonably assigned to Christian theology only if the situation in question is more or less general: the situation in which *most* people in a given time and place find themselves. But, as the poet e. e. cummings reminds us, you and I—and, as he clearly implies, everyone else—are not "most people." We are, each of us, a unique individual whose existential question about the meaning of ultimate reality for us takes a form more or less different from that of anyone else. And so if I am to express Christian faith to others, I have to go beyond anything that doing Christian theology, as such, can be reasonably expected to yield. I must take care to understand the others I would address for what they are individually, lest I fail to do all I possibly can so that the gift and demand of Christian faith really come home to them and they can make a responsible decision for or against its claim.

Finally—and, I trust, obviously—one must remember that, in the nature of the case, no one has an exclusive right to the label "Christian," pending the theological reflection ever required to vindicate the right.

Since theological reflection, as has been said, is always both unconcluded and inconclusive, and since the validity of our claims to validity is never a closed but always an open question, one may proceed to express Christian faith, or to bear Christian witness, without being in the least intimidated by anyone who kidnaps the label. This assumes, of course, that the three preceding considerations have indeed been kept in mind and that one has proceeded accordingly.

*4. Why does the Bible say, "because Christ died for us, our sins can be erased" (paraphrased)? Why couldn't God just do that before? He's all-powerful, right? Who said that he had to kill his only Son to forgive us? (Who said He only got one Son?) Or am I missing the point of the story? Maybe we can understand that God loves us through Jesus' suffering, and somehow that gets us forgiven.*

This is a complex question in fact, multiple questions—and I won't be able to do full justice to it—or to them. But here are some things to keep in mind in continuing to think about an adequate answer.

First, to say "the Bible says" is always to oversimplify, because the Bible is not so much one thing as many things, not simply *a* book, but rather a whole *library* of books, or, even better, *two* libraries, two collections of writings, which we respectively distinguish as the Old Testament and the New. So, while something like the questioner's paraphrased statement is indeed to be found in the Bible, we are less likely to be misled ourselves, or to mislead others, if we recognize that where it is found, more exactly, is in one or another of the writings included in the New Testament, and, more exactly still, in one or another of the many strands of tradition redacted, or edited, in one or another of the New Testament writings. In short, statements asserting the sacrificial character of Jesus' death, although definitely to be found in the Bible as well as in later Christian traditions, are one way, but nonetheless neither the only nor necessarily the most adequate way, of expressing Jesus' decisive significance for human existence. In fact, they are but one of many ways Christians have formulated the assertion concerning Jesus that is constitutive of Christian faith. To say this, of course, is to make use of the all-important distinction I introduced in answering the last question, i.e., the distinction between Christian faith itself, which alone is constant, and its many different expressions, which are—and, in the nature of the case, have to be—variable, and whose validity, as I argued, can never be a closed question, but always remains open.

The more specific questions the questioner asks in asking the main question indicate some of the reasons why many theologians, including myself, seriously question the adequacy of any statement asserting or implying that Jesus' death is, as has been said, the "meritorious cause" of the forgiveness of sins, and thus of our and all human beings' salvation. If Jesus had to die on the cross in order for humankind to be saved, then the love of God appears to be a conditional, not an unconditional, love, and either God's unsurpassable goodness or God's unsurpassable power—or both—clearly seems to be called into question. But, aside from reasons of this kind, there are also other—to my mind, at least as important—reasons for questioning the adequacy, and specifically, the appropriateness of any such statements.

I refer to the fact that one of the surest conclusions of New Testament scholarship is that the earliest Christian witness accessible to us through our own historical methods and knowledge have nothing whatever to say about the saving significance of Jesus' death. On the contrary, so far as these earliest traditions are concerned—I refer to the traditions lying behind and redacted in our Synoptic Gospels (i.e., Matthew, Mark, and Luke), what is significant about Jesus is, not his death, but his life: his own ministry of word and deed, in its immediate impact on those who encountered him and were open to his claim to bear God's decisive word to them in the last days of the world, before the imminent coming of God's reign. Moreover, it is clear beyond reasonable doubt that if some Christians then later expressed Jesus' decisive significance for us by making use of the sacrificial imagery of the Old Testament and Judaism to interpret his death, not all later Christians did so, or, if they did, they also made use of other, very different means for making the identical point. Thus Paul, for example, can focus, not on Jesus' death, as he certainly does in many places in his letters, but rather on Jesus' birth, as the decisive saving event. "But when the fullness of time had come," he writes to the Galatians, "God sent his Son, born of a woman, born under the law, in order to redeem those who were under the law, so that we might receive adoption as children" (4:4–5). Not a word is said here about Jesus' saving death, nor is it either asserted or implied that his birth is merely preliminary, simply the necessary condition of his subsequently having to die in order to achieve our salvation. No, this is another, totally independent way of making exactly the same point that is made—by, among others, Paul himself!—by talking about Jesus' dying, or having to die, in order for us to be saved.

I would like to pursue this line of argument. But I trust I've said enough to indicate my answer to the main question. As for the more specific question, Who said that God has only one Son? the answer, I think, must be that many, if not, indeed, most, of the writers whose work is accessible to us in or through the New Testament writings either said, or clearly implied, something that could be more or less adequately expressed by saying this, or something very like it. In other words, the assertion, implicitly or explicitly, in some terms or other, of Jesus' decisive significance, and therefore of his uniqueness among human beings, is in no way peculiar to this writer or that, but rather the common witness of all the New Testament writers as well as of the still earlier traditions, both oral and written, that they appropriated and made available. This is to imply, of course, that saying Jesus is God's only Son is but one of many ways of making the identical point about his decisive significance for us—by which I mean, not only for us as Christians, but for us as all humankind. But whether, or in what sense, this claim about Jesus is an exclusivist claim is another question that I cannot go into now, although I would certainly welcome its being pursued later in our general discussion. I may also refer you again to my book, *Is There Only One True Religion or Are There Many?*, which has not a little to say relevant to answering it.

## 5. When is war appropriate?

Like the notorious prosecutor's question, when did you stop beating your wife? this question is evidently what logicians call "a complex question." That is, it really involves two questions, because in asking one question, it assumes the answer to another. It assumes that war is appropriate in asking when it is so. Or is this only an appearance, because the questioner in asking the question really is open to, among other responses, "Never! War is never appropriate"?

Perhaps the questioner will in due course tell us. Anyhow, I assume that the context presupposed in asking the question is the context of Christian witness and theology, so that it could be more explicitly asked by asking something like, "When, if ever, is war appropriate, according to Christian witness and theology?"

Before speaking to the question, I should probably tell you that being a Christian *systematic* theologian, I'm only, in part, a Christian *moral* theologian. Although, even as a systematic theologian, I naturally have to concern myself with Christian action as well as Christian belief, I do not need to go into all of the details of particular moral questions, such as the question before us, in order to carry out my part of the theological task. So, in this answer, otherwise than in my answers to the preceding questions, I must be content, for the most part, to refer you to places where you may find the answer that I shall barely more than adumbrate in my own brief comments.

Students of the matter typically distinguish two main answers in traditional Christian witness and theology to the question, When, if ever, is war appropriate? One is the so-called *pacifist* answer, which is precisely an unqualified "Never!" because of God's commandment "You shall not kill." Thus it is like the answer of some so-called pro-life Christians today, who hold that abortion is never appropriate even in such extreme cases as have involved rape or incest. The other main answer is that developed in what is usually referred to as "just war theory," which I shall call, simply, the *just war* answer. Unlike the pacifist answer, it is not an unqualified "Never," but the qualified, "Whenever war is just, but only then." The whole point, then, of the just war theory in which this answer is elaborated is to spell out carefully and thoughtfully the conditions that have to be met in order for a war to be really a just war, as distinct from a war naturally claimed to be just by its proponents, so as to pay the tribute that even unjust action always pays to conscience, with its demand that we shall do justice and only justice in whatever we do.

I should perhaps add that although the pacifist answer has been given by some Christians from an early time and has continued to be the answer of particular Christian communities and churches—as well as, of course, individual Christians—right up to the present, it has been and continues to be the minority, not the majority, answer of the Christian community as a whole. Most Christians and churches at least since the fourth century CE have given some version or other of the qualified answer most fully worked out and argued for in just war theory. This is true, specifically, of the Reformed Church tradition, which includes the Presbyterian Church (USA) as well as of my own United Methodist Church, although it has to be said that both churches have also had important pacifist minorities, especially at times when the power struggle between nations has made the issue of war and peace a burning issue. I'm thinking especially of the late 1930s, when World War II became ever more inevitable, and all of the mainstream Protestant churches in the United States,

including the Presbyterian and the Methodist, had large and very influential pacifist minorities, if not—as it often seemed, at least—majorities.
At that time in our nation, the burden of representing and arguing for the
just war answer over against the near-dominant, if not dominant, pacifist
answer of many Protestant Christians fell almost solely on the great theologian Reinhold Niebuhr, whose work on this whole question is probably
the richest resource I can refer you to if you wish to pursue an answer to
it. Of particular value in this connection is the book edited by Harry R.
Davis and Robert C. Good, whose title tells you everything you need to
know about it: *Reinhold Niebuhr on Politics: His Political Philosophy and
Its Application to Our Age as Explained in His Writings.*[4]

I cannot go into the arguments, for and against, these two main
answers to our question. I must settle for a brief further word about just
war theory and then refer you to a couple other resources for your further
thinking about the question. You may infer from this, correctly, that my
own answer to the question, were I do develop it, would not be a pacifist,
but rather a just war, type of answer.

Just war theory is ordinarily developed in two main parts, traditionally called by their Latin titles, *Jus ad bellum* (which may be translated
somewhat freely, Justice in Going to War) and *Jus in bello* (or Justice in
Conducting War). The dominant concept in the first part is "just cause,"
since having a just cause is *the* condition that a nation has to meet if it is
to go to war justly. But other important conditions include the war's being
declared by a proper authority, the nation's having a right intention in going to war, the means employed being proportional to its end, and there
being a reasonable chance of its being successful. In the second part,
then, the concern is that justice also be realized in conducting the war,
by minimizing, so far as possible, its ferocity and its destructiveness, to
life, property, and resources. Thus the dominant concepts, or principles,
in this part are "discrimination," "proportionality," and also—in formulations of the theory since the Nuremberg trials of Nazi war criminals after
World War II—"responsibility." The first is concerned, above all, with dis-
criminating between combatants and noncombatants; the second, with
using no more force or causing no more destruction than absolutely necessary to attain the war's end; and the third, with individual combatants
having to take responsibility for their actions regardless of the commands
they may have received from their superiors.

4. New York: Scribner, 1960.

So sketchy an outline does scant justice to the complexity and depth of just war theory. And it gives no idea whatever of all the many questions that can and do arise not only in understanding exactly what it is that a particular condition of just war requires, but also, and most importantly, in actually applying the concepts, or principles, of the theory to the circumstances and possibilities of particular situations. But this is the best I can do, other than to refer you to some additional places where you may profitably pursue the question if you have an interest in doing so, as well as, of course, the time and the opportunity.

One such place, not surprisingly, is the Internet. Of the several things I checked, the best I found—and certainly a good place to begin— was the entry on Just War Theory in *The Internet Encyclopedia of Philosophy*.[5] So far as books are concerned, one of the best, almost certainly, is Michael Walzer's *Just and Unjust Wars*.[6] But there is a much shorter, more generally accessible book that you may well find to be more suitable to your needs—namely, Joseph L. Allen, *War: A Primer for Christians*.[7] I commend this book to you most heartily as simply a splendid book for its purpose, written by one of the genuinely well-furnished moral theologians I know. Among its other merits is that it distinguishes (and critically appropriates), not just the two traditional answers I have referred to, the pacifist and the just war answers, but also a third answer, which Allen calls "the crusade approach." Although taking account of this third answer does not, I think, significantly qualify anything I've said, it is characteristic of Allen as the scrupulous scholar he is to consider *all* the answers that could conceivably be relevant to answering the question responsibly.

## 6. Would you like to speak about the afterlife?

The honest answer, I suppose, is, "Not particularly!" But I hasten to add that this is not in the least because I do not recognize questions about the afterlife to be questions that any professional Christian theologian, not to say, any Christian, ought to be willing to go into, if anyone sincerely asks them. The simple fact of the matter is that talk about the afterlife, in one understanding or another, has been a part of the Christian tradition from its earliest stages, as well as of the wider Western cultural

5. Online: http://www.iep.utm.edu/justwar/.

6. Michael Walzer, *Just and Unjust Wars: A Moral Argument with Historical Illustrations*, 4th ed. (New York: Basic Books, 2006).

7. College Station: Texas A&M University Press, 2014.

and religious tradition by which all of us in our society and culture have somehow been shaped. Moreover, Christian witness and theology both have traditionally formulated the implications of Christian faith in ways involving—again, in one understanding or another—belief in an afterlife as an essential element in Christian belief. Still, it's clear from the historical record that the real use and meaning of talk about the afterlife has all along been more or less seriously problematic, so that questions about it can hardly fail to arise in any thoughtful mind, including, I should think, any thoughtful Christian mind. But this is all by way of saying that any such talk, as well as any properly theological talk about its meaning and validity, is bound to be difficult, particularly in the concluding minutes of any single, all too brief, theological conversation such as this.

Recognizing this, I shall respond to the question in two main parts. In the first, I shall simply state—all too summarily and dogmatically, I fear—the main things I try to keep in mind in thinking theologically about any talk about the afterlife, including the talk that I take to be typical of traditional Christian witness. In the second part, then, I will accept the opportunity the question as asked gives me of speaking—again, all too summarily—as I myself as a Christian am accustomed to speaking about the afterlife, in the straightforward sense of such life after death as I myself, as a Christian, hope and expect to be mine, along with any and every other creature of God, nonhuman as well as human.

The first thing I try to keep in mind is that, from at least the time of the New Testament writings on, there have been, not one way, but two ways—in fact, two very different, not to say contrary, ways—in which Christians have thought and spoken about the afterlife. The earliest such way is that of Jewish apocalyptic, with its talk about resurrection from the dead, or resurrection of the body, as well as a new heaven and a new earth when this old evil age has come to an end and the new age of God's coming reign has begun. Some such understanding as this is simply taken over, more or less uncritically, by most of the New Testament writers, following most of the still earlier writers whose work they somehow appropriate in their own. But in some of the New Testament writings—notably, the Fourth Gospel—this apocalyptic way of envisioning life after death as resurrection of the body is displaced by another, non-Jewish, Hellenistic, specifically Gnostic understanding for which the key concept is, not resurrection of the body, but immortality of the soul. The remarkable thing, however, is that both of these very different understandings in which different early Christians thought and spoke about the afterlife were eventually harmonized or worked together into what became the understanding of Christian orthodoxy. On this third, highly problematic understanding, the soul, being immortal or undying, goes immediately upon death either to heaven, where it rests in the hands of God until the final judgment, or to hell, where it already tastes the torments of God's punishment. (I should explain that I'm here following the Protestant version of the narrative, which intentionally rejects the third "receptacle" of purgatory so important in Roman Catholic piety and theology, as well as the other two receptacles referred to as "limbo"—i.e., the limbo of infants and the limbo of the fathers, meaning the righteous of the Old Testament, who prophesied Christ's coming but died before its fulfillment.) But, then, with the second coming of Christ and the last judgment, the bodies of all the dead, righteous and unrighteous, are to be raised and reunited with their souls, wherewith they will be finally judged together with those still living and consigned irreversibly either to everlasting blessedness or everlasting torment.

I can't go into any more detail, but I trust I've said enough to make clear two further things I try to keep in mind. First, neither of the understandings of the afterlife worked together into the eventual understanding of Christian orthodoxy is in any way original with Christian faith, but was simply taken over by Christians from the larger cultural and religious environment, Jewish or Hellenistic, in order to formulate their own understanding as Christians of the ultimate meaning of their lives. Then, second, there can be no doubt that, by contemporary standards of judgment, both understandings are properly classified as mythical or mythological in literary character. This in no way implies, I hasten to add, that they're simply false. It means only that in speaking about what they're really about—the ultimate meaning of our existence as human beings—they speak in terms appropriate enough to talking about the immediate realities of our ordinary experience but hopelessly inappropriate to talking about the ultimate reality of our existence: of ourselves, others, and the whole. They are just as misleading, indeed, as talk about God's transcendence as though it were a matter of immense spatial distance, as though God were simply another being among others, exalted only by being simply higher, or spatially "above" them. Here again, I have to be brief. My point, very simply, is that all traditional Christian talk about the afterlife, on any of the traditional understandings, is undoubtedly mythical, or mythological, talk and therefore has to be—in the term used by my revered teacher, Rudolf Bultmann—*demythologized*. That is to say, it has to be interpreted critically so as to bring out the self-understanding, or the understanding of existence, that it is really concerned to express, but that it as myth manages to express only most inappropriately.

But, then, so far as Christian witness and theology are concerned, the criterion by which Christians must judge the self-understanding, or understanding of existence, of any myth, including any myths about the afterlife, is the self-understanding, or understanding of existence, of Christian faith itself. I ask you to recall yet again the all-important distinction I introduced early on in our conversation, between *Christian faith itself*, on the one hand, and *its various, always only more or less adequate, forms and formulations*, on the other. As bound as we are to the first, I insisted, we are just as free from the second: free to make use of them or to set them aside, depending on whether, or how adequately and fittingly, they allow us to bear witness to the boundless love of God decisively re-presented to us through Jesus Christ. So far as Christian faith is concerned, then, it is solely this all-encompassing love that is both the beginning and the end of our lives and of everything else. And this means, I hold, that it is this love *alone* that is both the ground and the object not only of our trust and our loyalty, our faith and our love, but also of our hope. In other words, God's love alone is not only *why* we hope as Christians but also *what* we hope for. But, then, all the traditional understandings, or formulations, of Christian hope have to be judged by their appropriateness for expressing what Christian hope itself actually hopes for, not only in life, but also after life—namely, the pure, unbounded love of God, by which our lives and everything else, present as well as future, actual as well as possible, are everlastingly embraced and preserved.

This brings me to the second part of my answer to the question, in which I have promised to speak about the afterlife, as I, as a Christian, am accustomed to speak about it. I cannot help but recall in this connection a story my friend, the New Testament scholar Willi Marxsen, tells toward the end of his book, *The Resurrection of Jesus of Nazareth*. It is about his own theological teacher, Heinrich Rendtorff, who, when he was dying, asked his wife to listen quietly to what he had to say and then went on: "The last nights I have been thinking over and testing everything that we can know and everything that we have been told about what will happen to us when we die. And now I am certain of one thing: I will be safe." To which Marxsen adds: "Nobody could call Heinrich Rendtorff a representative of 'modern' theology. But he was a levelheaded man who always tried to confine himself to statements that he could justify. The only thing he was sure of on his deathbed was: I shall be safe."[8]

In somewhat the same way, the only thing I'm sure of, and therefore the only thing I speak of in speaking about the afterlife, is that I shall be safe—indeed, that all things shall be safe within the all-inclusive, never-ending love of God. This in no way implies, on my understanding, that I myself will somehow survive death as a subject and continue to enjoy for either a shorter or a longer future both myself and every other creature's being embraced by God's love. My *objective* immortality, or resurrection, in God's love is one thing; my own *subjective* immortality, or resurrection, or even my survival of death for some unspecified time, something else. But to avoid any misunderstanding, I neither deny our subjective survival of death nor have even the least interest in denying it, however problematic I continue to find all affirmations of it. This is especially true of affirmations of subjective immortality in the strict sense of the words, as distinct from merely subjective survival for some limited period after death. No, the only thing I would deny is the oft-heard claim, expressed or implied, that our subjective survival is in some way essential to the hope that is Christian hope itself, as distinct from some of the understandings of it in the Christian tradition. In my view, any such claim, fully thought out is quite simply idolatrous: setting up something besides God, instead of obediently surrendering to God *alone* as what we as Christians hope for. Whether or not we subjectively survive death, what we hope for, insofar as our hope is Christian hope, is not our own subjective survival or immortality but solely God's love for us, and, because of it, our objective immortality, or resurrection—our being forever safe—in God's love.

## Session 2

### 1. *Where is God in tough times?*

In answering this question, I simply assume, first, that by "God" is to be understood the God and Father of our Lord Jesus Christ, and so the One implied by "the greatest and first commandment," which reads, according to the formulation of Jesus' teaching in Matthew 22:37–38: "You shall love the Lord your God with all your heart, and with all your soul, and with all your mind." God is to be understood, in other words, as *the*

8. Willi Marxsen, *Resurrection of Jesus of Nazareth*, trans. Margaret Kohl (Philadelphia: Fortress, 1970), 188.

*all-worshipful One*, the one reality worthy of unreserved trust and unqualified loyalty, and hence *the all-surpassing, unsurpassable reality*, "than which"—in Anselm of Canterbury's words—"none greater can be conceived." And I assume, second, that by "tough times" is to be understood times that, for anyone trying to lead a human life, and for causes either more generally natural or more specifically historical, happen to be bad times rather than good, unfortunate rather than fortunate, and therefore troubling or demanding times, hard to live through.

My answer to the question, then, summarily is: *God is where God is in all times, tough or not tough—doing what God unfailingly does in every time.* I shall now briefly unpack this summary answer.

God unfailingly does mainly two things. First, God makes whatever comes to be really possible, in fact as well as in principle; and, second, God makes whatever comes to be both really real and abidingly significant. In doing the first thing, God may be said to create and emancipate, or providentially order, all things; and in doing the second thing, God may be said to consummate and redeem all things. Because, in both cases, God's doing extends to *all* things, God is rightly said to be, in the one case, *the* Creator, and, in the other case, *the* Consummator—all other things being, in their myriad different ways, also creators and consummators, although always only of *some* things, never of all.

But if God in tough times is where God is in all times, doing what God alone unfailingly does in every time, two implications follow necessarily.

First, there is no more reason, logically, to ask where God is in tough times than in any other times, there being no logical connection whatever between the times of our lives, tough or otherwise, and the whereabouts of God. This is true, at any rate, if God is to be understood as we assumed at the outset, i.e., as *the all-worshipful One* of "the greatest and first commandment," and thus as *the unsurpassable One*, "than which none greater can be conceived." To worship is to trust and to be loyal—ideally, to trust unreservedly and to be loyal unqualifiedly. But worship in this sense is authorized as a proper response only if the object of worship, of trust and loyalty, is worshipful—ideally, *all*-worshipful. And this the object of worship can be only if it is unsurpassable: absolutely unsurpassable, or unsurpassable by itself as well as all others, in all the respects in which anything can be so; and relatively unsurpassable, or unsurpassable by all others although not by itself, in all other respects. Although, for any believer in God conceived as all-worshipful and therefore unsurpassable, good times are rightly accepted as tokens or signs of God's reality and favor, they are in no way evidence, logically, of God's existence and activity and may not be taken, logically, to prove them. By the same token, bad times, or tough times, are in no way evidence logically of God's nonexistence or inactivity and disprove absolutely nothing that Christian witness and theology have any stake in affirming.

As for the so-called problem of evil, understood as being in some way a disproof of God as Christian faith understands God, it is, in point of fact, a pseudoproblem. It arises from a conception of God's "omnipotence" that is self-contradictory and therefore a pseudoconception only, altogether apart from the fact, or the extent, of evil in the world. Moreover, the only God about whose whereabouts the reality of evil could logically raise even the least problem, anyhow, is not the God and Father of our Lord Jesus Christ, not the God of "the greatest and first commandment," but an idol, a fetish, a non-God, or, what Paul dismisses as a "so-called god" (1 Cor 8:5).

It follows, second, then, that our possibility as human beings before God is exactly the same in tough times as in any other times. Because God remains present and active in every time, we have the same possibility in tough times as in any other times: the possibility that I speak of, following Paul, as obedient faith, which is to say, entrusting ourselves unreservedly to God's pure, unbounded love and then living in unqualified loyalty to the cause of God's love, loving God with the whole of our being by loving all whom God always already loves, to whom God is always already loyal—by loving our neighbors as ourselves.

I conclude by remarking that, if what I have said is sound, perhaps the most appropriate prayer for the present tough times, just as for any other times, is the so-called serenity prayer commonly attributed to the American theologian of the last century, Reinhold Niebuhr:

> God, give us grace to accept with serenity the things that cannot be changed, courage to change the things that should be changed, and the wisdom to distinguish the one from the other. Amen.[9]

On which I comment only that, if faith is what I've interpreted it to be—namely, the "obedient faith" of unreserved trust in God's love and unqualified loyalty to it—then it is, in its essence, submission to God as God. But if Niebuhr is right in assuming, as I judge him to be, that

---

9. Reinhold Niebuhr, *Justice and Mercy* (New York: Harper & Row, 1974), v.

there are "things that *should* be changed" as well as "things that *cannot* be changed," then, clearly, to obey God, and thus to submit to God as God, cannot be singular, but only dual. To act courageously and loyally to change the things that should be changed is no less to obey God, and so to submit to God as God, than to act serenely and trustfully to accept the things that cannot be changed.

2. *Who are God's "chosen people" today? What does that term mean in today's world?*

I shall answer these two questions in reverse order. So, first, What does the term "chosen people" mean in today's world?

As I've already explained, I can answer this question here only by taking the qualifying phrase, "in today's world," to mean, "from the standpoint of an adequate Christian witness and theology today." On this assumption, and in my own best judgment as a Christian and a theologian, I should say that the term "chosen people," used normatively, rather than merely historically or descriptively, is to be understood as designating any people—which is to say, any group of human persons—who, having been somehow called by God, have accepted God's call, and have therefore also been chosen by God through their own choosing. This assumes, of course, the scriptural distinction between being *"called"* by God and being *"chosen"* by God—as in the hard saying familiar to all of us from Matthew's account of Jesus' own preaching, "Many are called, but few are chosen" (Matt 22:14). Whereas the calling of human beings to obey, and thus to submit, to the gift and demand of God's pure unbounded love is, in all its modes, entirely God's work alone, God's choosing of human beings is not solely God's, because it is and must be mediated through each of their own free and responsible decisions to accept God's call. The term "God's 'chosen people,'" then, designates the people who are chosen by God, if they are, only through their own choosing.

Thus—to respond now to the first question—"God's 'chosen people' today" can only mean any and all persons today, here and now, *although only such*, who, having somehow accepted God's call to obedience, however it may have come to them, have thereby also been chosen by God. Of course, the only way in which God's call can be accepted, whatever the mode of its coming to any of us as an individual person, is through obedient faith: through unreserved trust in God's love, and unqualified loyalty to its cause. Simply to believe certain propositions to be true, or to perform certain actions that are good, is not to have faith in the sense required to accept God's acceptance. Therefore—as Jesus' parable of the missing wedding robe in Matthew 22:11–14 makes all too clear—it is always possible even for those who earlier responded to God's call to fail to accept it anew when it comes to them again, and thus *not* to be chosen through their own choosing, or, if you prefer, through their failure to choose positively. So the "chosen people" in one sense of the term may very well not be the chosen people in another sense—and, from my standpoint, the only sense that really counts, Christianly and theologically.

Two final comments: First, you may have noted that I've expressly allowed for there being plural modes, or ways, of God's calling human beings. In my view, simply to be a human being at all is already to have been called by God in one mode, what I distinguish as the "original," if also the merely *implicit*, mode of God's calling. But, then, any human being who is, in any way, religious, or has a live option to become such, is to be reckoned among the specially called, meaning by that the *explicitly* called: any and all who have not only received God's original though merely implicit call, but also God's explicit call, as re-presented, more or less adequately, through *some* religious concepts and symbols. Finally, then, there are those whom God has called not only implicitly, and even explicitly, also, but *decisively* as well—this being the claim that Christians make or imply for the mode of their own calling and also for that of any and all persons who have ever had a real option of becoming a Christian. Why? Well, because, to be a Christian is to understand oneself and to lead one's life decisively through Jesus, and, for Christians, Jesus is, as they confess, the Christ—by which they mean, simply, the decisive re-presentation of God's call to all human beings, and thus of the gift and demand of God's all-encompassing love of everyone.

But—to come now to my second comment—if there are at least these three distinct modes in which human beings may be and have been called by God; and if, accordingly, there are at least three main types of peoples, or groups of persons, who could, in their different ways, be said to be "chosen people," the principle still stands, that no one is chosen, whatever the mode of one's calling, or the group to which one thereby comes to belong, except through one's own choosing. And this means, as Kierkegaard likes to say, that we are chosen, if we are, always and only retail, never wholesale: not as any group, but always and only as single individuals, one at a time, each through her or his own free and responsible decision to accept God's calling, whatever the mode or modes through which God may call us.

3. *To experience a full and right relationship with God, is it necessary to be part of a religious community? Is there a difference in answering this question as between the Old and the New Testaments?*

This double question, which I've taken the liberty of rephrasing slightly to bring out what I understand to be the questioner's intention, is obviously closely related in certain ways to the one I've just responded to. So this seems to be a good place to try to answer it.

This I do summarily by saying yes to both parts: Yes, it is necessary, in an important sense, to be part of a religious community in order to experience a full and right relationship with God. And Yes, there is an important difference as between the Old and the New Testaments in answering this question. I shall now briefly elaborate this summary answer—beginning, once again, with the second part of the question and then proceeding to the first.

In talking about the relevant difference between the Old and the New Testaments so as also to answer the first part of the question, we are in particular danger of oversimplifying certain things that are more complex than we allow, thereby furthering misunderstanding rather than understanding. But fully recognizing this risk, I still think one can speak truly about an important difference between the Old and the New Testaments as they bear on answering our question. The difference, very simply, is the difference between being part of a religious community that is, in principle, at one and the same time, also a national or political community—in the case of the Old Testament understanding of Israel—and being part of a religious community that is, in principle, distinct from *all* other historical communities, national or political very much included—in the case of the New Testament understanding of the church, which is sometimes spoken of there, significantly, as "the *new* Israel." It was just this difference, of course, that occasioned the first great controversy in the early Christian community over whether it was necessary for gentiles—which is to say, all members of nations other than Israel—first to become Israelites before becoming Christians, just this being the significance of their submitting to the rite of circumcision.

But allowing that this difference remains, and that the church's longstanding, if not always wholly consistent, recognition of it is certainly relevant to answering our question, I would nonetheless argue that being a part of the religious community rightly identified as the Christian church is, in a sense, necessary to experiencing a full and right relationship with God. This is true, at any rate, if "God" means, as I simply assume, the One whom Christians mean when they speak of "the God and Father of our Lord Jesus Christ."

Still, there is necessary, and there is necessary—and being part of a Christian church is necessary to a full and right relationship with this God only if—in a phrase of John Wesley's—there be "time and opportunity." In other words, it is necessary in a *conditional* sense only. Wesley drove this distinction home by appealing to the situation of the thief dying on the cross, for whom there simply was no "time and opportunity" to become a part of any religious community, including the religious community that is the visible church of Jesus Christ. But, then, was Jesus' promise to the thief vain? No, Wesley insisted; for all that was necessary in an *unconditional* sense was the thief's obedient faith, his obedient trust in God and loyalty to God in accepting Jesus' promise. Being part of a religious community—by constantly making use of its distinctive means of salvation through faith and then joining in continually administering these means to others through bearing witness—being part of a religious community in this sense follows necessarily from the obedient faith through which alone anyone is saved solely by God's grace through faith. But the necessity in this case is always conditional only, always provided that there be "time and opportunity"; and it is in *this* sense—although *only* in this sense—that I answer yes to the first part of the question, also.

*4. In our society, both sacred and secular, we generally speak of life and death separately, e.g., life is one thing, death another. Is there a more correct way to think of them in Christian theology? Is life one thing and death another?*

Although I happen to have had the opportunity to talk about this question briefly with the person who submitted it, I must confess I'm still perplexed by it and fearful of missing its point. But, for what use it may be, I'll make three points of my own by way of response, and then leave it to our general discussion to produce a proper answer.

First, it's one thing to speak of things "*separately*," something else again to *distinguish* them. In both cases, one's point in speaking, presumably, is to deny that the things in question are simply identical, or one and the same. But it's being misled and misleading to suppose—as even the philosopher David Hume once notoriously allowed himself to do—that any things that can be distinguished can also be separated. That people in our society, sacred and secular, generally speak of life and death as *distinct* I, too, would take to be true. But that they thereby take them to be *separate* seems to me to be another, and distinct, claim for which I find no compelling evidence.

On the contrary—and this is my second point—anyone in our society who has been educated in the so-called life sciences as they're now conventionally taught, for the most part, in our schools, colleges, and universities will surely have learned that, although life and death are certainly distinct, they're also inseparable, since to live is to die, dying, and so death, too, being entirely of a piece with living. Consequently, wherever Christian witness and theology have critically appropriated the Christian tradition in the light of modern scientific understanding, including that of the life sciences, there is a recognition, however consistently or inconsistently worked out, that death, for all of its difference from life, is insofar an integral part of it, all prescientific notions to the contrary notwithstanding. I have in mind, for example, the notion that we find in the stories of human origins in the book of Genesis that death is not properly of a piece with, or a part of, life, but is rather utterly contrary to it, being a divine punishment arbitrarily called down upon the first human beings (and, curiously, all of their progeny as well!) because of their disobedience to God's command.

As I see it, then, if there is a more correct way to think of life and death in Christian theology today, it's almost certainly due to theology's having allowed itself to learn from the best scientific knowledge now available to us, instead of being content simply to hand on the prescience of earlier human generations. In other words, it is to science, more than to theology, that we owe the corrections that some Christians and theologians, also, may have eventually learned to make in traditional Christian teaching on this whole subject.

Even so, my third point is that the ultimate justification for any such revisionary theological understanding as the questioner would presumably take to be "more correct" cannot be simply that it agrees with modern scientific understanding about the inseparability of life and death, or, if you will, of living and dying. No, this revisionary theological understanding is finally to be justified, if it is, only by the kind of properly religious, indeed, Christian, understanding of life and death to which Paul bears witness in at least some—although certainly not all!—of the things he has to say about them. I'm thinking not only of his powerful assurance in Romans 8:38–39 that "neither death, nor life," any more than "anything else in all creation, will be able to separate us from the love of God in Christ Jesus our Lord"; I'm thinking, above all, of what he says to the Romans in the fourteenth chapter of that same letter: "so then, whether we live or whether we die, we are the Lord's" (vv. 7–9).

*5. So much is said about Christian forgiveness. I believe in a loving and forgiving God, but the extent and capacity of God's love is beyond human comprehension. Does God want me, a human being created in the image of God, to forgive those who have hurt me, who continue to choose evil over good, and who are unrepentant? Does God forgive them? What if I won't—or can't?*

On my analysis, there are two closely related questions here. I shall take them up in order, as follows.

First, does God want me to forgive those who have hurt me, continue to choose evil over good, and are unrepentant? My response, unhesitatingly, is, Yes, God does want you to forgive those who have hurt you, and so on, and God wants this precisely because you are, as you say, a human being created in God's image. I have no hesitation in giving this answer because to give any other would require me to contradict what I take to be essential elements in the normative witness of the Christian community. If anything is clear to me from the gospels' accounts of Jesus' preaching, it is that forgiveness is always in order toward those who have sinned against us, and that the forgiveness we owe them has no limits. The love of our neighbor as ourselves to which we are called is consistently expounded to include both love of our enemies and willingness ever to forgive any and all who have need of our forgiveness.

But having said this, I would be the first to insist that nothing is more essential theologically than to have a right understanding of what is, and is not, meant by the "forgiveness" to which we're called as well as by the "love" of which it's an expression. On what I take to be such a right understanding, for one to love another—whether we're talking of God's love of others or of the love to which God calls all who are created in God's image—for one to love another, always involves two things: first of all, to accept the other unconditionally, for what she, he or it actually is, thereby allowing the other to make a difference to oneself and what one

156

is to be and do; and then, secondly, to act toward the other, on the basis of such acceptance, so as to realize, as far as possible, the other's own true good, consistently with one's similar obligations to all the others affected by one's actions. Forgiveness, then, is simply loving in this same twofold way any and all who have acted hurtfully and unrepentantly against one, not allowing their offenses to qualify in any way one's accepting even them unconditionally for what they are and then acting so as to bring about, so far as possible, what is good for them, too.

This, stated all too briefly, is the understanding of "love" and "forgiveness" on the basis of which I have responded unhesitatingly, Yes, God does want you to love your neighbor as yourself and, as an essential expression or form of such love, to forgive anyone and everyone who, for whatever reason, stands in need of your forgiveness. But, given the fact that the terms "love" and "forgiveness" may be understood in other, sometimes very different senses from those I've tried to clarify, I have no trouble understanding how my response to the question might appear more problematic than I take it to be.

But what about the second question? Granted that God does indeed want me to forgive any and all who are in need of my forgiveness, what if I won't—or can't—forgive them? On what I take to be an adequate Christian theological understanding of human existence, there is good news and bad news. The bad news is that, notwithstanding God's call to each of us, in some mode or modes, to live as God's beloved children—which very much includes God's wanting us to love our neighbors and to forgive without limits any who may have offended against us—notwithstanding our all having been thus called by God, we have each always already rejected God's call, freely choosing to live contrary to it. Consequently, it's true of everyone of us that we won't—i.e., *will* not—love our neighbors as ourselves, including our enemies, and hence *will* not forgive any of them who stands in need of our forgiveness. Moreover, as long as we persist in our disobedient choice, we not only *will* not love and forgive others; we also *can* not love and forgive them. Because we *won't* love and forgive, we *can't* love and forgive, either. But, of course, the good news of the gospel, as Christians understand it, is that what is impossible for us is nevertheless possible for God—that because God has always already loved and forgiven all of us, each of us, despite her or his persistent disobedience, ever remains God's beloved child who, as such, ever has the possibility of trustfully accepting God's love and loyally loving in return. In other words, each of us, although a sinner, is always already a *forgiven* sinner, who therefore needs only to accept her or his being forgiven through obedient faith in order to be able to love and to forgive others, as God wants us to do. In this sense, God's demand is but the flip side of God's gift. And not the least of the ways in which we accept God's gift is by obeying God's demand that we forgive one another as God has forgiven us all.

*6. I resent noisy fundamentalists hijacking the name "Christian" and wonder whether they don't do more harm than good in communicating the Christian gospel.*

The question here, I take it, is this: Is it possible that those who hijack the name "Christian" do more harm than good in communicating the Christian gospel?

My answer—again unhesitatingly—is, Yes, it certainly is possible that those who hijack the name "Christian" do more harm than good in communicating the gospel. I'm assuming, naturally, that what is meant in context by "hijacking the name 'Christian'" is claiming explicitly or implicitly that one's own way of being Christian is the only way rightly so named. But you'll have noted, I'm sure, that both my reformulation of the question and my answer to it allow for the possibility—which I trust the questioner, also, would wish to allow for—that "noisy fundamentalists" are by no means the only, even if, perhaps, the noisiest, Christians who make or imply such an exclusivist claim.

More than this, however, I will not say here by way of responding to the question, since it's close enough in meaning to a question I responded to at some length in Session 1 (Question 3) that I have no hesitation in referring all of you to that question and to my response.

*7. Many "fundamental" Christians seek the kingdom of God as a physical place after death. Many who attend mainline churches also struggle with the concept of what occurs after death and how our living "now" impacts what happens "then." Can you speak to your understanding of "the kingdom of God" and its impact on us as a people of faith and/or the emphasis the Christian religion should place on "the afterlife"?*

This is another question I take to be close enough in meaning to one I responded to at length in Session 1 (Question 6) that an extended answer here hardly seems called for. Whereas that question asked, "Would you *like* to speak about the afterlife?," the present question asks whether I *can* speak about it (italics added). And, of course, I should like to think that what I said in answering the earlier question is sufficient evidence that I indeed can—that I *am* able to speak about the afterlife, however adequately.

But you perhaps noted that there's one thing the current question asks about that I did not specifically go into in my earlier response— namely, how I understand the concept or term, "the kingdom of God." So just a brief further word on my understanding of how "the kingdom of God" is understood by what I take to be normative Christian witness and an adequate Christian theology.

The Greek term translated by our English phrase "the kingdom of God," is, as is said, "*systematically* ambiguous," in that it can express both of two different, if also closely related, in fact, correlative, concepts. It can thus refer both to the *rule* or dominion exercised by God and to the *reign* or domain over which God rules. On my understanding of how these two concepts are to be used normatively by Christian witness and theology, the rule or dominion of God is simply God's pure, unbounded, all-encompassing love of all things, whereby anything that is alone becomes possible both in principle and in fact and whereby anything that is alone is really real and of abiding significance. Correlatively, then, God's reign or domain is simply *all* things: everything whatsoever, both possible and actual, that is embraced or encompassed by God's love.

So, on my understanding, to ask, as the questioner does, about the "impact" of "the kingdom of God" on us as a people of faith, is to ask about nothing else than the "impact" of God's boundless, all-embracing love on us as people who trustfully accept God's love and loyally live accordingly, loving God and all that God loves, which, of course, is everything and everyone—or, to avoid misunderstanding, anything and anyone. In the same way, to ask about "the emphasis the Christian religion should place on 'the afterlife'" can only be to ask about the emphasis Christians should place on God's all-encompassing—*and* never-ending—love; for to be embraced everlastingly by that love is, as I understand it, the only "afterlife" that Christians have either the right or the responsibility to emphasize.

*8. If you have been taught that intercessory prayer works if you have enough faith, why is it that it seems a magical incantation and not really faith—especially when nothing happens?*

This question raises several important theological issues—from What is the right course to follow when what you've been taught proves to be either patently false or unfalsifiable and therefore meaningless? to What is really faith, as distinct from magic? and, not least, What is the point of intercessory prayer if, on at least some understandings of it, it seems to be quite pointless and/or a matter of practicing magic instead of really living by faith? Obviously, we could spend our entire time in this session on any one of these issues—to say nothing of the others the question also raises. So I shall respond to it by saying only a few things about just one of them—leaving it to the subsequent discussion to bring out anything else that can and should be said to respond to the question.

The issue to which I shall speak is the third I specifically mentioned: What is the point of intercessory prayer? The issue of the point of prayer is probably most commonly raised when persons ask, Does prayer work? and, in the case of intercessory prayer, Does petitioning God on behalf of others work? The answer the questioner confesses to having been taught—along, I suspect, with many of the rest of us—was, "Yes, intercessory prayer works if you have enough faith and keep on praying." But wherein, exactly, does the working of prayer consist? Supposing that, if one has enough faith, one's prayers for others *will* work, what would be the evidence that, in point of fact, one *has* had enough faith and that one's intercessory prayers *have* worked? Would the evidence be that the others for whom one had prayed actually received what one had asked for on their behalf? And is this why, when "nothing happens," as the questioner puts it, it seems that one's incessant intercessory prayers *haven't* worked and are therefore pointless and/or just a magical incantation?

If the answer is Yes, then the underlying theological issue, clearly, is, What is the point of intercessory prayer? If it's not effective as, in William James's memorable words, "an effort to lobby in the courts of the Almighty for special favors," then what, exactly, is its point, and why do we continue to engage in it—and to enjoin one another (not to mention bringing up our children!) to do so? If intercessory prayer is not a reliable means of getting what we want, what good is it?

There's an old position on this issue that I take to be—or, at least, to point to—the right theological position; and I want now briefly to develop it by way of focusing our discussion. Simply put, the position I'm prepared to defend is that *prayer generally, and petitionary and intercessory prayer in particular, are a means of salvation* or transformation, or, if you will, a means of grace.

The difficulty with this simple formulation, of course, is that there are so many things that have been said to be "means of salvation." If the term is most commonly applied in a Christian context to such things as preaching the word and administering the sacraments, it has also been applied to the faith through which the grace mediated by both word and sacraments alone becomes effective in our lives. But then it is also often applied to the representative ministry of the church and, by further extension, to the visible church itself, which, in the well-known formula of the Roman Catholic Church's Second Vatican Council, is defined as "sacrament of the salvation of the whole world" (*sacramentum salutis totius mundi*). More than that: in much contemporary theology, the application of the term has been extended still further to include Jesus Christ himself, who is said to be the *primal* sacrament, or means of salvation, the church then being distinguished as the *primary* means, and all other such things as the church's word, sacraments, and ministry being distinguished as *secondary* means. My own way of making essentially the same point is to say that faith in God through Jesus Christ, although in its own way a *means* of salvation and therefore not constitutive of salvation, but only representative of it, nonetheless *is* the constitutive such means for Christians—which is to say, the means that constitutes anything and everything else as properly Christian—while all other so-called means, be they the primary means that is the visible church itself or the secondary means that the church in turn constitutes, are in no sense constitutive but rather *representative* means of salvation even for Christians.

Now, clearly, "prayer," as we ordinarily understand it, is—if a means of salvation at all—but one of many such representative means that we as Christians recognize and use. I say, "as we ordinarily understand it," because, as we all know, the term "prayer" can also be used in extended senses—so extended, indeed, that Paul can exhort the Thessalonians, "Pray constantly," or, as the King James Version has it, "Pray without ceasing." In the same vein, the great theologian of the ancient church, Origen, can say that "the whole life of the saint [is] one great unbroken prayer," and Bishop John A. T. Robinson can write in our own time, in *Honest to God*, "Prayer is the responsibility to meet others with all I have, to be ready to encounter the unconditional in the conditional, to expect to meet God in the way, not to turn aside from the way. All else is exercise towards that or reflection in depth upon it." Clearly, "prayer" is being used in all these cases in so broad a sense that it covers the whole of our Christian existence as an existence in faith working through love and love seeking justice, and is thus merely another word for our proper worship, or service, of God.

But, as we most commonly use the term, "prayer" has the much narrower meaning illustrated paradigmatically by what goes on, or should go on, in the corporate worship of the gathered church. Far from referring to the whole of our existence and activity as Christians, it refers to one activity alongside others, the significance of which—as of all such special "religious" activities (which, of course, are the "all else" of which Bishop Robinson speaks)—is in some way to re-present the ultimate reality understood and responded to in different ways through Christian faith and witness. In that sense, prayer is the re-presentation through appropriate concepts and symbols of the understanding of God, our neighbors, and ourselves to which we are brought insofar as we understand them in the light of God's decisive word to us through Jesus Christ. Prayer in this sense, in other words, is our response or "Amen" to the truth disclosed to us through God's decisive revelation through Christ as mediated through the visible church and all of its other secondary means of salvation. Prayer is our acknowledgement in an outward visible way of the reality of God, our neighbors, and ourselves as this ultimate threefold reality is decisively re-presented to us through Christ and the church.

Thus our prayers of adoration primarily re-present our understanding of God, while our prayers of confession primarily re-present our understanding of ourselves before God, in face of God's liberating judgment against our sin. On the other hand, our prayers of thanksgiving explicitly express both—both our understanding of God as the primal source and final end of all that we are and have, and our understanding of ourselves as the grateful recipients of all God's gifts—while our prayers of petition further re-present our understanding of ourselves, and our prayers of intercession re-present our understanding of our neighbors. In the "second" commandment that is like "the greatest and first," you'll remember, we're charged with loving our neighbors as ourselves (Matt 22:38–39). Well, I hold that petitionary prayer, in the usual sense, is one of the ways we go about fulfilling the commandment to love ourselves, even as intercessory prayer—which is really only petitionary prayer for others—is one of the ways we go about loving our neighbors as ourselves.

But how so? *Why* do we pray for ourselves and our neighbors? *To what end* do we pray? Here is where I always remember one of my favorite theologians, Martin Luther, who was the first to help me answer these questions, although I have since learned that essentially the same teaching is to be found already in Augustine (from whom Luther may very well have learned it) as well as in the sermons of the chief teacher of my own church tradition as a United Methodist—John Wesley. In his commentary on the Sermon on the Mount, and specifically on Matthew 6:7–13, Luther writes (and I quote him at length):

> Therefore Christ says now: 'Your heavenly Father knows what you need before you ask for it' [vs. 8]. It is as if he would say: 'What are you up to? Do you suppose that you will talk [God] down with your long babbling and make him give you what you need? There is no need for you to persuade him with your words or to give him detailed instructions; for he knows beforehand what you need, even better than you do yourself.' . . .
>
> But you may say: 'Since [God] knows and sees all our needs better than we do ourselves, why does he let us bring our petitions and present our need, instead of giving it to us without our petitioning? After all, he freely gives the whole world so much good every day, like the sun, the rain, crops and money, body and life, for which no one asks him or thanks him. He knows that no one can get along for a single day without light, food, and drink. Then why does he tell us to ask for these things?'
>
> The reason [God] commands it is, of course, not in order to have us make our prayers an instruction to him as to what he ought to give us, but in order to have us acknowledge and confess that he is already bestowing many blessings upon us and that he can and will give us still more. By our praying, therefore, we are instructing ourselves more than we are him. It makes me turn around so that I do not proceed as do the ungodly, neither acknowledging this nor thanking [God] for it. When my heart is turned to [God] and awakened this way, then I praise him, thank him, take refuge with him in my need, and expect help from him. As a consequence of all this, I learn more and more to acknowledge what kind of God [God] is . . . .
>
> You see, a prayer that acknowledges this truly pleases God. It is the truest, highest, and most precious worship which we can render to him; for it gives him the glory that is due him. . . . [A] Christian heart is one that learns from the word of God that everything we have is from God and nothing is from ourselves. Such a heart accepts all this in faith and practices it, learning to look to [God] for everything and to expect it from him. In this way praying teaches us to recognize who we are and who God is, and to learn what we need and where we are to look for it and find it. The result of this is an excellent, perfect, and sensible

[woman or] man, one who can maintain the right relationship to all things.[10]

"By our praying, therefore, we are instructing ourselves more than we are [God]. . . . Praying teaches us to recognize who we are and who God is, and to learn what we need and where we are to look for it and find it." Or, as John Wesley puts it, "The end of your praying is not to inform God, as though he knew not your wants already; but rather to inform yourselves. . . . It is not so much to move God, who is always more ready to give than you to ask, as to move yourselves, that you may be willing and ready to receive the good things [God] has prepared for you."

In sum: we pray because we are human beings who, as Paul says, do not know how to pray as we ought (Rom 8:26). We pray because in this way, through the means of salvation that prayer is, we may be saved from the unbelief—or, if you will, the unfaith, the lack of obedient trust in God and loyalty to God and to all to whom God is loyal—to which we are continually tempted by our life in this world.

But here I would remind you that the primary emphasis in the classical Protestant doctrine of the priesthood of all believers is not that we are each our own priest before God, but that we are each to be priests of God *to and for one another*. Therefore, when I say—following Luther and Wesley—that we pray to instruct ourselves, I mean also, and primarily: *we pray to instruct one another*—wherein, incidentally, the reason is to be sought for learning how to pray in the church's school of prayer, through her treasury of prayers and her prayerbook. In this sense, *we pray to bear witness*—to re-present to one another and to all the truth decisively disclosed to us through God's word in Jesus, so that, again and again, we can each make this truth our own through faith. We pray for ourselves and our neighbors in order to bear witness: to re-present to one another the truth about our existence disclosed to us through Jesus Christ. God gives us both ourselves and our neighbors to love in and through God's love, and, in God's decisive word to us through Jesus, God discloses both ourselves and our neighbors in the light of God's all-encompassing love, under its gift and demand. By means of our prayers of petition and intercession, we re-present our reception of God's gift of ourselves and our neighbors, so as to make it really ours, so as to take full responsibility for it, so as also to obey God's demand.

10. Jaroslav Pelikan, ed., *Luther's Works*, vol. 21, *The Sermon on the Mount and the Magnificat* (St. Louis: Concordia, 1956), 143–45.

But if prayer is rightly understood, not as an ineffective means of lobbying with God for special favors, but as, in this sense, a means of salvation, how effective a means is it? Otherwise put: Does prayer used as such a means work? Does *something* happen, after all? I deeply believe it does; for when we learn to pray as we ought, making use of prayer as the means of salvation it properly is, it is bound to be effective for us as the pray-ers, and we have every reason to hope and pray that our prayers may also become an effective witness, and insofar an effective means of salvation, for others.

## Session 3

*1. What is the purpose and mission of the church in the world as we experience it now?*

There are different ways, all more or less adequate, of thinking and speaking about the purpose and mission of the church in—and, as I would want to add, *for*—the world. But, for our purposes here, I'll simply follow Paul's lead (in 2 Cor 5:17–21) and say that the church's purpose and mission is the one God gave it in reconciling the world with Godself decisively through Christ. In one and the same event, God, through Jesus, revealed God's world-embracing, all-reconciling love and also established the church—namely, by entrusting to us, as Paul says (meaning, to us as Christians, as those who are "in Christ"), the "message" and "ministry" of reconciliation. So the church's purpose and mission in and for the world at all times and in all places is so to bear this message as to perform this ministry—so to bear witness to God's self-revelation through Christ as to be God's own servant, the servant of God's world-embracing, all-reconciling love, in and for the world.

And when I say yet a second time, "God's *world*-embracing, *all*-reconciling love," I mean exactly that. Notwithstanding all the many differences between any one of God's creatures and any other, all are the creatures of God's love, with each and every one of which God is always already, "eternally," reconciled, because God is always already, "eternally," love: in Luther's phrase, "sheer love," "nothing but love." The first commandment says it all—the commandment that is first, as Luther quipped, just because it doesn't command anything! No, it *promises* something—and is, in fact, the mother of *all* promises: "I am the LORD your God!"

And, like all of God's promises, this primal promise is irrevocable: once made, it can never be taken back, and we can rely on it unreservedly. This means that none of us human beings, whoever we are, can ever live her or his life outside the bounds of God's boundless love for all of us. The only question ever is whether we're willing, each of us, to entrust ourselves to this love and then to live in loyalty to its cause, loving one and all of our neighbors as ourselves in our returning love for God; or whether, on the contrary, we forget or choose to ignore God's promise and try to make it all on our own, in distrust and disloyalty, estranged from God, our neighbors, and ourselves. The purpose and mission of the church in carrying out its servant task is always so to proclaim its message, so to bear its witness, that every human being is confronted, and *re*-confronted, with this question and can responsibly answer it, for her- or himself.

But now it's of the utmost importance to understand just how the church, how we as Christians, are to proclaim our message, or bear our witness. And to this end, I'm going to appeal to the authority of an injunction usually but, it seems, mistakenly, attributed to Francis of Assisi: "Always preach the gospel, and, if necessary, use words." My way, as a theologian, of trying to think and act on this shrewd injunction is to distinguish between two ways, or forms, of bearing Christian witness that I call, respectively, "*explicit* witness" and "*implicit* witness," always insisting that the second way, or form, is certainly no less important, even if no more, than the first.

By "explicit witness" I mean witness by means of *words*, which, in the case of the kind of witness the church is entrusted with bearing, are properly *religious* words. In my view, *religion* designates what the anthropologist Clifford Geertz calls "a cultural system," by which he means a set of concepts and symbols that a group of people use in order to communicate, to think and to speak together, about the things that are of concern to them, that they have a more or less vital interest in. A religion, then, is just such a set of concepts and symbols, and so, in that broad sense, is the "words," in which the members of some human group think and speak about what Paul Tillich calls their "ultimate concern," or that most vital of their vital interests—namely, their interest in the meaning of their lives within the all-encompassing whole of reality of which they know themselves and all others to be parts. How, given this ultimate reality, are they authorized to understand themselves and lead their lives accordingly? So, viewed in this way, the Christian religion provides the words, the language, through which Christians think and speak about their "ultimate concern" in order to communicate explicitly to and for all others as well as themselves what they've been entrusted to say to the world, to all women and men, by God's decisive act through Jesus Christ.

But, as we say, "Actions speak louder than words," and this is nowhere truer or more important than in connection with religion. I say, "in connection with religion," because the whole point of religion as explicit witness to the ultimate meaning of human life is to be a means to something beyond itself, to mediate a certain kind of action, a certain way of understanding who we really are and are authorized to be and then leading our lives accordingly. In this sense, the whole point of religion, or of "talking the talk," if you will, is to "walk the walk," so as thereby to bear *implicit* witness to God's boundless and all-inclusive love, not only through religion, but through literally everything that we think, say, and do—secular as well as religious.

Ever since I first read it as a student, I've never forgotten a statement of the American theologian Alexander Miller. "To give men bread," he says, "is not to affirm that they live by bread alone, but to witness that we do not." Yes, giving bread to the hungry is a good example of what I mean by "implicit witness." But, as the years have gone by, I have become only the more confident that the witness borne by the simple act of feeding the hungry goes even further, attesting to them and to others that, in the final analysis, *they* do not live by bread alone, either, nor does anyone else.

I wish I had time to elaborate on "implicit witness" by going into some of its other implications –like, for example, that there are also representative forms of bearing implicit witness just as there are such representative forms of bearing explicit witness through the forms of religion. Alongside sanctuaries in which the pure word of God is to be preached and the sacraments rightly administered, or church school buildings and schools of theology in which the meaning of valid Christian witness is to be communicated through teaching and learning—these being what I mean by representative forms of the *explicit* witness of the church— Christians have also built and maintained homes for the elderly and orphans, shelters for battered women and the homeless, as well as hospitals, colleges, and universities—all of which are representative forms of the church's *implicit* witness. They, too, preach the gospel, but for the most part they don't use words—not, at any rate, religious words.

But, having given this one example of some of the other things that would be very much worth our thinking and talking about, I need to move on, especially since I've as yet said nothing about an important part of the question as it's actually asked.

Up to this point, I've talked only about the purpose and mission of the church in and for the world in general, at any time and in every time. But as important, and even necessary, as it may have been for me to do this, the questioner's interest, clearly, is in the world more particularly, "as we experience it now," in our time. So I must say something, at least, by way of acknowledging her or his interest, even if, unfortunately, it's already too late to say anything like what could and should be said.

Of course, how "*we*" experience the world now calls for me to say more than I would be willing to say, anyhow. The most I feel comfortable talking about, really, is how "*I*" experience the world now, as sensible as I am that I'm hardly alone in experiencing it as I do.

As I experience the world now, anticipating that others' experience would, to a greater or lesser extent, confirm mine, I conclude that carrying out the church's purpose and mission in our time faces at least two fundamental challenges, which I have called elsewhere respectively, "the challenge of emergent plurality" and "the challenge of persistent inequality"(cf. above, 3. "Being a Christian Today").

By the first I mean the challenge posed to us as Christians by the fact that, as the process of globalization advances, the world more and more becomes, in the phrase of Marshall McLuhan, "a global village," to the extent that the actual plurality of human cultures and religions, which has always been there, but has, for the most part, been hidden from ordinary persons, is now more and more out in the open, so that we all can see it. We're more and more aware, all of us, that, far from being the only way of understanding human existence and leading human lives, our Christian way is, in reality, but one way. Hence the urgent question that now faces Christian systematic theology: Is there only one true religion, or are there many? which some of you may recognize as the title of one of my own more recent books. To answer this question at all adequately and honestly, however, requires that one enter upon the project called "interreligious dialogue," which in turn calls for yet more changes in our wonted ways of pursuing our purpose and mission as Christians in and for the world—such as, for instance, a new, nondogmatic openness to the adherents of other religions, and also to the adherents of secular, nonreligious understandings, that takes seriously the possibility that the claims they make for their understandings may be just as valid as they think they are.

Please don't misunderstand me: I'm not saying that we as Christians must now all become "religious pluralists," who confidently claim that there are, in fact, many true religions, or, in any case, more than one, and that traditional Christian claims to the contrary simply have to be given up. As much as I agree that this is certainly one possible responsible answer to the question, I don't at all agree that it's either the only or the most adequate answer. My only point is that the challenge of emergent plurality is real, and that one of the unmistakable evidences of its reality is what I think and speak of as "the challenge of pluralism," meaning by that phrase the growing number of Christians and theologians who have taken a pluralist position in the Christian theology of religions.

As for the other challenge of persistent inequality, I mean only that, for all of the rapid social and cultural change brought about, first, by modernization, and then, more recently, by globalization, the "inequality gap" between the haves and the have-nots, in our own nation and in the other nations of the world, far from closing, persists, and, if anything, appears to be widening. I hasten to say that the continuing, even growing inequality that I judge to be of major concern here is not, in the first instance, the inequality *in results,* in income and wealth, that is obvious to all of us—not least in our own country, where "winner-take-all politics" has more and more become the *only* politics, whichever the party. Rather, it's the inequality *in opportunity* from which so many suffer, who, for want of resources that the rest of us take for granted, never even have a fair chance to run the race of life.

But, of course, to recognize such inequality is to acknowledge injustice, and not only the injustice of one individual's denying to another some opportunity that is rightly her or his as a child of God. No, it's to acknowledge the injustice built into our society and culture themselves, because, or insofar as, their very *structures* are unjust—denying to some their just due while awarding to others more than their fair share. But, on my understanding, to love our neighbors as ourselves is always and without exception to do justice, to give to one and all what is due them as united with us by God's all encompassing love. And for us now, today, in our time and place, to do justice means, in turn, to enact just social and cultural structures, within the security of which all individuals have the opportunity to love their neighbors as themselves by also giving them the opportunities that only individuals can give to one another.

This implies, I think, that our implicit witness as Christians of giving bread to the hungry of the world as we experience it now has to involve such things as our seeing to it that there's a reliable supply of bread to give them; that it's baked with ingredients, and packaged and distributed, under conditions that guarantee, as nearly as possible, that it will nourish their bodies instead of poisoning them; that there are therefore laws and regulations, and policies and procedures of enforcement governing the bread industry—in sum, that we as Christians now can bear our implicit witness that none of us lives by bread alone only by becoming engaged *politically* in creating, maintaining, and, where necessary, transforming all the relevant social and cultural structures, especially those of government and the state. Such political engagement, I believe, is as necessary to bearing Christian witness *implicitly* in and for the world as we experience it now as entering upon the project of genuine interreligious dialogue is to bearing our witness *explicitly*.

## 2. Does God make things happen that may not be good for everyone?

No, God does not make things happen that may not be good for everyone. This is so, as I see it, for two reasons.

First, God doesn't *make* anything happen, if you mean by making something happen, making something to be what it actually is. God, as Kierkegaard puts it, is "the actuality of the possible," which is to say, God's role as Godself something actual is to make everything else, not what it actually is, but what it possibly can be—can be both in principle and in fact. "Anything's possible," we say, "but only some things are probable." Only some of the things that can be, or could be, in principle, at *some* time, are also probable, or likely to happen, in fact, at this, that, or the other *particular* time. But if they're possible in either sense, either in principle or in fact, at some time or at any particular time, it's always only because God is actual and, as actual, makes them possible. In this sense, in the sense of making whatever happens possible, God is rightly said to create whatever happens, and thus to be *the* Creator (capital *C*)—"*the* Creator" because the *first* or *primal* creator, and therefore the *universal,* creator: the creator of all the other creators, that are, at best, only *second* or *secondary* creators, or *particular* creators, even if, in their creaturely ways, they are *co*-creators *with* God.

But why, you may ask, does God only make things possible, not actual? I answer: because to be actual, whether God or any creature of God, is insofar freely to create oneself, to be, in the old Scholastic phrase, *causa sui,* cause of oneself, or self-caused. Although God is *the* Creator, the first or universal cause of all things, Godself as well as everything else, God is not and cannot be the *only* creator, or the *only* cause of anything, because everything, from God all the way down, so to speak, can be what it actually is, and thus more than what it possibly can be, only through itself, only through its own *self*-causation, its own *free* self-creation.

I realize, of course, that it's common enough for the unlearned as well as the learned to think and speak very differently, as though the relation between God and God's creatures could be something other than the genuinely social, bilateral relation it actually is—as though it were, in fact, a nonsocial, unilateral relation. But, of course, if you think about it, a one-sided relation is really no relation at all; and any God whose creatures did not also create themselves would not have any creatures to be the God of.

So must one judge, at any rate, if one takes seriously the witness of Christian faith that God is nothing but love, sheer love, and therefore is and must be really, internally related to a world of creatures who are the objects of God's love, and who, as such, must be, in their own way, also creators: creators of themselves, creators of others, and, in one respect, creators even of something in God. Were creatures anything other or less than this, they wouldn't be anything at all. For to make a difference to oneself and to things other than oneself, and insofar to create them, to create something even—indeed, above all—in God, is simply what it means to be something at all.

The first reason for my negative answer to the question, then, is that God doesn't make anything happen, God makes everything possible, and that means—as the English clergyman and author Charles Kingsley puts it—God makes things make themselves.

But I said there's a second reason why God does not make things happen that are not good for everyone. If God is the God necessarily presupposed and implied by Christian faith and witness, then God is the One, in Anselm of Canterbury's phrase, "than which none greater can be conceived," the Unsurpassable One, who is supremely great in goodness as well as in power and wisdom. As supremely great in goodness, God not only does not, but also cannot, do anything but what is good, and good for everyone. But what, exactly, does God do?

I've said that God's is the actuality that makes everything possible, both in principle and in fact. But, being unsurpassably good, God's actuality thereby imposes a certain order on things such that always, in any situation, there's an optimum ratio between possibilities: between the opportunities for good, on the one hand, and the risks of evil, on the other. By "good," I mean harmony, as the mean, or balance-point, between unity and difference that avoids both excess of difference, and so conflict, chaos, and unbearable frustration, at the one extreme, and excess of unity, and so tedium, boredom, and intolerable monotony, at the other. "Evil," then, means just the loss or lack of harmony instanced by either of these opposite excesses or extremes: either too much unity and too little difference, or else too much difference and too little unity.

But you'll note, I hope, that I've not said that God's actuality so orders things that only good things happen or even that in all situations, more actual good happens than actual evil. This I could not say without backing into saying that God makes things happen in the very sense I've been at pains to reject. No, I've said only that, thanks to the actuality of God, there's always an optimum ratio of *possibilities* of good to the *possibilities* of evil, in the sense that were the ratio other than it is, were God to allow God's creatures either less or more freedom than they, in fact, have to create themselves and one another, and thereby to make a difference also to God, there would be more risks of evil happening than opportunities for good to happen.

This order that God imposes in making everything possible is what we usually call "natural law," or "the laws of nature." But real and effective as such natural laws are, they in no way preclude things happening that may not be good for everyone. We could think otherwise only if, once again, we were to slip into supposing, wrongly, that God makes everything happen, whereas God's role, as I've argued, is to make everything possible, or, as we may also say, God creates everything to create itself. But because every creature, made possible by God, makes itself actual, God, although *the* Creator, neither is nor could be the *only* creator; and evil, in one form or another, is therefore ever a possibility both in principle and in fact. Indeed, the same essential conditions that make good possible—namely, God's universal ordering of all things and the freedom of each and every creature itself to be a creator—these same essential conditions make evil possible as well.

So things happen that may not be, and are not, good for everyone. But the cause of their happening is never God, whose ordering of all things is always unsurpassably good for all. The cause of things happening that are not good is God's creatures, more exactly, their free decisions, whose complex intersections, being of necessity matters of chance as well as of order, may always bring forth evil as well as good. If their decisions happen to harmonize, the outcome is good, but if they fail to harmonize, it's not good, it's evil.

I should probably add that the line of reasoning I've just outlined entitles me to think and to say that the traditional problem of evil, which so many on both sides of the issue take to be a real, and even an extremely serious, problem for Christian belief in God, is nothing of the kind. In reality, it's a pseudoproblem, which arises only because people again and again slip into supposing, mistakenly, that because God is rightly understood to be *the* Creator, God therefore has to be somehow the *only* creator. Once recognize, however, that the relation between God and God's creatures, if real at all, can only be a genuinely social, bilateral relation between real individuals on both sides, and that, therefore, there must, in the very nature of the case, be a plurality of creators, each making some difference, however great or small, to the way things actually go—once recognize this, and consistently follow through on it, and the so-called problem of evil is exposed as something that no one needs to worry about. Anyone is entirely free to believe in a God who is both unsurpassably good and unsurpassably powerful without in the least having to deny or even question that evil is anything but real and, by the very nature of things, ever a real possibility. Because there are and must be multiple creators besides God, which are always only surpassably, not unsurpassably, good and powerful, things can always happen that are not good for everybody. But—to say it one last time—it's never God who makes them happen.

### 3. What do we mean when we say Jesus "lives"?

We mean, or, in any case, should mean, I think, two things.

First of all, and fundamentally, we mean that the final end of Jesus, like everyone and everything else, is not simply to slip into nothingness, but to belong to God, to live everlastingly in and through God's love. On the understanding of God that I take to be implied by Christian faith and witness, God is, in Luther's phrase, "sheer love," or, if you will, "nothing but love." If "love" is used, then, in anything like its ordinary meaning, this can only imply that everything whatever makes a difference to God, and that, because the difference it makes is *to God*, it is and must be an *everlasting* difference, just as everlasting, indeed, as God Godself is. Another, somewhat more technical way of saying this is that God, being God, and thus sheer love, is really, internally related to the objects of God's love, which is to say, to everything other than God. By a "real, internal relation" is understood a relation where one term makes a difference to the other term. For example, my coming to know that $2 + 2 = 4$ makes a difference to me as a subject coming to know this, but it makes no difference at all to the equation as the object I come to know. Whether I come to know it or not, it will ever be just what it is, always true, never false. But, then, far from being the God of the classical Christian theologies that have held that God cannot be really, internally related to anything beyond Godself, since that would implicitly qualify or deny God's perfection, God, in my view, is related to God's creatures in both ways. In one respect, God is really, internally related to all things; and, in another respect, God is only logically, externally related to all of them—such a merely "logical, external relation" being the contrasting kind of relation, where one term does *not* make any difference to the other—as in my example a moment ago, where my coming to know that $2 + 2 = 4$ makes no difference whatever to the equation, for all the difference it makes to me. Although being sheer love, God is and must be really, internally related to everything, *that* God is and is nothing but love is not, and cannot be, itself really, internally related to anything, lest it be, to that extent, relative, dependent, changeable—in a word, unreliable, not to be confidently trusted without reservation or loyally served without qualification.

In sum, both are true—everything makes a difference to God, and yet nothing makes an *existential* difference to God, in the sense of a difference as to whether or not God exists and exists as the God who is nothing but love and to whom, therefore, all things make a difference.

To say that Jesus "lives," then, is to say, first of all, that Jesus, like everyone and everything else that has ever been other than God, lives everlastingly in God. Of course, the early Christian way of saying this was to use late Jewish, or more exactly, Pharisaic, terms so as to speak of God's having raised the crucified Jesus from the dead or of Jesus' having been exalted to God in heaven after his death. But the necessary assumptions and consequences of this mythological way of speaking can no longer be regarded by us today as credible, and the only viable alternative, so far as I've ever been able to discover, is to say something more or less like what I've just said.

But there's a second thing we mean when we say that Jesus lives—namely, that he is ever and again really present in his body the church and in its witness of faith, both explicit and implicit, and that he therefore also lives in the hearts and lives of all for whom, through obedient faith working through love, he is ever and again of decisive significance. I mean, of course, of decisive significance for each of them as individuals in their understanding of themselves and others in relation to the mysterious, all-encompassing whole within which all of us live and move and have our being. To be sure, if we're right in believing as Christians that the first and fundamental sense in which Jesus lives is that he lives in and for God, that he abides everlastingly, together with all that is past, in God's unending love, then his living as the risen Lord in no way depends on us but solely on God's consummation of his life together with all lives and all things in God's own life. But what, if anything, Jesus is to become *for us*, for each and every one of us who is given to encounter him through the church and its witness, in every way depends on us: on how we, individually—*each of us freely and responsibly*—choose to live when faced with the decision with which he confronts us, not only or primarily by his death, but by his life, or, if you will, by his life including his death. Will we accept through our own obedient trust and loyalty the gift and demand of God's all-encompassing love that Jesus decisively re-presents to us? Or will we reject it, looking to something besides God's love for the final meaning of our lives? How we each answer this question will indeed decide Jesus' meaning for us, and that means, I think, whether or not he will also live in us, in our individual hearts and lives, even as he lives everlastingly in God's.

*1. Some say that all will be saved. Is that true? And is there a time limit on salvation?*

I should note, at the outset, that I've taken the liberty of thus combining two questions about salvation that were submitted for this session.

Of course, the question logically prior to both questions is, What is salvation? Or what do we properly mean, as Christians, when we use the term "salvation"? To this question I answer briefly and summarily as follows.

"Salvation," like many other Latin derivatives ending in -*ation*, is an abstract noun formed from a present participle designating a process—in this case, the process of saving, or delivering, someone or something by rescuing or preserving her, him, or it from harm. In the context of Christian witness and theology, *salvation* properly means the process whereby God, as Christians understand God decisively through Jesus Christ, saves, or delivers, human beings, and any other beings endowed with the same kind of moral freedom and responsibility, from the grievous harm of sin and its consequences.

By "sin," then, Christians understand, first of all, the act or state of a morally free and responsible being, human or of some other kind, who rejects instead of accepts God's primal promise to be our God: to love and to accept one and all of us unconditionally, as God's own dear children, requiring us only obediently to accept God's acceptance by trusting in God's promise without reservation and then loyally serving the cause of God's love without qualification. It's from sin in this sense of distrust in God's love and disloyalty to it, together with the consequences of sin, that Christians understand God, decisively through Christ, to save us. And in the churches of the Reformation, commonly called Protestant, Christians have witnessed, in the words of the New Testament (Eph 2:8), that we are "saved by grace through faith"—and, more exactly, that all human beings, and any other beings there may be who are also morally free and responsible, are saved *by* grace *alone* and *through* faith *alone*.

(By the way, the point of the Protestant exclusive particle "alone" is never to rule out everything else from having any role at all to play in the process in question. Its point is always only to rule out anything else's ever playing a *primal*, or *primary*, role. So to say, for example, that we're saved *by* "grace alone" is not at all to deny that things other than grace are involved in the process of salvation—most notably faith, *through* which we are saved. It's only to assert that nothing else that may be involved— even faith—is involved *primally* or *primarily*, as grace alone is and can be—grace being the sole factor upon which any other factor that may be involved, in turn, depends.)

And this, of course, is also the rationale for the distinction made by using the two prepositions, "by" and "through"—*by* grace but *through* faith. Our faith is involved in the process of our salvation as necessarily as God's grace is. But it is involved as the means *through* which, as distinct from grace as the power or agency *by* which, our salvation occurs—by which, indeed, even our faith itself, as the means of our salvation, is alone made possible. It is by God's grace or acceptance alone that we're enabled to accept God's acceptance through faith alone.

But with this much by way of answering the logically prior question of what we as Christians properly mean by "salvation," we should be able to answer our two questions—beginning with, Is it true, as some say, that all will be saved?

Because our faith, though but the means through which God saves us, is always also involved, and necessarily involved, in the process of our salvation, we're never entitled to say, as some do say, that "all will be saved." As certain as we may be, even must be, that God's promise of unconditional love and acceptance is indeed made to all, and is never revoked or taken back in the case of any, we ever remain uncertain in every individual case, including our own, whether God's promise to be our God is actually accepted through obedient faith, or rather rejected by disobedient sin: by distrusting instead of trusting the God who makes it, and by being disloyal instead of loyal to that God's cause in the world.

In other words, while we as Christians can and must speak of a universal *possibility* of salvation, we cannot and should not speak, as some do, of "universal salvation" itself. Because the second depends, as we've seen, not only, even if first of all, on God's unconditional acceptance of all women and men by grace, but also on every one of them individually freely and responsibly accepting God's acceptance through their own obedient faith—because this is so, Christian witness and theology can no more affirm the actuality of universal salvation than they can deny its possibility, as is done, in fact, by the counterposition to "universalism" that I speak of, for want of a better term, as the position of "double destination," with its assertion of either heaven or hell, either eternal salvation or eternal damnation.

As for the second question, Is there a time limit on salvation? my answer, for reasons I've already given, can only be, Yes, there is. Although there neither is nor can be any time limit on God's promise, and thus on God's unconditional acceptance of each and every one of God's creatures in each and every situation, the process of salvation, as I've argued, also involves, and necessarily involves, each morally free and responsible creature's actually accepting God's promise through her, his, or its own obedient faith. And there's always a time limit on our making any decision, including the decision of faith: of deciding whether to accept God's promise of acceptance or to reject it. When I'm confronted with a needy neighbor who calls to me for help, there's always a time limit on my response: either I respond with such help as I'm able to give or I don't, and to put off the decision is only a way of rejecting the neighbor's call instead of accepting it. But we have it on the highest authority that what's at stake in every such confrontation with a neighbor in need, and thus in every such decision, is nothing other or less than our salvation: "Truly, I say to you, as you did it, or did not do it, to one of the least of my brothers and sisters, you did it, or did not do it, to me" (Matt 25:31–46).

In answering in this way, of course, I'm assuming that the decision of faith, and thus for or against the salvation that, thanks to God's grace, is always already a possibility for any being who faces the decision—that this decision of faith can never be made once for all, but has to be made and remade ever and again anew, in every new moment of one's life—as soon and as long as one is a morally free and responsible being at all. But there's always, in the nature of the case, a time limit on making any decision, including the decision of faith, and in this sense, although only in this sense, I say there is and must be a time limit also on salvation each time one is faced with the decision for or against it.

5. *In a talk you once replied to the question, "How does one pray to a process God?" I would like you to answer this question again and explain your views about how God is part of or subject to process.*

On my analysis, there are two main questions here. The first I take to have two parts: (1) How does one pray to God Christianly, or as a Christian? and (2) What difference does it make to pray in this way if God is rightly conceived as "a process God"?—by which I take the questioner to mean, as a so-called process theology (or process philosophy) conceives God?

Of course, the prior question is, What is it to pray, anyhow? Or what do we mean by "prayer"? At the risk of oversimplifying, I would say that "prayer" has been commonly used, not only in a Christian context, but also in the context of theistic religions generally, in both a stricter sense and a broader sense. In its stricter sense, it refers to explicitly religious thought, speech, or action, either public or private. A good example of public prayer in this sense is what is likely to go on in any ordinary service of worship in this or any of the other Christian churches in this community on Sunday morning. And a corresponding example of private prayer would be what is typically thought, said, and done in the devotions or meditations of an individual person or a group—a family, say.

But "prayer" has also commonly been used in a broader sense to include the whole of the worship or service of God, implicit as well as explicit, both of religious communities and of their individual members. We may recall in this connection the sage advice attributed to Francis of

Assisi that I cited earlier, "Always preach the gospel, and, if necessary, use words."

But if this will serve as an all-too-brief clarification of what it is to pray in general, what is it to pray Christianly, in particular? Christian prayer, I think, is defined by two characteristics: first, it's properly addressed to the One whom Jesus and the early apostolic Christian community call "Father"; and, second, it's, for that reason, properly offered "through," "in the name of," or "for the sake of" Jesus Christ our Lord. This means that whatever else praying as a Christian is, it can never be a matter, either of informing God of what God would otherwise not know, or of importuning God to do what, but for one's praying, God's unwilling to do. If we pray Christianly, or as Christians, we pray, as Luther, for one, teaches, not to instruct or persuade God, but to instruct and persuade ourselves. Our praying, he says, "teaches us to recognize who we are and who God is, and to learn what we need and where we're to look for it and find it."

But, even on this understanding of what it is to pray Christianly — which, by the way, is fully and explicitly shared by the chief teacher in our own Methodist tradition, John Wesley—to do any such thing makes no sense unless it makes a difference to God, unless God Godself is genuinely affected by whatever we think, say, and do. The minimal condition of our praying, as of our living at all, is that it make a real and permanent difference, that it have an ultimate significance, that, in this sense, it be "heard" by God.

To realize this, however, is to realize the difference it makes to pray to God Christianly if God is rightly conceived as at least some "process theologies," or "process philosophies" conceive God. The difference it makes—to answer now the second part of our first question—is that the centuries-long disconnect between praying to God, on the one hand, and conceiving God theologically, or philosophically, on the other, is at last overcome. One's praying as a Christian can be fully accounted for and supported by the way one conceives God theologically or philosophically, rather than contradicted and undermined by it.

I'm well aware that the importance of this difference may be hard to appreciate fully, perhaps, even to understand, unless one has at least some familiarity with the learned traditions of Christian theology, as distinct from the more popular conceptions of God that tend to prevail in ordinary Christian faith and witness and in the religious life they serve to mediate. But the fact is that one of the chief defining characteristics of the conception of God common to most classical Christian theologies, as well as most classical Western philosophies, is that the unique transcendence, or eminence, of God, as compared with everything else, is conceived to require God's being absolutely independent of all things. God, therefore, is in no way really, internally related to God's creatures, although they're all really, internally related to God, hence their absolute dependence on God. This radically one-sided conception of God, which Christian theology took over uncritically fairly early on from Greek philosophy, has always been a profound problem for it, because it's always made impossible anything like a clear and coherent understanding of God as the boundless love that Jesus and the apostles, and also Paul and John, call "Father." A love to which nothing whatever can possibly make any difference is, in fact, love in name only; and any talk of our praying to it, in any of the senses of "prayer" we've taken account of, is simply meaningless.

But, on the conception of God worked out by the "process" theologies and philosophies that I take the questioner to have in mind, the unique transcendence, or eminence, of God is not one-sided, but *two*-sided, or, as one of these process philosophers, Charles Hartshorne, puts it, God's is a "*dual* transcendence." This means that, just as God, in one aspect of God's being, is—as classical theology rightly teaches—uniquely independent of God's creatures, in the other aspect of God's being, God is uniquely dependent on them. Although no creature makes any difference whatever to God's *existence*, and thus to God's always existing and existing somehow as God, all creatures do make a difference to God's *actuality*, and thus to just how God exists in relation to just these creatures instead of others that God could have created. So, on this conception, everything makes a difference to God, even if nothing makes an *existential* difference to God, in the sense of a difference as to whether or not God always exists and exists as the Unsurpassable One that God alone is.

But, then, praying as a Christian also makes a difference to God, and, far from being pointless, worshiping and serving God in all the senses we took into account in our analysis of the term "prayer" can at last be conceived to have a point.

This brings us to the other main question, which I restate in this way: How, in your view—which is to say, in my view—is God seen to be "part of" process or "subject to" it?

Let me say, first, that, in my view, God is not to be seen as properly "*part*" of process at all, for the very good reason that God is properly viewed as "*the whole*" of process. The easiest way to grasp the unique difference between God and everything else, I believe, is to distinguish between "whole" and "part," or "all" and "some." Whereas anything other than God is included in God as a part of God, God Godself is not such a part, but is the all-inclusive whole of which all other things are parts. In the same way, whereas anything other than God is really, internally related to only *some* things, even as only some things are so related to it, God is really internally related to *all* things, just as all things are so related to God. Of course, "whole" and "part" are distinct and insofar not simply one thing but two. But there's no *dualism* of two things here, which each could be said to be "part of." No, there's simply a *duality* of two things, one of which includes the other, which is included in it. Because the whole includes the part, even as the part is included in the whole, God is not properly "part of" process but is the whole of it—all processes other than God's own process being included in it as its parts.

But, as should now be clear, for the part to be included in the whole is for it to make a difference to the whole, even as for the whole to include the part is for it to be insofar "subject to" the part—in the sense that it would be a different whole without the part or with another part instead. So this is how, in my view, God is "subject to" process, meaning by that, subject to any and all processes other than God's own, all of which are included in God's process as "part(s) of" that one all-inclusive process. To include is to be insofar really, internally related to, to be dependent on, and, in that sense, "subject to" whatever is included.

But here I must remind you of the point I made earlier, that, although everything other than God, being included in God, makes a difference to God, nothing makes or conceivably could make an *existential* difference to God. It neither makes nor possibly could make any difference whatever as to whether or not God always exists and exists as God. In that all-important respect, God is *not* "subject to" process, being related to it only logically, externally, and so being absolutely independent of it.

In sum, that God is and always is *somehow* as God, is, in my view, a necessary truth—as necessary as 2 + 2 = 4. But just *how* God is as God, is, and can only be, a contingent truth. In this respect, but *only* in this respect, God is correctly said to be "subject to" process.

*6. A really simple and accurate definition of what it means to "abide in the Spirit" would suit me well.*

"To abide in," in the sense in which I take it to be used in this phrase, means such things as "to dwell in," "to make one's abode, or dwelling place, in," "to remain in," "to stay in," "to continue in," "to keep on in." So "to abide in the Spirit" means, simply, to do such things as these "in the Spirit."

By "the Spirit," then, I understand the active presence and power of God, or, if you will, the empowering presence of God's love, empowering, or enabling, us to live our lives as creatures and to lead our lives as human beings. This I take to be the meaning, or the point, of the short, summary definition of the Spirit in the Nicene Creed as "the Lord, the giver of life": the One who, in the beginning, gives us and all creatures our lives, and hence who is the primal source of our *existence as such*, but also, and above all, the One who, in the end, gives us *new* life, and hence is also the primal source of our *authentic existence* in obedient faith working through love.

This may make more sense to you if you simply reflect on how it is in our relations with other persons, family and friends, whose love for us empowers us or enables us to lead our lives. Our ability to entrust ourselves to them and to return their love for us by loving them, and by loving and serving others, is precisely their gift to us, the gift of their love for us. And to abide in their love is to accept their gift and to keep on accepting it as we lead our lives on into new situations in the future, with the new challenges and opportunities they bring with them. On the understanding of Christian faith, the primal, underlying power by which all of us are empowered to live and to love is the power of God, present and active in our lives as God's Spirit.

Two more points, very briefly. One is that living in the Spirit, and so also abiding in the Spirit, is always to be thought of, following Paul, in both indicative and imperative terms, as both asserting what we already are and calling us to become what we're always still to be. So Paul says to the Galatians, "If we live by the Spirit, let us also walk by the Spirit" (Gal 5:25). In other words, we can only *be* in the Spirit by *abiding* in the Spirit, and that means by thinking, saying, and doing all that we think, say, and do in the Spirit's power, in the power of God's abiding love. And that's the other point: the chief defining characteristic of living in the Spirit by abiding in the Spirit, and so also walking in the Spirit, is, quite simply, love—in the sense of loyalty to God and hence loyalty also to all to whom God is loyal, and therefore the acceptance of one's neighbors as oneself and the active service of all creaturely needs in which such acceptance finds expression. Paul speaks in this connection of "the fruit of the Spirit," which is to say, in his terms, "love, joy, peace, patience, kindness, goodness, faithfulness, gentleness, self-control" (Gal 5:22–23).

So what my "simple and (I hope) accurate definition of what it means 'to abide in the Spirit'" comes to is this: in the abiding power of God's love, to keep on keeping on in faith working through love by bearing just such fruit.

## Session 4

1. *Could you speak to the issue of "reconciliation" as it relates to individuals, groups, our nation, and the world?*

I'll be glad to speak briefly to the issue of reconciliation, although I should say for the record that my expertise is not primarily that of a moral theologian, such as the question mainly seems to call for, but that of a systematic theologian. This helps to explain why I have not thought all that much about the issue as it relates to groups, nations, and the world, not, at any rate, since interest in and talk about "truth and reconciliation" in South Africa and elsewhere were fairly common some years ago. Also, while I have close friends who have been working for some time as volunteers in justice-and-reconciliation programs, especially among youthful offenders in Boulder and elsewhere in the Denver metropolitan area, I have no firsthand experience of their efforts, and those of others, at reconciling offenders and offended and reuniting offenders with the larger community from which their offenses have estranged them.

I should also say, I think, that while I've long recognized the importance of "reconciliation" as a religious or theological concept, I have also had some of my deepest difficulties with the tradition of Christian witness and theology at the point of how this concept has been—and widely continues to be—misused, or, I would say, abused, in thinking and speaking about the relations between human beings and God. In fact, few things in much conventional Christian preaching and teaching more turn me off than continuing talk of God's needing somehow to be reconciled to sinners, and so also theories of the atonement that represent Jesus' crucifixion as the "meritorious cause" of God's at last being free to be reconciled to us. I hope you don't misunderstand what I'm saying. One of my own all-time favorite formulations of the whole meaning of

Jesus Christ turns on the concept or term "reconciliation." I refer to Paul's formulation in 2 Corinthians 5:17–21:

> So if anyone is in Christ, there is a new creation: everything old has passed away; see, everything has become new! All this is from God, who reconciled us to himself through Christ, and has given us the ministry of reconciliation; that is, in Christ God was reconciling the world to himself, not counting their trespasses against them, and entrusting the message of reconciliation to us. So we are ambassadors for Christ, God making his appeal through us; we entreat you in Christ's stead, Be reconciled to God!

You'll have noted, I trust, that, in Paul's understanding, it's in no way God who needs to be reconciled to the world; it's in every way the world that needs to be reconciled to God. God, for God's part, is, as Paul Tillich likes to say, "*eternally* reconciled." And so, through Christ, God has now acted decisively to overcome the world's estrangement and has given to us, which is to say, to all of us who are in Christ, who are Christians, the "ministry and the message of reconciliation." And "all this," Paul insists, "is from God."

But lest I get carried away and fail to respond to the question asked, let me say very simply and directly what I'm able to say about the issue of "reconciliation."

First of all, *reconciliation* is yet another word of Latin derivation that it pays to pronounce now and then otherwise than we usually pronounce it—namely, as "*re*-conciliation," so as to remind ourselves that it refers to a process of *repeating* something, doing it *again, another* time. In this case, it is the process of "conciliating" that is to be repeated, or done again, the process, in other words, of uniting, bringing together (our English word *council* has the same root). But this uniting, bringing together, needs to be done *again*, because of some intervening separation, estrangement. Those who were once united, brought together, have in the meantime become separated, estranged, and therefore now need to be *re*-united, *re*-brought-together, *re*-conciled.

Also to be learned simply by consulting the dictionary is that a near synonym of the verb "to reconcile" is "to pacify," which, in its Latin root, *pacificare*, means literally *to produce, bring about,* or *make peace,* by bringing an end to hostility, by overcoming estrangement, by reuniting those who are separated. It's important to reflect on this connection between reconciliation and peacemaking, I think, because we have it on good authority—the authority of widespread, repeated human experience—that there can be no peace and therefore, given this connection, no reconciliation, either, where there is not also truth and justice. To call for peace, the while ignoring the falsehood and injustice corrupting human relationships at every level—individuals, groups, nations—is to call for peace where there is no peace and can never be any peace until the reasons for its absence are forthrightly identified and faced up to. And this brings me to the one other thing I want to say in response to the question. In the understanding of Christian faith, these reasons for the persistent absence of peace and the urgent need for reconciliation in all human relationships are to be found, at bottom, in the threefold estrangement of each of us as an individual human being from God, others, and ourselves. Although we're essentially united with all three, the truth about each of us as we actually exist is that we've become separated from them. By rejecting instead of accepting our absolute dependence on God's love for us, we've become estranged not only from God but also from one another and from who we ourselves are and are meant to be. Whatever else must be done, then, to deal with the issue of reconciliation at all the different levels and in the quite specific forms in which it always confronts us (and there are always many things to be done), we must ever accept for ourselves what Paul calls the message and ministry of reconciliation. By ever heeding his word, "Be reconciled to God!"—to the God who is always already reconciled to us—we acknowledge our own estrangement and the deepest reason for it, and so may begin, once again, the process of overcoming it, of becoming reconciled to God, our neighbors, and ourselves.

This means, above all, playing our own part in carrying on that message and ministry of reconciliation, which God through Christ has entrusted to each and every one of us insofar as we are in Christ. And make no mistake about what it means to play that part: not only to bear witness explicitly to the decisive significance of what God has done through Christ, but also, and just as importantly, to bear witness *implicitly* by a whole life of faith acting in love and incarnating itself in justice whenever there is, as Mr. Wesley says, "time and opportunity."

## 2. What is grace?

Grace, Luther teaches—and I concur—is well rendered by the Latin word "*favor*," whence, of course, our English word, "favor." Much the same meaning is also expressed by our other word, "regard," the two phrases, "to look with favor on" and "to have regard for" coming to pretty much the same thing. More recently, with the further development of psychology and psychiatry, and other forms of psychotherapy, some theologians—most notably, perhaps, Paul Tillich—have rendered the biblical words traditionally translated by our English word "grace" with the therapeutic term "acceptance," with its positive overtones of "acknowledging," "confirming," and "validating," as distinct from such still more positive expressions as "approving," "endorsing," and "being pleased by." I can properly accept someone or something for what she, he, or it really is and act accordingly, and yet withhold my approval or endorsement and even be more pained than pleased by whom or what I accept.

In any case, the term "grace" is rightly used, I think, to designate what Luther insists is a "foreign" or "external," good, by contrast with a "domestic," or "internal," good. To make sense of his language in drawing this contrast, you have to assume what he assumes—namely, that we as human beings always live our lives in relation to, and in dependence upon, others: others who are not ourselves, but distinct from and beyond us, and are therefore, in that very broad sense, "external" or "foreign" to us. We're especially dependent on how others think of us, or judge us, and we want ever so much to enjoy, as we say, their good opinion or favorable judgment. This is true not only in our relations with our fellow human beings, but also, and above all, in our relation with God. But, then, the good we seek in others' good opinion or favorable judgment of us is nothing internal to us, and, in that broad sense, "domestic," but something external to us, and, in that equally broad sense, "foreign," just as we speak of the external affairs of a nation-state as its "foreign affairs," by contrast with all that goes on within its borders, which we call its "domestic affairs."

So, if "grace" rightly means God's favor or regard toward us, it names a good that is "external" or "foreign" in this sense: a good from beyond ourselves that is nonetheless a good *for* ourselves—indeed, the greatest good of all for us. To enjoy God's favor or regard is to enjoy, not just one of God's many goods or gifts to us, but God's sheer all-accepting love itself. Here's how Luther puts it:

> [God] scatters His gifts broadcast among the multitude; but He does not therefore regard them. His good things are merely gifts, which last for a season; but his grace and regard are the

inheritance, which lasts forever, as St. Paul says in Romans 6:23: 'The grace of God is eternal life.' In giving us the gifts He gives only what is His, but in His grace and His regard of us He gives us his very self. In the gifts we touch His hand; but in His gracious regard we receive his heart, spirit, mind, and will.[11]

You can bring Luther's point home to yourself, I suggest, if you reflect on your own personal experiences with others. If you find yourself uncertain, for example, about just how you stand with another person whose good opinion of you you covet, but from whom you've had no recent word, and, in that state of mind, go to the mailbox only to find a letter from her or him, you can't wait to open the envelope. But, then, when you read what she or he says, even if it may make you ashamed of some of the things you've said or done earlier, you suddenly realize that she or he has accepted you for who you are, and that the sheer fact of the letter is the explicit promise of her or his acceptance. In that instant, you experience the grace of that other person, and like all of your experiences of grace, it literally makes *you* a new person. Knowing yourself now to be, as we say, in her or his "good graces," you find yourself living quite literally in a new world. Your whole day's different, and different, most of all, because you experience a strange new freedom, both from yourself and everything else, and also for them—a freedom to be more open and accepting of others as well as yourself than you've been able to be before.

What we as Christians mean by Jesus Christ is, quite simply, the one who is, for us, like that letter: the word, the explicit promise, that the mysterious, all-encompassing whole of things of which we and all others are parts is neither an empty void nor an unreconciled enmity, but a boundless, unconditional acceptance that ever wills to set us free, to live in and for what Paul calls "the glorious freedom of the children of God." And this is what we properly think and speak of whenever we greet one another and would say to one and all, "Grace to you and peace from God our Father and the Lord Jesus Christ."

### 3. Does nature have free will?

Assuming what's usually meant by "free will," I would have to say, No, nature in general, or simply as such, does not have free will. Why not? Well, because what we ordinarily mean in speaking of "free will" is

---

11. Jaroslav Pelikan, ed., *Luther's Works*, vol. 21, *The Sermon on the Mount and the Magnificat* (St. Louis: Concordia, 1956), 324–25.

"rational choice," which, so far as we're able to judge, is a property of only *some* natural things, in no way of all. Indeed, it's a property of a vanishingly few things in nature, in contrast with the vast number of natural things that show no signs of being qualified by it.

In point of fact, if one holds, as I do, that "rational choice," properly so called, is one of the possibilities of the distinctive capacity that some have spoken of as "the symbolic capacity," then the only things in nature of which we can confidently take it to be a property are the natural things we distinguish as "human beings." They alone, so far as we can tell, naturally come to think and speak in general concepts and symbols at the high level instanced, not only by regularly playing all the various "language games" that so interested the philosopher Ludwig Wittgenstein, for one, but also by doing such other familiar and related things as making maps, drawing pictures, and writing and reading musical notation. Exercising "free will," I suggest, is yet another property of human beings—although, as it appears so far, only of human beings—that evidences the same capacity to use general concepts and symbols at this high level. We can rationally choose because we can think and speak in concepts and symbols that enable us to distinguish norms or standards and to establish rules to govern our believing and acting—rules that we can then choose either to follow or not to follow.

This implies, I more and more think, that natural things such as we ourselves are insofar as we are human beings may be said to have the power of "rational choice" and/or "free will," just because, but only because, we also command the pertinent concepts and symbols: because we have the concepts of rational choice and free will, and because we know how properly to use the corresponding terms.

But if nature generally does not have "free will," because natural things in general show no signs of having the "symbolic capacity" that alone makes rational choice a possibility for them, this is not to say that nature in general does not have freedom in some sense other than the highly specialized sense of "rational choice." On the contrary, one may very well argue, and I do argue, that any natural thing whatever has, and must have, freedom in the more general libertarian sense of self-causation or self-determination: of never being what it actually is solely by the causation or determination of others, but of always also causing or determining itself, thereby making its own unique difference to the whole ongoingness of things (or, if you will, the whole "process" of things). But, more than that, I argue that it's in this same sense of self-causation or self-determination that, not only everything in nature, but what Thomas Jefferson called "nature's God" as well—indeed, nature's God, above all—is rightly said to be free. In this sense, this more general sense of self-causation or self-determination, everything that is so much as conceivable as a concrete, singular thing—from God all the way down to the least particle in "God's nature"—if I may use the counterpart term to Jefferson's—is free, and must be free.

So my metaphysics—and I believe the metaphysics necessarily presupposed and implied by the Christian witness of faith—is a metaphysics of freedom, which I have sometimes summarized in two propositions: (1) Nothing whatever, not even God, can wholly determine the being of something else; and (2) Everything whatever, even God, is in part determined by the being of other things. You can see from this, I hope, why a metaphysics of freedom for which everything, even God, is free is also, unavoidably, a metaphysics of sociality, for which to be anything whatever concrete and singular, from the Greatest to the least, is at once to cause or determine both oneself and others and to be caused or determined by them. But the utterly universal freedom that makes such utterly universal sociality possible is a *metaphysical* freedom, not the *moral* freedom we properly mean by "free will" or "rational choice."

*4. What's the best way to study scripture? Where do I start? How much every day? With a group or individually? What sources do I use?*

The best way to study scripture is the same way you would study any other written text that said something you wanted to understand. There may be good reasons, particularly for Christians, to think of scripture as special, even indeed as the sole primary source and norm of what they, as Christians, are to believe and to do. But this in no way means that scripture, in any of its parts, in any of the individual books or writings bound between its covers, is not a collection of writings individually written, preserved, and eventually brought together by human beings, in essentially the same ways any other writings have been written, preserved, and, in due course, collected into a single volume. Inspired writings they may be, but they require to be studied in exactly the same ways you have to study any other written text in order to understand what it has to say.

To be sure, people write things, just as they say things, or communicate things in any other way, not just for one reason, but for various reasons, in order to answer different questions and to say different things in doing so. Moreover, people who study writings commonly want to study them for different reasons, to put different questions to them, in order to get different answers, and this they may do whether or not their reasons, their questions, the answers they seek, are the same as, or quite different from, those of the writers of the writings themselves. One student—a professional historian, say—may study a writing only in order to discover what it can tell her or him, if anything, about the particular time and place in history in which it was written—which is something very different, presumably, from what the writer of the text itself wanted to say by writing it. But another student may study the very same writing in order the better to understand her or his own individual life here and now today: what its possibilities are, and its limitations—in short, in order to learn whatever she or he can learn about how best to understand her- or himself and to lead her or his own life as a human being. Some such reason as this, in fact, is why most of us have an interest, insofar as we do so, in studying writings in philosophy and religion, poetry and drama—in what we call the humanities generally.

So when I say that the best way to study scripture is in the same way you would study any other written text if you would understand it, I in no way mean to ignore, much less to deny, this plurality of ways of possibly studying it. I mean only that once you have become reasonably clear about why *you* want to study scripture, what question *you* want to put to it, the kind of answer *you* are looking for in studying it, the best way for you to proceed is in exactly the same way in which you would proceed to study any other writing for the *same* reason, asking the *same* question, and looking for the *same* kind of answer.

If we ask, then, what's the best way for Christians *as Christians* to study scripture, I know of no better answer than the one given in what once was the Collect for the Second Sunday in Advent in the old Book of Common Prayer of the Episcopal Church, which reads:

> Blessed Lord, who has caused all holy scriptures to be written
> for our learning: Grant us to hear them, read, mark, learn, and
> inwardly digest them, that, by patience and comfort of your holy
> word, we may embrace and ever hold fast the blessed hope of ev-
> erlasting life, which you have given us in our Savior Jesus Christ,
> who lives and reigns with you and the Holy Spirit, one God, for
> ever and ever. Amen.

If this Collect's to the point, as I take it to be, the purpose for whi. God has caused all holy scriptures to be written is "our learning." Ar the end to which we are to learn, by hearing the scriptures, reading ther marking them, and inwardly digesting them, is to "embrace, and ev hold fast, the blessed hope of everlasting life which [God] has given in our Savior Jesus Christ." And if we ask, what is "everlasting life? v have the witness of the Fourth Gospel, above all, to tell us: "And this everlasting life, that they may know you, the only true God, and Jesus Christ whom you have sent" (John 17:3).

In other words, we're to study scripture as Christians as a word addressed to us, to each of us as an individual person, by asking the question about the ultimate meaning of our life, and by looking for the answer that scripture has to give to this question. The way in which I as a Christian theologian have learned to say exactly this, in terms that I judge to be appropriate and credible in our situation today, is to say with Rudolf Bultmann and others that we're to study scripture as Christians by interpreting its meaning existentially: by putting to it our own existential question as human beings about how we're to understand ourselves and lead our lives in the world within the all-encompassing reality of the whole, the whole decisively re-presented to us through Jesus as the pure, unbounded love of God.

But once we've determined to study scripture in this way, we should go about it just as we would study any other writing in that same way. And this means, above all, that we must study it as at once a historical document and as a piece of literature—employing all the means of studying it and following all the methods for doing so familiar to and used by any and all other students of history and literature.

I can't go into all that this involves without exceeding the limits I have to observe in answering our question. But I can make the most essential point by saying, simply, that no one's born knowing about the proper means and the right methods of historical and literary studies; one has to learn them, and this means that one has to undertake one's study of scripture not only in the company of others, in some group of fellow students, but that one needs to be sure to include in one's group at least some who, having been around the course a time or two before and learned a few things, are in a position to teach one those things, or, better, to help one learn them. Any wise person always seeks to do her or his own thinking and learning with more minds than just her or his own, and that means, always in a group. But no mind's so precious in any group as that of an experienced, proven student of the same subject matter, the honorific name for whom is scholar-teacher.

This means, for all practical purposes, that one will need to rely on sources, written or otherwise published, if not directly available in person, other than the primary sources of the scriptures themselves. But unless you belong to an awfully small minority, you're going to be inevitably dependent on such other, so-called secondary, sources, anyhow. Unless you can study the scriptures, if not in their original autographs, then at least in the languages in which they were originally written, without having to consult English dictionaries and lexicons at every turn, you'll simply have to rely, to a greater or lesser extent, on secondary sources, if only on the English translation that will be your only access to them.

So far as the other parts of the question are concerned, I don't know what to say about how much scripture you should study every day. This is yet another "complex question" that simply assumes an affirmative answer to the prior question: Should I study some scripture every day? My honest answer is, I don't know whether you should or not, and much less do I have any notion of how much you should study if you should do so. If you really want to find out what scripture has to say to you about how God has given and called you to understand yourself and lead your life decisively through Jesus, then the proper answer, presumably, is that you should study scripture as often and as much as will be necessary actually to find that out.

As for where you start, I should say anywhere that promises to facilitate attaining your objective. Christians obviously have good reasons to give a definite priority to the writings collected in what we know as the New Testament, since it's in them alone that Christian witness, explicitly as such, is to be found in scripture. But wherever you start, you need very much to keep in mind one of the most elemental rules of studying any writing as a historical document and a piece of literature—the rule, namely, that you're to study it always and only in its own proper context, studying its parts always and only within the whole to which they properly belong.

And here it's of the utmost importance never to forget that scripture as a whole, or even the New Testament as a whole, is *not* the proper context of any writing in scripture, much less of any of the parts of any of its writings. When Mark, for example, composed his Gospel by collecting and editing traditional materials from a still earlier time, he did not compose it with an eye to what Matthew, Luke, and John would have to say, or in any other way as a part of the later whole that we call "the New Testament." And the same is true of every other writing contained in the New Testament canon, as well as, of course—the necessary changes being made—in the Old Testament canon. So no New Testament writing is properly studied within what some speak of as a "canonical context." To proceed otherwise is simply not to study any New Testament writing in *its* proper context, and therefore not really to study *it* after all.

### 5. Did Jesus descend into hell? What did he do there?

As with other talk about hell in traditional Christian witness and theology, the assertion that Jesus descended into hell is a mythological assertion that demands to be "demythologized," even as it itself invites "existentialist interpretation." By this I mean that it's to be taken as a symbolic way of saying something about the reality of our existence as human beings, but only in terms that tend more to obscure what's being said than to disclose it—and, into the bargain, are no longer even intelligible to modern women and men such as ourselves. It's simply a fact that we no longer live and think in a three-story world, with heaven above as a place to ascend, or go up, to and hell below as a place to descend, or go down, to.

So my answer to the question can only be, No, Jesus did not descend into hell, nor did he do anything there, since there was no there there in which to do it (with apologies to Gertrude Stein!). Consequently, for Christians to continue talking about Jesus' having descended into hell is, at best, seriously misleading, unless they make clear that they're saying something symbolically that they're always willing to put in other, very different, terms, so that it will be expressed more adequately and that women and men today can understand it and make the decision it calls them to make.

I may add just this word about the clause in the Apostles' Creed that is the main source in our Western Christian tradition for the assertion that Jesus descended into hell. First appearing in the Creed only at the beginning of the fifth century CE, this clause was the latest addition made to it and has also proved to be the most vulnerable to theological objections. In modern times, it has sometimes been made optional or simply eliminated, being conspicuously absent, for example, from the Creed now used by the United Methodist Church. But problematic as it certainly is, the mythological claim that Jesus descended into hell has been shown to be symbolically significant by Christian graphic artists with their sometimes powerful depictions of his triumph over Satan and his release from Satan's power of those who have already died. And these, by the way, are just the things that Jesus would have done in hell had there been any there there for him to do them in.

### 6. Who created hell?

The first thing that, for whatever reason, popped into my mind when I read this question was the famous line in Jean-Paul Sartre's play, *No Exit*: "Hell is other people." But, then, I thought, if that line's right, the answer to the question is, *Other people created hell*. From the standpoint of Christian faith and witness, as I understand it, however, this answer could never be the whole of a good answer to our question, or even the most essential part of a good answer. For, on a Christian understanding, anything created is always the work of three types of creators, of which "other people" are but one of the three.

To be sure, if by "*creator*" we mean the God whom Christians think and speak of as "*the* Creator" (capital C), the primal and universal creator, but for whose unique creative activity nothing would or could be created at all, then there's only one type of creator and only a single, unique instance of that type. But to be *the* Creator in this sense is one thing, to be the *only* creator, something else. To be *the* Creator, as God alone is, is to be, in Kierkegaard's phrase, "the actuality of the possible," to make all things possible both in principle and in fact, and yet to make nothing actual. Why not? Because the only way in which anything can ever be made actual, whether it be God or anything else, is to make itself actual, to create itself, to be, as the Scholastics said, *causa sui*, cause of itself, or self-caused. This means that there's always just so much that any creator can do when it comes to creating others. God as *the* Creator can make all things possible, in principle as well as in fact. And creatures of God, who are also, in their ways, creators, can make their contribution to God's making all things possible in fact as well as in principle. But only the individual things themselves can make themselves actual, each by its own individual act of self-creation.

So if hell has been created—and, on a Christian understanding, anything other than God has to have been created—hell has been created by these same three types of creators that are involved in the creation of everything else. God as *the* Creator of all things has created hell by

making it possible, in principle as well as in fact; other people have created hell by making their contributions to God's creating it in fact as well
as in principle, which is to say, in more traditional terms, by tempting
their fellows to sin instead of helping to deliver them from it; and hell
has created itself, in the sense that anyone actually in hell is there, finally,
thanks only to her or his own act of sin, of rejecting God's promise to be
our God in distrust and disloyalty, instead of obediently accepting it in
unreserved trust and serving its cause with unqualified loyalty.

But just what does the term "hell" properly refer to when we speak
of someone's actually being in hell? In most traditional Christian witness
and theology even today, "hell" is thought and spoken of mythologically,
in mythical concepts and terms, as designating a special region of the
world-whole reserved as the place of eternal punishment for sinners, at
least, incorrigible sinners. But if it's the very nature of mythology to represent—or, really, *mis*represent—existential realities as though they were
simply additional empirical, or quasi-empirical, realities, this whole traditional way of thinking and speaking about hell, or about anything else
mythologically, has to be demythologized. By this I mean—just as Rudolf
Bultmann, the theologian to whom we owe the term "demythologizing,"
always meant—that mythology itself invites, or demands, that its terms
always be so interpreted as to disclose the existential realities that its talk
of them as though they were simply other empirical facts obscures.

This, by the way—this invitation or demand that mythology itself
issues, to interpret its terms existentially—is the most important reason
why demythologizing, or existentialist interpretation, is a necessary theological task for us—not the fact, although it definitely is a fact, that, for
more and more women and men today, mythology is no longer a credible,
or even intelligible, way of thinking and speaking about their existence.

But—to return to the main point—to demythologize talk about hell,
or actually being in hell, is to expose the real reference of "hell" to the
existential state or condition of being in sin, of being oneself a sinner,
who, in her or his own individual case, through her or his own moral
freedom and responsibility, has actualized the possibility of sinfully rejecting God's promise to be our God instead of obediently accepting it.
*Sin and its consequences*: that's what "hell"'s rightly understood to refer
to, just as "being in hell" properly means having to suffer them, and also
to forfeit, as long as one persists in one's sin, one's possibility of being the
authentic human being that God has created one to be.

I should add that it's in a corresponding way that "heaven" is to be understood as *faith and its consequences*, even as "being in heaven" rightly means enjoying them, and also being free to enjoy them as long as one abides in faith by again and again becoming anew the human being that God ever wills one to become.

So I say that it's not just other people who create hell, as much as they always play their part by being sinners themselves and tempting their brothers and sisters to sin. Nor is hell created simply by God, even though God alone can make it, just like anything else, possible both in principle and in fact—and, as we must never forget, also suffer with each and every sinner as soon and as long as she or he, being in the state or condition of sin, is suffering in hell. The devil, Luther used to say, is God's devil. And I like to say, in the same vein, hell is God's hell, because no sinner ever suffers hell alone, but always and only *with* God, who suffers with her or him. Still, the most essential part of a good answer to our question, although even it's only part of the answer, is that hell's created, in the sense of being made actual, only by each individual sinner her- or himself, through the misuse of her or his own moral freedom and responsibility.

### 7. Why doesn't Jesus just come now and take us to heaven?

My first impulse is to answer, simply, Because there isn't any place called heaven from which Jesus could come and to which he could take us, whether now or at any other time. Why not? Well, because the whole way of thinking and speaking assumed by the question is mythological, and this means two things: that it systematically misrepresents what it's really talking about—the reality of our own human existence and its possibilities—by talking about it in terms properly used to talk about other, very different things; and that it simply demands to be demythologized, or invites demythologizing, not only or primarily because it no longer makes sense to us today to think and speak in this way (although it doesn't!), but also, and above all, because it's a systematically misleading way of talking about who we really are and how we're to understand ourselves and lead our lives as human beings in the world.

But first impulses often need to be resisted, so I want to say more than simply this. I want to say that already in the New Testament writings themselves, the particular mythological way of thinking and speaking that the question assumes—namely, the way biblical theologians take to be distinctive of late Jewish apocalyptic—is only one way of trying to grasp and express the decisive significance of Jesus. If you turn to the Gospel of John, you'll find another very different way of thinking and speaking: so different, in fact, that one may say that John, meaning the author of this gospel, had already demythologized the apocalyptic concepts and symbols used by most of the other New Testament writers, including Paul. Whereas Paul still thinks and speaks in terms of apocalyptic's two ages of the world—the present old age, which is nearing its end, and the future new age, which has already begun with Jesus' coming and especially his saving death, and yet will not be fulfilled until his visible coming again—John completely, and deliberately, breaks with this whole way of thinking and speaking. Thus he has the disciple Judas (not Iscariot) ask Jesus, "Lord, how is it that you will reveal yourself to us, and not to the world?" only to receive Jesus' answer, "Those who love me will keep my word, and my Father will love them, and we will come to them and make our dwelling place with them" (John 14:22–24).

My point, in short, is that if you don't make certain assumptions, such as the question makes, you have no reason to ask certain questions, including it, and that, already in the New Testament, in the Gospel of John, we have at least one great Christian teacher and theologian who does not make, but explicitly rejects, the assumptions made by the question. For John, there's no point in asking why Jesus doesn't just come now and take us to heaven, because Jesus has already come, and with the Father whom he reveals, makes his dwelling place in the hearts and lives of all those who, through faith, keep his word.

### 8. Is baptism necessary for salvation?

No, baptism is not necessary for salvation. If we're saved, as I, as a Protestant Christian, confess we are, "by grace alone through faith alone," then nothing's necessary for our salvation, or anybody else's, except, first, the grace of God *by* which alone we're saved, which is to say, God's all-encompassing, unconditional acceptance of all God's creatures, including even sinners such as ourselves; and, then, second, and in absolute dependence on God's grace, our own obedient faith as the single individual each of us is, *through* which alone any of us is saved, which is to say, our own individual acceptance of God's acceptance through unreserved trust in it and unqualified loyalty to it.

The point of baptism, then, is in no way to satisfy some additional condition necessary to salvation, but to bear witness, in its particular way as a sacrament, or sacramental action, to the only conditions that are necessary: God's grace, *by* which alone we are saved, or even have the possibility of salvation, and our own obedient faith, *through* which alone that possibility can become an actuality in our own individual case. This means that the persons we as Christians baptize do not become beloved children of God only because we baptize them; we only baptize them because they always already are God's beloved children, in order, by this "means of salvation," to call each of them by name ever to be and to become who they really are: to actualize in their own individual case the possibility of salvation that's always already theirs because of God's boundless and indefeasible love. As the New Zealand Prayer Book translates Psalms 145:9, "You Lord are good to all of us: and your mercy rests upon all your creatures."

## Session 5

*1. How do we explain to our children why babies die?*

Very carefully—by which I mean, in such a way as not to say or imply things by our explanation that if you think about them, are really inconsistent with Christian witness and its claim to tell only the truth about human life. The last thing we as Christians ever want to do in raising our children is to deal with any serious problem so as, however unintentionally, to place a stumbling block in the way of their coming in due course to a sound understanding of Christian faith and a true understanding of their own lives as human beings.

This means, I think, that in any case where what we believe and understand simply as and because we're Christians is insufficient of itself to enable us to explain something to someone, we unhesitatingly look elsewhere for the best explanation we can find, leaving no doubt in anyone's mind that this is exactly what we're doing. Just as in trying to meet any other human need, we do the best we can: we give the best explanation we know to give without in any way invoking the authority of Christian witness and theology for the validity of what we say. Think of how much trouble we as Christians could have saved ourselves and countless others if only we'd been guided by this rule! If we'd either left such genuinely "disputed questions" as arose unanswered, as questions that we as Christians as such have no authority to answer, or else made clear to one and all that we were depending on resources in answering them beyond any available to us simply as Christians—if only we'd proceeded in this way, think of the difference it would have made to our painful controversies over such church-dividing issues as contraception, abortion, and gay ordination, to mention just a few of the hottest issues currently in dispute.

But now the relevance of these very general comments to the specific case of being asked to explain to our children why babies die seems to me to be this: contrary to what many suppose, including many Christians, there's simply no properly Christian answer to this question. There's nothing that my being a Christian, as such, authorizes me to say that would explain why babies die, any more than my being a Christian enables or entitles me to explain any other actual thing. Things happen! And not everything that happens can be explained, beyond giving the kind of explanation that it belongs to the special sciences, not to Christian faith, witness, or theology, to give. All that I or any other Christian can do to explain the death of babies to our children is to mediate to them as fittingly to their situation as one can the explanation offered by the relevant special sciences—all the while being clear oneself, and, so far as possible, also making clear to the children, that one is not giving them a properly "Christian" explanation because there's simply none to give.

I'm well aware, of course, that many Christians, together with many non-Christians, believe very differently, because they assume uncritically that God cannot be *the* Creator unless God is the *only* creator, the only one, finally, who does anything, or makes any difference, and whose doing, therefore, is the sufficient cause of everything that's done. But this assumption, I'm persuaded, is profoundly misguided, implying, as it does, that the relations between God and God's creatures are not the genuinely social, bilateral relations that Christian faith and witness clearly imply them to be. Far from being the only creator, God creates every creature to be a creator, to make a real difference to the whole ongoingness of things, however large or small the difference may be and whether it's for good or for ill.

In other words, the idea of the unsurpassable power, or "omnipotence," of God, as it's technically called, is not the absurdity of one individual's having all the power there is, but the clear, coherent idea of an individual's having all the power that could conceivably belong to any one individual consistently with there being other individuals all also having some power, however minimal. Only this second understanding of "omnipotence" is compatible with the claim that God is pure, unbounded love of others who are exactly that: real others bound together both with God and with one another by relations that are really, not merely verbally, social. Creatures are not puppets dancing at the end of God the puppeteer's strings; they're one and all real agents, creators in their own right: in the right secured to them by God's creating each of them to create itself.

In any case, to explain to our children that babies die because, being omnipotent, God, for whatever reason, causes them to die is exactly the kind of wrong explanation that I began by saying we must be very careful never to give. Make no mistake about it, the cost of giving this explanation to our children, or to anyone else, for that matter, will prove exceedingly high. Far from helping them toward eventually acquiring a sound understanding of Christian faith and a true understanding of themselves, this explanation can only be an obstacle in the way to their ever acquiring either.

*2. What is the best thing to say to a young wife and her children to explain why they have lost their husband and dad?*

How I will respond to this question should be clear from how I've just answered the last one. The underlying issue's the same, and the dangers of slipping into giving the wrong explanation just as serious. There's simply no properly "Christian" explanation of why anyone dies; and the best thing for a Christian to do in a situation in which anyone needs or asks for an explanation is simply to make that as clear as she or he possibly can in the circumstances, and then, if pressed, mediate, or pass on, the only kind of explanation that's ever possible, which is to say, the kind given most authoritatively by the relevant special sciences.

But, of course, no science explains the death of a particular individual person like just this individual woman's husband and her children's father. The sciences can illuminate the fact of his death, insofar as they can do so, only in exactly the same way they can illuminate any other particular fact: by explaining why a certain *general kind* of fact, as distinct from this fact in particular, is most likely to have happened as it has. And that, of course, is why simply passing on a scientific explanation of a certain kind of death is not calculated to be all that helpful to persons asking, not why husbands or fathers die in general, but why *my* husband or *my* father has died.

So any Christian may be pardoned for not being at all confident about just how to proceed in a situation such as our question asks about. There're simply some things that can't be explained, and if it's true, as I think Christian faith and witness necessarily imply that it is, that God is not the *only* creator, even if *the* Creator, the only *primal*, universal, unsurpassable creator, then there's a fixed limit on explaining *anything whatever that actually happens, any actual thing.* Because God's role as the Creator is not to make anything actual, but to make everything possible both in principle and in fact, so that each and every thing can alone make itself actual—or, if you prefer, because God creates everything to create itself, and everything does so—for this reason, there can be no explanation of *any* actual occurrence *as actual.* It happens! It makes itself!

But if none of us as a Christian can ever be certain about the best thing to say in the situation assumed by our question, none of us should ever be in doubt about the worst thing to say. One of my all-time favorite poems puts it better than I can, although, since it's a German poem, I can only share it with you through my poor English translation. Its author is the contemporary German Swiss pastor and poet Kurt Marti, from a 1972 book of his poems called *Funeral Discourses*, and its title is simply a line from the German Lutheran theologian, Christoph Blumhardt:

*We are people who protest against death.*

the lord our god
is in no way pleased
that gustav e. lips
died in an auto accident

first of all, he was too young
second, a tender husband to his wife
third, a playful father to two children
fourth, a good friend to his friends
fifth, filled with lots of ideas

what's to be done now without him?
what's his wife without him?
who plays with the children?
who takes the place of a friend?
who's going to have the new ideas?

the lord our god

is in no way pleased

that some of you thought

he would be pleased by such a thing


in the name of him who raised the dead

in the name of him who died and rose again:

we protest against the death of gustav e. lips[12]


### 3. What do you think of "contemporary" worship, so called?

What I think of so-called contemporary worship may well not be all that worth thinking about. I'm not a practical theologian, any more than I'm a historical theologian, or even a moral theologian; I'm a systematic theologian, and so my opinions in the area of practical theology, which is the area in which this question belongs, are pretty much that—opinions. And we all know what opinions are generally worth: as we say, "a dime a dozen." But with that disclaimer, which I hope you'll all take seriously, I'll speak briefly to the question.

I think that in a proper sense, everything about the church's life, including its worship, ought always to be "contemporary"—*in time with* any of the historical situations in which it finds itself. The church is given and called decisively through Jesus Christ and the Holy Spirit, to be God's servant to the world, which is to say, to any and all human beings who are able to benefit from the church's service—from what Paul calls its ministry and message of reconciliation (2 Cor 5:17–21). But if the church is to perform this service, it must ever take care to see that the witness it bears is a *valid* Christian witness, which demands always two things: that it be *adequate to its content*, so that it says by word and deed what, though only what, it's authorized to say; and that it be also *fitting to its situation*, so that the women and men living in that situation are able to hear and understand its witness and can therefore responsibly make the decision it gives and calls them to make. To be fitting to a situation, however, the church's witness has to be insofar contemporary with that situation—to be so formulated and specified in that situation's terms that, as nearly as possible, persons living in that situation are enabled to live the Christian

---

12. Translated by the author from Kurt Marti, *Leichenreden* (Darmstadt: Luchter-hand, 1972), 22–23.

life in and for it, instead of being required to believe and to act, and so also to worship, as if they were living in some situation other than their own.

The great problem, of course, is that persons can live more or less at the same time and in the same place in history, and in that sense be, as we say, contemporaries, and yet really live in very different situations socially, culturally, and reflectively. A good theologian friend of mine, whenever asked about his place on the spectrum of theological positions, used to say, "I reckon I've got to be smack in the middle of contemporary theology, because, whenever I look, there're always other theologians both to the left of me and to the right!" But, as the years have passed, I myself have realized more and more that most of the Christian theologians that I see to the left and right of me who have lived during roughly the same years I've lived are not really my contemporaries at all, but, as I've come to think and say, my "contemporary ancestors"—and this they are, I've learned, whether or not they think of themselves as "conservatives" or as "progressives." Most of the "liberals" I know are what I can honestly think of only as "*old* liberals."

But, then, something like this condition is replicated at all levels of the church's life, right down to the local church and its way of publicly worshiping God, along with everything else it does or tries to do. The forms of worship that some in the congregation take to be "contemporary," others judge to be either long out of date or else so far ahead of their time as to be, as we say, "way out" for yet other members of the community. So, as far as I've ever been able to tell, there's no easy way, if there's any way at all, to get around the fact that one member's "contemporary" is another's "traditional," and vice versa.

Nor is our past record of trying to solve problems of this kind, considering the Christian church generally, all that encouraging. Instead of remembering how Paul responded to the slogan of some of the advanced movers in his churches at Corinth, that "All things are lawful"—namely, by reminding them, "but not all things are beneficial," "not all things build up"—champions of the contemporary only too often become a stumbling block to their weaker brothers and sisters, conscience-bound, as they are, by tradition. On the other hand, champions of tradition all too often confuse its timeless substance with its temporary forms and wind up denying the freedom rightly claimed by those who would be "contemporary" to judge by *their own* conscience instead of somebody else's conscience in the past (1 Cor 10:21–30).

Even so, the demand remains that the church's witness must ever be as fitting to the situation in and for which it must be borne, as it is adequate to its own content as Christian witness. And this means that the church's public worship, also, remains ever subject to this demand: this demand to be, in a proper sense, "contemporary," hard as it is to obey.

*4. Why is it true, if it's true, that one group or another has persecuted the Jewish people since the time of Jesus?*

As a historical question about the reasons or causes of certain developments in history, this question should be answered either by a secular historian or a historical theologian or church historian with specialized knowledge of the developments in question. As a systematic theologian, I do not have such expertise. All I can do is say, briefly, what I believe to be true as a lay historian in order to respond to the question as best I can.

I shall simply assume a rather broad meaning of "persecution," including ethnic or religious prejudice and social ostracism, or other social disadvantages, as well as well as official, legal forms of persecution.

The statement asked about is, I believe, largely true, although it's arguable that persecution of the Jews antedated the time of Jesus, witness the story lying behind the Jewish Festival of Lights (Chanukah). And while persecution certainly occurred after Jesus' time, if not exclusively at the hands of Christians, it was primarily Christians who were the persecutors, at least after Christianity became the state religion of the Roman Empire early in the fourth century CE. We know from the New Testament, however, that Jews, for their part, also persecuted Christians. But once Christianity became an established religion, Jews were certainly by far more the persecuted than the persecutors.

We also know from the New Testament, however, that conflict between the synagogue and the church began early, and is reflected in the New Testament writings. The Gospel of John has even been judged "anti-Semitic" by some critics because of its author's use of the term "the Jews" and of the picture he paints of those he so designates. Careful scholars, however, recognize that what this author means by "the Jews" is simply "the world," the world that God loves and to which the Son of God is sent, but that does not receive, but rather rejects, the Son's mission to reveal his Father. On the other hand, there's no doubt that countless readers were taken in by John's unfortunate use of terms and used his language to justify things that he hardly intended. But in the other gospels, also, there are clear signs that Christians have already stereotyped the Jews as "the enemy." Indeed, according to some New Testament scholars, there is convincing evidence that the whole portrayal of the Jews, especially the Pharisees, in the gospel traditions is more legend than historical reportage, motivated by the early church's own later polemic against the synagogue. Another powerful motivation in its presentation of the Jews, presumably, was its desire to shift responsibility for Jesus' death more to them, so as to exculpate the Roman authorities that the church was eager, if not to please, then certainly not to displease.

Anyhow, once the idea gets abroad that "the Jews" are "Christ-killers," Christian persecution of the Jews can appear to many as justified—notwithstanding overwhelming evidence that Jesus was, in fact, crucified by the Roman occupation authorities, not by the Jews—witness simply the mode of his execution: crucifixion. That the Jewish authorities may have connived in this is entirely possible. But the responsibility for Jesus' death falls squarely on Roman shoulders.

Underlying all such factors was the understanding on the part of Christians that the church as the "new Israel" had superseded Israel as the chosen people of God. The very distinction, "old covenant/testament"/ "new covenant/testament" expresses this supersessionism, and, given the assumptions of the times, that, if you had power to enforce your own beliefs and values by persecuting minorities having different beliefs and values, you were justified in using it—given these assumptions, persecution of the Jewish minority by the Christian majority was as close to being inevitable as makes no difference.

### 5. What's the difference between Catholics and Methodists?

It's not easy to say, because there are, in fact, many differences between these two communities of Christians. Most of these differences are differences between Catholics, on the one side, and Protestants, on the other. This is because Methodists are one of the communities included within the more inclusive communion of Protestant Christians. If by "Catholics" we mean, as we ordinarily do, "Roman Catholics," then, as that name indicates, Roman Catholic Christians are united in being members of one institutional church, whose headquarters are in Rome, Italy. At the very head of their church is the figure they call "the Pope" (meaning the Father). Roman Catholics believe that this figure, the Pope, is, under Christ, the final authority in their church, in that his judgment concerning what Christians are to believe (and not to believe) and to do (and not to do) is overriding, or final. Methodists, being Protestants, do not acknowledge this supreme authority of the Pope. They appeal, instead, to the supreme authority of scripture. But please do remember the first thing I said in answering your question: there are many differences between Roman Catholics and Methodists, not all of which are connected to this one fundamental difference.

### 6. Why are there so many different churches?

There are, as you may have suspected, many reasons for there being so many different churches. But probably the most basic, or important, reason is that people generally, and, therefore, Christians generally, are simply different. They don't all believe exactly the same things, or believe them in exactly the same ways. And the same is true of what they do—of their actions, of the things they think it proper for Christians to do, or of the ways they think these things should be done. When these differences, then, are or become great enough, and when Christians mistakenly assign more importance to their differences than to what unites (or should unite) them, they may reach the point where separation from those who differ from them may seem to be the only, or the best, thing to do. As time passes, however, many of the differences between Christians have come to seem less important to some of them, and the ever-present sense that they are, at bottom one, and therefore should be one, has led them to explore possibilities of reuniting with their fellow Christians. They are one, namely, in their faith in God as they know God through Jesus and in their call to love God and to love their neighbors as they love themselves.

### 7. Will my dog be in heaven?

If by "being in heaven" you mean, as you well may, "being everlastingly held in God's unbounded love," then, Yes, your dog will be in heaven. Why? Well, because your dog, just like you and everything else there ever was, is now, or ever will be is and always will be held forever in God's love. Many Christians have believed, and some believe still, that only human beings, not animals, are included in God's love. But I think that Psalm 145 from the New Zealand Prayer Book says it exactly right: "The Lord is good to all of us: and his mercy rests upon all of his creatures." What makes us as human beings different from other animals and other creatures is not that we alone are included in God's love, but that we are able to know, as they do not, that this is true of us and of all things and to allow knowing this to shape our entire lives. So even now we're able to live knowing ourselves to be God's beloved children, And this is the other closely related thing we may well mean by "being in heaven": knowing that just this is who we really are.

*8. Jesus gives us eternal life. But what happened to the people before Jesus came?*

Jesus gives us eternal life by revealing or making known to us that eternal life is God's everlasting gift to us—and to everyone else. As the verse from the Psalms I just cited says, God is good to all of us, and God's mercy is over all that God has made. If eternal life means, as I believe it does, the life that each of God's creatures has everlastingly in God's love, then all people, together with all of God's other creatures, are given eternal life because they're given the gift of God's love.

The problem with people, however—unlike the animals and other creatures that don't have this problem—is that they have to receive God's gift of eternal life in God's love through their own freedom and responsibility as human beings. You know how it is: you can offer your friendship to someone by doing whatever you can to be her or his friend. But if she or he doesn't *accept* the gift of your friendship, it's as though you'd never given it—not so far as *you're* concerned, of course, but so far as the other person is concerned. Unless and until she or he accepts your gift, your having given it is wasted on her or him. So what we people, unlike our animal fellow creatures, often need most is for someone to make known to us that we've already been given a gift, although we ourselves have to accept it before it can do us any good. For us as Christians, Jesus is the one who makes just this known to us in a decisive way in the case of God's gift of God's love for us all: for all who lived before Jesus came and for all who will live thereafter, including all of us who are living now. Our part in this as Christians is simply to help Jesus help others to know that they, too, have always already been given this gift, but that they themselves also have to receive it before God's giving it, and Jesus' making it known, will make any difference in their lives.

*9. Describe or talk about your faith: the profound, basic trust that shapes the way you live. What are the sources of that life-shaping faith? What or who are the resources that help you resist drifting away from the faith-shaped way of living in good times or tempting you to abandon it in bad times?*

There are circumstances in which I would not hesitate to describe or talk about my own faith. But both as a Christian teacher and as a Christian theologian, which are the two closely related, and yet distinct, roles that I understand myself to be playing here, in these sessions of asking and answering questions, I find it more fitting to do something else: to describe or talk about what I think my own or anyone else's personal faith *ought to be* if it is to be Christian faith, instead of some other faith. So, by your leave, I'll proceed to answer the question with this shift of focus: from what my faith *actually is* to what it *should be* if it's the Christian faith I claim it is by identifying myself as a Christian and giving others to recognize me as such.

Christian faith, as I understand it, is a way of living out the obedience to which all human beings, in every time and place, in every moment and in every situation, are always already called—if not *explicitly* called through some particular religious community and its tradition, then at least *implicitly* called simply through their lives as human beings, through their encounters with their neighbors and with their own individual destinies in the world. Christian faith's not the only way of living out this obedience to which all are called, but it's one way; and for those who've been called to follow this Christian way—as they believe, *decisively*—through Jesus, it's the best way they know, and they unhesitatingly commend it to others accordingly: as "good news" for them, too.

But what is the obedience to which Christians understand themselves, along with everyone else, to have always already been called at least implicitly, even before receiving their decisive call to be Christians? If I answer assuming what the question asked of me assumes, I can only say that it's "the profound, basic trust that shapes the way [one lives one's life]." But as much as I certainly agree that the original obedience to which all human beings are always already called is indeed, and first of all, a profound, basic, life-shaping *trust*, I would want to add that it's also, and just as importantly, a profound, basic, life-shaping *loyalty*. We're all called not only to entrust ourselves without reservation to the all-encompassing whole of reality from which we and all things come and to which we and they all return, but also to serve that whole of reality loyally without qualification by loyally serving all of its parts as we serve ourselves. "You shall love the Lord your God with all your heart, soul, mind, and strength; and you shall love your neighbor as yourselves."

So trust *and* loyalty, confidence *and* faithfulness—these are the *two* aspects of the obedience to which, not only we as Christians, but also every other human being, are always already called, if only implicitly, as soon and as long as we're human beings at all.

If one asks, then, what are the sources of a faith that's a Christian faith? one source, certainly, is our experience of the all-encompassing whole of things, of which each of us is a part, and whose gift and demand to us as human beings have always already been presented to us implicitly through our own experience and reason simply as and because we're human. Before any of us ever receives a special, explicit call, including the decisive call to be a Christian, each of us has always already been *implicitly* called to the obedience of faith: to unreserved trust in, and un-qualified loyalty to, the ultimate whole of reality of which we and others are one and all parts.

But this implicit source is not, and could not be, the only source of a properly *Christian* faith. No, there can be Christian faith, properly so called, only through the special experience of Jesus Christ, which is to say, only through the man Jesus experienced as explicitly, indeed, decisively, *re*-presenting, or presenting *again*, our original call to obedi-ence: our call to unreserved trust and unqualified loyalty that's always already come to each and every human being simply as and because that's who she or he is. Because Jesus is an actual person of the historical past, however, the only way anyone could have such a special experience of him after his death is through the witness of his contemporaries: those who lived and walked with him, and whom Christians are accustomed to single out as "the apostles." They alone are what Søren Kierkegaard calls "*firsthand* disciples," all the rest of us Christians being at best "disciples *at second hand*." And we've become even that only through our believing acceptance of the apostles' witness to Jesus as the decisive revelation of God, the decisive re-presentation of the meaning of ultimate reality for us, which he discloses as nothing but love, sheer, all-accepting love.

So the other, explicit source of Christian faith, in addition to its im-plicit source in our individual human experience of the ultimate reality of our own existence, is our experience of Jesus himself, as he's proclaimed to us through the witness of the apostles. Their witness is mediated to us, in turn, by all the intervening generations of their successors, gath-ered together in this and all the other Christian churches. This means, of course, that the apostles, and all the apostolic churches in communion with them, are also, in their ways, explicit sources of properly Christian faith. They are, we may say, its explicit *primary* and *secondary* sources respectively, Jesus Christ himself being rightly distinguished from both as their sole explicit *primal* source.

But, instead of saying this, it might be better to take advantage of the distinction the question itself makes, between "sources" and "resources," and say, rather, that everything other than our common human experience of ultimate reality, on the one hand, and our specifically Christian experience of Jesus through the apostolic witness, on the other, is more appropriately thought of as a "resource" than as a "source" of properly Christian faith. Of course, as is clear from the words themselves, "resource" and "source" are very closely related in meaning. But assuming that one way of distinguishing them is to say that a "resource," properly so called, is a way or means of retrieving, or putting ourselves back in touch with, one or the other of the two sources of our faith, we may say, appropriately enough, that everything else I've mentioned, is a resource for returning again and again to one or the other of these two sources: either to our common human experience of ultimate reality—of ourselves, others, and the all-encompassing whole of which we're all parts—or to our specifically Christian experience of Jesus as decisively re-presenting the meaning of that ultimate reality for us as nothing but love.

But our question doesn't ask just about resources generally, it asks about resources that specifically help a Christian to resist drifting away from her or his faith-shaped way of living in good times and to resist the temptation to abandon that way of living in bad times. Judging from my own experience, I can only say that every Christian is almost certain to have her or his own collection of resources for just these circumstances in which any Christian is likely to find her- or himself in the different situations of life. In any case, I know I have such a collection, even though I question whether anyone else could profitably make it her or his own without critically appropriating it. Suffice it to say, therefore, that in principle, any of the resources on which a Christian is, in the nature of the case, always dependent for being able to retrieve the two sources of her or his faith can always be drawn upon also to provide help for living the Christian life in the different kinds of times in which we're called to live it.

If my own experience is any guide, however, paramount among all such resources are any that forcefully remind us that there's never a time in which we do not have the possibility of Christian faith: of entrusting ourselves without reservation to the mystery encompassing us and everything else as the boundless love of God that Jesus discloses it to be, and of then doing all that in us lies to live loyally to that love and to all who, as much as ourselves, are lovingly embraced by it. I think especially in this connection of the witness borne by a Christmas sermon of the great seventeenth-century English preacher and poet John Donne, which I have used more than once to bear my greetings to family and friends at Christmastide. "God," Donne says, "made sun and moon to distinguish seasons, and day, and night, and we cannot have the fruits of the earth but in their seasons. But God hath made no decree to distinguish the seasons of his mercies. . . . All occasions invite his mercies, and all times are his seasons."[13]

Because there're no seasons to God's mercies, there're also no seasons—no good times or bad—to our possibility to live as the human beings God created us to be. Because all times are God's seasons, we're always free in any situation in which we find ourselves to entrust our lives to God's unbounded love for us all, and to spend our lives, whenever there is time and opportunity, loyally serving as ourselves any whom God gives us to love.

> Grant us grace, our Father, to do all of our work as workers who need not be ashamed. Give us the spirit of diligence and honest inquiry in our quest for the truth, the spirit of charity in all our dealings with our fellows, and the spirit of gaiety, courage, and a quiet mind in facing all our tasks and responsibilities; through Jesus Christ our Lord. Amen.[14]

13. Evelyn M. Simpson, ed., *John Donne's Sermons on the Psalms and Gospels: With a Selection of Prayers and Meditations* (Berkeley: University of California Press, 1963), 182.

14. Composed by the author.